AF560776

WOMEN EMPOWERMENT

MYTH OR REALITY

BOOKS BY THE SAME AUTHOR

1. Indian Philosophy: Nyāya Vaiśeṣika and Modern Science (Sterling Publishers, New Delhi, 1984)
2. Parmārtha Pathika (ed.) (Parmārtha Niketana Rishikesha, 1985)
3. Education Policy and Administration (Deep & Deep Publications Pvt. Ltd., New Delhi, 1994)
4. Distance Education in 21st Century (Deep & Deep Publications Pvt. Ltd., New Delhi, 2000)
5. Environment and Ancient Sanskrit Literature (Deep & Deep Publications Pvt. Ltd., New Delhi, 2003)
6. Human Resource Development and Ancient Sanskrit Literature (Deep & Deep Publications Pvt. Ltd., New Delhi, 2003)
7. Good Governance and Ancient Sanskrit Literature (Deep & Deep Publications Pvt. Ltd., New Delhi, 2003)
8. Women Development and Empowerment: Organisation and Structure (Deep & Deep Publications Pvt. Ltd., New Delhi, 2003)
9. Education and Socio-Economic of Women Development and Empowerment (Deep & Deep Publications Pvt. Ltd., New Delhi, 2004)
10. Violence and Protective Measures for Women Development and Empowerment (Deep & Deep Publications Pvt. Ltd., New Delhi, 2004)
11. Ancient Sanskrit Wisdom: Modern Science and Beyond (Deep & Deep Publications Pvt. Ltd., New Delhi, 2005)
12. Ancient Sanskrit Wisdom: Current Problems and Solutions (Deep & Deep Publications Pvt. Ltd., New Delhi, 2005)
13. Human Values and Education (Deep & Deep Publications Pvt. Ltd., New Delhi, 2005)
14. Stress Management and Eduction (Deep & Deep Publications Pvt. Ltd., New Delhi, 2005)
15. Higher Education in the 21st Century: Organisation, Administration and Functions (Vol. I) (Deep & Deep Publications Pvt. Ltd., New Delhi, 2005)
16. Higher Education in the 21st Century: Quality and Excellence (Vol. II) (Deep & Deep Publications Pvt. Ltd., New Delhi, 2005)
17. Higher Education in the 21st Century: Extension Education Services (Vol. III) (Deep & Deep Publications Pvt. Ltd., New Delhi, 2005)
18. Violence Against Women: Issues and Perspectives (ed.) (Deep & Deep Publications Pvt. Ltd., New Delhi, 2006)
19. Yoga Education: Philosophy and Practice (Deep & Deep Publications Pvt. Ltd., New Delhi, 2007)
20. Human Values: Principles and Practices (Deep & Deep Publications Pvt. Ltd., New Delhi, 2008)
21. Women Health Education (Deep & Deep Publications Pvt. Ltd., New Delhi, 2008)
22. Distance Education: Principles, Potentialities and Perspectives (Deep & Deep Publications Pvt. Ltd., New Delhi, 2009)
23. Educational Administration and Management: An Integral Approach (Deep & Deep Publications Pvt. Ltd., New Delhi, 2009)

WOMEN EMPOWERMENT

MYTH OR REALITY

DR. ARUNA GOEL

Honorary Director, Centre for Women Studies and Development, Panjab University, Chandigarh (1.3.2004-31.7.2008)
Former Chairperson of Women Study Centres in all Universities in India as a Member of UGC
Former Member of the Society of Indian Advanced Studies, Shimla
Former Member of Sahitya Academy (Sanskrit Board) Government of India, New Delhi
Chairperson, Deptt. of Correspondence Studies, P.U., Chandigarh
Former Member of UGC
President Awardee with a Cash Prize of Rs. 5 lacs on 15th August, 2008.
Fellow, P.U., Chandigarh
Professor of Sanskrit, P.U., Chandigarh

DEEP & DEEP PUBLICATIONS PVT. LTD.

F-159, Rajouri Garden, New Delhi-110027

WOMEN EMPOWERMENT
MYTH OR REALITY

ISBN 978-81-8450-182-7

Typeset by S.S. COMPOSERS
3190, Mohindra Park, Shakur Basti, Delhi-110034.

Printed in India at MAYUR ENTERPRISES,
WZ Plot No. 3, Gujjar Market, Tihar Village, New Delhi-110018.

Published by DEEP & DEEP PUBLICATIONS PVT. LTD.
F-159, Rajouri Garden, New Delhi-110027.
Phones: 25435369, 25440916
E-mail: ddpbooks@yahoo.co.in • ddpubs@gmail.com
Showroom:
2/13, Ansari Road, Daryaganj, New Delhi-110002 • Telefax: 23245122

Contents

Preface

Gender equality is an issue of primary importance to the welfare and progress of all nations. It is fundamental to achieving people-centered development. What humanity needs is a world that is free, fair and equal; a world that will have no discrimination, violence, or exploitation, a world where opportunity and prosperity are shared by all. So, why is violence against Women and discrimination so widespread all over the world? It is because discrimination begins in the minds of people, where gender-bias becomes a habit in thought and action. These have over centuries developed deep-rooted cultural traditions which regard women as subservient, the girl-child as a liability, and discrimination as normal. The root of all prejudice is ignorance. Education, greater awareness, public policy and the media can play an important role in eradicating such prejudices. Recent work has brought out very clearly that women's literacy and educated participation of women in decisions within and outside family strongly influence the relative respect and regard for women's well-being.

As pointed out in one of the UN publications "In every country, whether it is new or long established, whether it is underdeveloped or highly developed, any programme of economic or fiscal development, of improvement in education, health, labour and social conditions and of reform and reconstruction in any of the women services can only succeed if it is supported by machinery and method established under sound principles of public administration and adapted to the circumstances of the country concerned."

The intention of policy-makers and planners to promote Women Development and Empowerment is to be ensured by Organisations entrusted with this work. This requires an ideal structure, material and personnel so that the intentions of policy-makers are translated into action. There is also a need of constant organizational analysis based on method study, work measurement and manpower planning. In this Book, "Women Empowerment—Myth or Reality", we have engaged our attention not only on existing framework but also what these should be based on research and analysis so that in the 21st century we can feel proud in achieving our cherished goal of Women Development and Empowerment.

A question arises as to how the developing countries can translate their aims and objectives enshrined in their constitution as well as legislation for Women Development and Empowerment suffering from abject poverty, disease, squalor, hunger, unemployment, low status and other socio-economic ailments. It requires an overhaul of the old administrative structures and creating a new administrative set-up required for socio-economic development of women. Organizations are not mere structures but action systems. Action system is a structured device through which resources are mobilized and transformed by the use of certain skills and technology to produce pre-designed output. The prevailing administrative system dealing with women development and empowerment is a basic aid to the achievement of women welfare objectives. If the design is unsound, the achievement of objectives is likely to fall short of expectations. Administration can provide the means whereby the most effective use can be made of the knowledge and skills of the personnel engaged in different activities. The benefits of modern science and technology can reach the women only if services for women are properly planned and effectively implemented. An increase in the scientific nature of determination is an important factor in raising its efficiency.

The Beijing declaration paid particular attention to the right against discrimination and inequality that pose severe threats to the health, education and employment of all women. At the core of the equality is the recognition that access to primary health care, including reproductive health, basic education, employment is indispensable to the social rights of women. While entering the 21st Century, the empowerment of women in health, education and employment must be an integral part of the sustainable human development programme. Psychological factors associated with health differ widely among men and women. There are qualitative differences in social roles of men and women. Often power and resource control lies in the hands of men, and women are victims of violence, discrimination and harassment. The unequal gender treatment in matters of education, recreation, health, medical care and lodging in regard to male and female children, is still continuing, in rural India.

In India, women-friendly development remains a myth. The indicators for women's development present a pathetic picture despite all the rhetoric. It is quite frustrating to see the clock turn back in our country. The glorious traditions of more than century and a half of the nineteenth century, the Gandhian ideology of women's emancipation, the guarantees, provided by the Constitution of India for gender equality, everything goes in vain, widening the gap between rhetoric and reality.

Plethora of Laws have been enacted to empower women. However, laws are not always enforced and women are often unaware of their legal rights. Women's lack of decision-making powers, whether at the highest level of government or in the household, underlies many of the issues prevalent today, including the gender disparities seen with regard to women's access to education, better paid work and health care.

Empowerment of Women would ultimately depend upon the change in social value system, attitudes and social structure prevalent in the country which can be injected through socio-economic inputs. In addition, women themselves have to change their attitudes towards women. This would necessitate co-ordinated and concerted efforts on the part of women institutions, political leaders, social reformers and other intellectuals as well as social reformers of social strata, including women themselves.

> This beautiful world designed by the Almighty
> Is culturally evolved by innumerable
> Generations of people, in the course of millions of years.
> No one has the right to destroy it
> Let us preserve it for your enjoyment and
> For future generations.
>
> —Vethathiri Maharishi

We are sure that new millennium would usher an era where women can enjoy the life in full and in all fields to ensure socio-economic justice. To awaken people, it is the women who must be awakened. Once she is on the move, the family moves, the village moves, the nation moves.

The speed with which women empowerment is progressing would take too long or may reverse in course of time. The need is that the legislature, Government, Judiciary must work earnestly, sincerely and with dedication to remove the present myth of women empowerment into reality. Most of the people quote some examples of women who had or are occupying high offices in politics are only marginal and may not be equated with women empowerment. Women in villages, urban slums, tribal areas and to some extent even in cities are far from achieving empowerment in true sense of the term. Daily Newspapers, TV, periodicals are full of daily reporting problems of rape, dowry, atrocities, violence, beating, etc. women which is a reflection of great shame on policy-makers and administrators. Therefore, there is a need of understanding the meaning of women empowerment, its characteristics and methods of achieving it.

The Book, "Women Empowerment : Myth or Reality" is supplemented with facts, charts and tables.

It is hoped that this book would be of great use to women in general to help them to avoid violence against them and improve their status. It would also be of great source for policy-makers, planners and administrators to take realistic decisions about women. It would serve a great purpose to those who are engaged in the study and research of gender issues. The chapters of the book reflect the contents covered in this book.

I am sure that the book would be of great use to all interested in women empowerment.

Chandigarh

ARUNA GOEL

1

Introduction

"... the principle which regulates the existing social relations between the two sexes—the legal subordination of one sex to the other—is wrong in itself, and now one of the chief hindrances to human improvement; . . .it ought to be replaced by a principle of perfect equality, admitting no power or privilege on the one side, nor disability on the other."

—J.S.Mill and Hariet Taylor Mill

The Status of women varies enormously from one part of the world to another. However, nowhere do women enjoy equal status with men. But in the developing countries like Africa, the Middle East, Asia and Latin America, the Status of women is so low as cannot be imagined by women in the developed countries. Status is a relative term. In sociological expression, it denotes neither rank nor hierarchy but only position *vis-a-vis* others in terms of rights and obligations. In the ultimate analysis, status is "the conjunction of positions a woman occupies . . . as a worker, student, wife, mother . . . the power and prestige attached to these positions and the rights and duties she is expected to exercise." Women's status can then be analysed in terms of their participation in decision-making, access to opportunities in education, training, employment and income. In recent years, there has been an increasing recognition of the interface between women's ability to control their fertility and their exercise and enjoyment of other options in life.

State's response to women issues has been mixed and ambivalent, it has been both a process of progression and retrogression. The last twenty years show a record of the state laws and policies ostensibly to improve the situation of women. At the same time their inability to effectively address the issue of equality between men and women, the manner of approaching women's issues within them and the gap in the implementation, raises doubts about the state's intentions to actually improve the status of women. This also points to the problematic nature of relationship between women's movement and the state. Women's groups and women's movement have approached the state and pressurised it to frame pro-women laws and policies. While the state has framed seemingly pro-women laws and policies, these have actually helped women very little and more importantly, have not helped to break sexual stereotypes and male-dominance, rather as argued in the previous chapters most of the state policies have reinforced these tendencies. Neither have these policies been able to achieve the objective of equality. Thus, women continue to have contradictory experiences with regard to the state policies towards them.

The role of the home-maker is still assigned primarily to women not only through conventions and customs but in some cases also in Law. In actual practice, there is a big gap between women's role and status that has been granted to her in theory and by law and the one that she enjoys in real day-to-day life. In spite of the laws that have been passed the position of women is still not at all satisfactory particularly of women in the rural areas. It is too early to judge whether the practical application of these new laws will satisfy the intentions behind their enactment. If the courts interpret the law, according to the traditional principles of the supremacy of man and if governments do not move to give authority and to implement the new laws, the spirit and interest of the reform will be largely nullified. Meaningful interpretation and implementation of the acts will require reform fundamentally affecting the society, which cannot be expected merely as a consequence of the legal reform itself. National Perspective Plan For Women has rightly commented that there is often a wide gap between the Legislative Intent and the use of laws and legal processes in reality. While Parliament and State Legislatures respond to public opinion by enacting legislation conducive to the attainment of equality, considerable time is lost in framing rules, appointment of functionaries, settling up legal institutions, etc.

CHANGING STATUS OF WOMEN

Women, as an independent target group, account for 495.74 million and represent 48.3 per cent of country total population, as per the 2001 Census. Empowering women as a process demands a life-cycle approach. Therefore, every stage of their life counts as a priority in the planning process. Depending upon the developmental needs at every stage, female population has been categorized into 5 distinct sub-groups (population as projected for 2001). They include:

- Girl children in the age-group 0-14 years who account for 171.50 million (34.6 percent), deserve special attention because of the gender bias and discrimination they suffer from at such a tender age;

- Adolescent girls in the age-group 15-19 years who account for 52.14 million (10.5 percent) are very sensitive from the view-point of planning because of the preparatory stage for their future productive roles in the society and family, respectively;
- Women in the reproductive age-group 15-44 years numbering 233.72 million (47.1 percent) need special care and attention because of their reproductive needs;
- Women in the economically active age-group 15-59 years, who account for 289.40 million (58.4 percent), have different demands like those of education/training, employment, income generation and participation in the developmental process, decision-making, etc.; and
- The elderly women in the age-group 60 + years numbering 34.87 million (7.0 percent), have limited needs mainly relating to health, financial and emotional support.[1]

The constitution of India was ahead of its time, not only by the standards of the developing nations but also of many developed countries, in removing every discrimination against women in the legal and public domain of the Republic.

CONSTITUTIONAL GUARANTEES TO INDIA'S WOMEN

The concern in safeguarding the rights and privileges of women found its best expression in the Constitution of India.

Fundamental Rights

Article 14: "The State shall not deny to any person equality before the law or the equal protection of the laws within the territory of India."

Article 15(1): "The State shall not discriminate against any citizen on grounds only of religion, race, caste, sex, place of birth or any of them."

Article 15(3): "Nothing in this article shall prevent the State from making any special provision for women and children."

This article empowers the state to make affirmative discrimination in favour of women

Article 16(2): "No citizen shall, on grounds only of religion, race, caste, sex, descent, place of birth, residence or any of them, be ineligible for, or discriminated against in respect of, any employment or office under the State.

Directive Principals of State Policy

Article 39: "The State shall, in particular, direct its policy towards securing—

(a) that the citizens, men and women equally, have the right to an adequate means of livelihood;

(b) that there is equal pay for equal work for both men and women;
(c) that the health and strength of workers, men and women, and the tender age of children are not abused and that citizens are not forced by economic necessity to enter vocations unsuited to their age or strength."

Article 42: "The State shall make provision for securing just and humane conditions of work and for maternity relief."

Article 51A(e) imposed a fundamental duty on every citizen to renounce the practices derogatory to the dignity of women.

In our opinion, the national objective of integrating women into the process of development at all levels and the constitutional guarantees given to them require social acceptance of the multiple roles of women as home-makers, mothers, and socially and economically productive individuals. It is therefore imperative that society in general and the state in particular provide the necessary conditions and support to enable women to perform their various roles successfully. Marriage and motherhood which contribute to the continuation of the nation should not become disabilities in the gainful participation of women in the economic process. Without the type of supportive services and institutionalized aids suggested here, these dual roles will continue to impose tremendous strain on the physical and mental resources of women and affect the welfare and development of children.[2] We therefore recommend the adoption of a well-defined policy, through a Government Resolution, to fulfil the Constitutional directives and government's long-term objective of total involvement of women in national development. The policy will have to be implemented carefully so that women are not excluded from any occupation except those from which they are debarred by law, without specifying clearly the basis of unsuitability. It is also necessary to create a cell in the Ministry of Labour and Employment, at both the Central and State levels, to deal with problem of women.[3]

DEMOGRAPHY AND VITAL STATISTICS

Women Population

There has been a slight increase in the total female population of the country, from 407.1 million (48.1 percent of total population) in 1991 to 495.7 million (48.3 per cent) in 2001. While the percentage increase of 0.2 is very marginal, increase in term of absolute numbers was 88.6 million as against 77.1 million between 1981 and 1991. The growth rate of female population for the 1991-2001 decade was 21.79 percent, which was 0.86 percentage points higher than that of the total population. Yet, the demographic imbalances between women and men continue to exist till date. (Refer Table 1.1)

If demographic balances were affected by economic factors, then poor states of Orissa, Bihar or Madhya Pradesh would have recorded the worst

TABLE 1.1

Sex Ratio (1981-2001)

Census	*Sex Ratio*
1981	934
1991	927
2001	933

Note: Sex Ratio: Females per thousand males.
Source: Census of India, 2001, Provisional Population Totals, Registrar General and Census Commissioner, GOI, New Delhi

sex ratios. On the contrary, it is the prosperous states of Haryana, Punjab and Delhi that are among the worst. Better sex ratios are noted among the southern states, some hill regions and states with large tribal populations. Kerala (1071), Pondicherry (1007) are the only States/UTs where sex ratio is tilted in favour of the females.

Comparison over the decade 1991 to 2001 based on rank analysis shows that ranks of Maharashtra, Madhya Pradesh, Punjab, Goa, Gujarat and Himachal Pradesh have droppted by 2 or more places, while it has improved in the States of West Bengal, Manipur, Arunachal Pradesh, Mizoram, Meghalaya and Nagaland. (Refer Table 1.2)

This clearly points to the fact that economic growth may not necessarily bring about an improvement in the status of women. This, in turn, can be attributed to the discrimination the girl child faces and the consequential problems of poor health and nutritional status. Added to these are the problems of female fortified and female infanticide, the incidence of which is on an increase.

Expectation of Life

The life expectancy at birth among females has been steadily improving over the years from 23.3 in 1901 to 65.3 in 2001 and has surpassed that of men since the eighties. Male life expectancy in 2001 is 62.3 years. The urban female life expectancy is higher at 68. The rural-urban difference is the highest in Madhya Pradesh (8.6) and the lowest in Kerala (1.0). (Table 1.3)

The life expectancy indicator highlights that number of older women will be on the rise. Many of them will be widows and living alone given the increasing tendency of nuclearisation of families. The absence of social security measures for them on the one hand and the declining support structures from family and society on the other, indicate the plight of these already low status aged women.

Female Infant Mortality Rate

In many States, the number of infant deaths among girls exceed that of boys due to discriminatory child care practices. The worst case is that

TABLE 1.2

Sex Ratio in 6+ Age group Ranks in 1991 and 2001 and Decadal Differences (1991-2001) among States

Rank 2001	*States/UTs*	*Adult 2001*	*Sex Ratio 1991*	*Rank 1991*	*Differences 2001-1991*
1.	Sikkim	858	860	2	2
2.	Haryana	869	862	3	7
3.	Punjab	886	883	6	3
4.	Arunachal Pradesh	888	829	1	59
5.	Uttar Pradesh	895	867	5	28
6.	Nagaland	899	865	4	34
7.	Bihar	916	899	7	17
8.	Madhya Pradesh	917	926	12	-9
9.	Maharashtra	923	931	12	-8
10.	Rajasthan	925	908	9	17
11.	Assam	926	910	10	16
12.	Gujarat	927	936	14	-9
13.	West Bengal	929	907	8	22
14.	Mizoram	932	911	11	21
15.	Tripura	947	940	15	7
16.	Goa	964	967	19	-3
17.	Karnataka	966	960	18	6
18.	Meghalaya	974	947	16	27
19.	Orissa	976	972	20	4
20.	Andhra Pradesh	980	972	21	8
21.	Himachal Pradesh	981	980	23	1
22.	Manipur	981	955	17	26
23.	Tamilnadu	992	978	22	12
24.	Kerala	1071	1049	24	22
	India	934	923		11

Source: Annual Report of women and Child Development, Department, Ministry of HRD (Govt. of India).

TABLE 1.3

Life Expectancy at Birth (1981-2001)

(In Years)

Year	*Female*	*Males*
1981-85	55.7	55.4
1989-93*	59.7	59.0
1996-2001	65.3	62.3

* Based on the Sample Registration System.
Source: Ibid., Estimates.

of Haryana, where the gender difference in IMR is 19. This is followed by Punjab, Rajasthan and Tamil Nadu. Contrarily in Orissa, where infant mortality rates are the highest (96), girls have marginally higher chance of survival than boys.

Maternal Mortality Rate

In India the Maternal Mortality Rate (MMR), which is calculated as the number of maternal deaths per 100,000 live births, is among the highest in the world and therefore a matter of great concern. It has come down from 468 in 1980 to 407 in 1988. (See Table 1.4)

TABLE 1.4

Maternal Mortality Rate (1990-1998)

(Per lakh live births)

Year	*Maternal Mortality Rate*
1980	468
1993	437
1998	407

Source: Ibid.

There is wide range of variation in MMR across regions and States—from 28 in Gujarat to 707 in Uttar Pradesh.

Mean Age at Marriage

Similarly, the effective mean age at marriage for females has also increased from 18.3 years in 1981 to 19.5 years in 1997. The Child Marriage Restraint Act, 1976 which raised the age of marriage for girls from 15 to 18 years has no doubt, helped reduce child/early marriages and the consequent early pregnancies and birth of premature babies at the same time, education and employment of women/girls has also played a very important role in raising the age of marriage. (Refer Table 1.5)

TABLE 1.5

Mean Age at Marriage (1981-1997)

(in years)

Year	*Females*	*Males*
1981	18.3	23.3
1991	19.5	23.9
1997	19.5	N.A.

Source: Sample Registration System Bulletins for respective years, Registrar-General and Census Commissioner, GOI, New Delhi.

Women's Health and Family Welfare

Lack of adequate resources prevents women belonging to poorer households from availing health services for themselves. Undernourished, ill-fed and overworked, most women from such households are extremely vulnerable to ailments and diseases, which do not get properly diagnosed and treated. Poor sanitation, unhygienic surroundings, difficulty in procuring safe drinking water are some of the factors that affect the general health of women.

Every second woman in India suffers from some degree of anaemia. 2 percent of them are severely anaemic, while 35 and 15 percent have mild and moderate anaemia levels respectively. Here again, the inter-State differences are very pronounced.

While the Birth Rate has declined by 7.8 points from 33.9 in 1981 to 26.1 in 1999, the Death Rate has also declined by 3.8 points from 12.5 in 1981 to 8.7 in 1999. (Refer Tables 1.6 and 1.7)

TABLE 1.6

Birth Rate (1981-1999)

(per thousand)

Year	*Birth Rate*
1981	33.9
1991	29.5
1999	26.1

Source: Ibid.

TABLE 1.7

Death Rate (1981-1999)

(per thousand)

Year	*Females*	*Males*	*Total*
1981	12.7	12.4	12.5
1991	9.7	10.0	9.8
1999	8.3	9.0	8.7

Source: Ibid.

However while the female death rate has come down by 4.4 points from 12.7 in 1981 to 8.3 in 1999, the male death rate has come down by 3.4 points,, i.e. from 12.4 in 1981 to 9.0 in 1991.

Female Literacy

Literacy or the ability to read and write is the first step towards formal education. Female literacy has been steadily improving over the years. The proportion of women who are literate has increased by 15 percent over the last decade from 39.29 percent in 1991 to 54.16 percent in 2001. Yet, even today, 193 million women are illiterate in India.

Gender gap in literacy continues to be very high at 22 percentage points. The gaps are even more glaring among disadvantaged groups such as scheduled castes and tribes. Among scheduled castes (SCs), 50 percent males are literate while only 24 percent females can read and write. Similarly, among scheduled tribes (STs), 41 percent and 18 percent, males and females respectively are literate.

Urban-rural differences are significant, with urban females almost matching up to rural male literates, especially among SC/STs. The female literacy rate for rural areas is only 47, while it is 73 in urban locations. Bihar and Jharkhand, the two poor literacy states in rural areas (30) perform relatively better in urban areas. They are at third and eighth ranks respectively.

TABLE 1.8

(In Percent)

Census	*Females*	*Males*	*Persons*	*Male-female gap in literacy rate*
1981	29.76	6.38	43.57	26.62
1991	39.29	64.13	52.21	24.84
2001	54.16	75.85	65.38	21.69

Note: The literacy rates relate to the population aged seven years and above. The 1991 census rates exclude Jammu and Kashmir.

Source: Census of India 2001: Provisional population Totals, Registrar General and Census Commissioner, GOI, New Delhi

The gross enrolment ratio for girls both at primary and middle levels have also increased from 64.1 in 1980-81 to 85.2 in 1999-2000 in respect of primary level and from 28.6 to 49.7 in respect of middle level during the same period. Between 1990-91 and 1999-2000, the GER of girls at the middle level has also increased from 47.8 to 49.7.

The number of women in higher education which includes colleges, universities, professional colleges of engineering, medicine, technology,, etc. has also increased form 1.32 million (33.0 percent) in 1990-91 to 3 million (39.8 percent) in 1999-2000 (Table 1.9). The number of women enrolled has shown an increase in both absolute and relative terms.

Work and Employment

While the female work participation rate increased from 19.7 per cent in 1981 to 25.7 per cent in 2001, still it is much lower that the male work participation rate in both urban and rural areas (Table 1.10). There are wide

TABLE 1.9

Enrolment of Girls in Graduate/Post-Graduate/Professional Courses (1990-91 to 1999-2000)

(Figures in Million)

Levels	*1990-91*		*1996--97*		*1999-2000*	
	Women	*Total*	*Women*	*Total*	*Women*	*Total*
Graduate	1.14	3.29	1.82	4.87	2.66	6.51
(B.A./B.Sc./B.Com)	(34.7)		(37.4)		(40.9)	
Post-Graduate	0.12	0.35	0.17	0.54	0.22	0.55
(M.A./M.Sc./M.Com.)	(32.8)		(30.5)		(39.6)	
Ph.D./D.Sc./D.Phil	0.01	0.03	0.01	0.04	0.02	0.05
	(26.2)		(29.2)		(35.4)	
B.E./B.Sc (Eng)/	0.03	0.24	0.05	0.33	0.08	0.36
B. Architecture	(10.9)		(14.9)		(22.0)	
M.B.B.S.	0.03	0.08	0.04	0.12	0.05	0.14
	(34.3)		(35.4)		(37.8)	
Total	1.32	3.99	2.09	5.90	3.03	7.61
	(33.0)		(35.3)		(39.8)	

Source: Selected Educational Statistics for respective years, Department of Education, Ministry of Human Resource Development, GOI, New Delhi.

regional variations amongst the major states, ranging from as high as 34 per cent in Mizoram to as low as 4 per cent in Punjab, as per the 1991 Census. (State-wise data for the 2001 Census is not yet available) (Table 1.10)

Women's share in the organised work-force has also shown an increasing trend, from 2.8 million (12.2 per cent) in 1981 to 4.8 million (17.2 per cent) in 1999. Between 1991 and 1999, rise in the percentage points of women was 3.1 in contrast, the share of men has been declining. However, women's participation in the organised sector is still very low, as compared to men. (Table 1.11)

Similarly, women's employment in the public sector has also recorded an increase from 1.5 million (9.7 per cent) in 1981 to 2.8 million (14.5 per cent) in 1999 (Table 1.12). However, it is still much lower than that of men. (Table 1.12)

Just as in the case of women in Public Sector, they also hold a low-key with only 14.6 per cent of the total 10.7 million employees in Government in 1997. No doubt, there has been an increasing trend in the representation of women in Government, as it rose from 11.0 to 14.6 per cent between 1981 and 1997, but at the same time, their representation can be rated as very low, when compared to the number of educated women. (Table 1.13)

TABLE 1.10

Works Participation Rates by Sex (1981-2001)

(In per cent)

Census	*T/R./U*	*Females*	*Males*	*Persons*
1981	Total	19.7	52.6	36.7
	Rural	23.1	53.8	38.8
	Urban	8.3	49.1	30.0
1991	Total	22.3	51.6	37.5
	Rural	26.8	52.6	40.1
	Urban	9.2	48.9	30.2
2001	Total	25.7	51.9	39.3
	Rural	31.0	52.4	42.0
	Urban	11.6	50.9	32.2

Source: Census of India, 1991, Series 1 and Census of India, 2001: Provisional Population Totals, Registrar General and Census Commissioner, GOI, New Delhi.

TABLE 1.11

Women in the Organised Sector (1981-99)

(Figures in Million)

Year	*Women*	*Men*	*Total*
1981	2.8 (12.2)	20.1	22.9
1991	3.8 (14.1)	23.0	26.7
2001	4.8 (17.2)	23.3	28.1

Source: Director-General of Employment and Training, Ministry of Labour, GOI, New Delhi

TABLE 1.12

Women in the Public Sector (1981-99)

(Figures in Million)

Year	*Women*	*Men*	*Total*
1981	1.5 (9.7)	14.0	15.5
1991	2.4 (12.3)	16.7	19.1
2001	2.8 (14.5)	16.6	19.4

Source: Director-General of Employment and Training, Ministry of Labour, GOI, New Delhi

TABLE 1.13

Women in the Government (1981-97)

(Figures in Million)

Year	*Women*	*Men*	*Total*
1981	1.2 (11.0)	9.7	10.9
1997	1.6 (14.6)	9.1	10.7

Source: Director-General of Employment and Training, Ministry of Labour, GOI, New Delhi.

DECISION-MAKING

(i) Administrative

The representation of women in the decision-making levels through the Premier Services viz; the Indian Administrative Service (IAS) and Indian Police Services (IPS), which stood at only 5.4 per cent in 1987 increased marginally to 7.6 per cent in 2000. However, the figure is still very low, requiring not only affirmative action but also special interventions to help raise the number of women at various decision-making levels. (Refer Table 1.14)

TABLE 1.14

Representation of Women in Premier Services (1987-2000)

Service	*1987*		*1997*		*2000*	
IAS	339 (7.5)	4.204 (10.2)	512	4,991 (10.4)	535	5159
IPS	21 (0.9)	2418	67 (2.2)	3045	110 (3.3)	3301
Total	360 (5.4)	6622	579 (7.2)	8036	645 (7.6)	8460

Note: Figures within parentheses indicate percentage to total.
Source: Department of Personnel and Training, GOI, New Delhi.

The 73rd and 74th Constitutional Amendments in 1993 have brought forth a definite impact on the participation of woman, in terms of absolute numbers, in grassroot democratic institutions viz. Panchayati Raj Institutions (PRIs) and Local Bodies (Table 1.15). In fact, these amendments have helped women not only in their effective participation but also in decision-making in the grassroots democracy. Of the 475 Zilla Parishad in

TABLE 1.15

Women in Panchayati Raj Institutions (1995-2001)

(Figures in thousand)

Year	*Women*	*Men*	*Total*
1995#	318 (33.5)	630	948
2001@	725 (26.6)	1997	2722

Source: Ministry of Rural Development, GOI, New Delhi

the country, 158 are being chaired by women. At the Block Level, out of 51,000 members of Block Samitis, 17,000 are women. In addition, nearly one-third of the mayors of the municipalities are women. In the elections to PRIs held between 1993 and 1997, women have achieved participation even beyond the mandatory requirement of $33\frac{1}{3}$ per cent of the total seats in states like Karnataka (43.45 per cent), Kerala (36.4 per cent) and West Bengal (35.4 per cent). However, the all India figure for women show that their representation in 2001 is still low.

Although the number of women in Parliament has increased from 59 in 1998 to 70 in 2001, their share continues to be very low representing only 8.5 per cent (Table 1.16) of the total members in Parliament in 2001.

TABLE 1.16

Representation of Women in Parliament (1998-2001)

Year	*Women*	*Men*	*Total*
1998	59 (7.2)	761	820
1999	67 (8.5)	723	790
2001	70 (8.5)	750	820

Note: Figures within parentheses indicate percentage to total.
Source: 1. Election Commission of India.
2. National Informatics Centre, Parliament House, New Delhi.

The number of women in the Central Council of Ministers continues to remain extremely low, but with a marginal increase of 0.8 percent between 1995 and 2001 (Table 1.17). Of these, 2 are of Cabinet rank and 6 are of the rank of Minister of State, and of these, 2 are holding Independent Charge. These trends point out very clearly to the need for affirmative action

TABLE 1.17

Representation of Women in the Central Council of Ministers (1985-2001)

Year	*Women*	*Men*	*Total*
1985	4 (10.0)	36	40
2001	8 (10.8	66	74

Source: National Information Centres, Parliament House, New Delhi

besides addressing these issues in a systematic and expeditious way so that women's concerns gain political prominence and a fairly representative number of women are in position not only at grassroot level, but also at the state and national levels.

To sum up, Table 1.18 presents the status of women including that of the girl child along with the progress made by them over a period of two development decades (1981-2001) as reflected in the 21 Selected Gender Development Indicators. (Table 1.18)

A quick review of the progress made by women has not only focused light on the gains but also brought forth to surface certain critical areas of concern relating to women by Draft Tenth Plan requiring attention of the Government during the Tenth Plan. They include: increasing burden of poverty; unequal access to primary health care, under/malnutrition, high rates of illiteracy and lack of training; lack of access and control on assets and resources; inequalities in sharing of power and decision-making; lack of access to information and media; increasing violence against women, adolescent and the girl child persisting discrimination against the girl child, etc. Keeping these Issues/Concerns in view, the Tenth Plan suggests the following approach not only to strengthen, but also to speed up, the on going process/efforts of empowering of women.

STRATEGIES IN THE FIVE YEAR PLANS (See Chart 1.1)

Over the years the planning strategies on women and children in the country has evolved from 'welfare' to 'development' to 'empowerment'.

The approach in the **First Five Year Plan** (1951-56) was to provide adequate services to 'promote the welfare of women' so that they can play their 'legitimate role in the family and the community'. It was noted, 'the position and functions of women differ to a great extent in different communities, and therefore, community welfare agencies will have to work out their programmes and activities according to the specific requirements in which they work'. The Plan document further noted that special organizations on the part of the Central or State Governments for promotion of the welfare of women had not yet been developed and therefore stressed

TABLE 1.18

The 21 Selected Gender Development Indicators: 1981-2001

S.No.	Indicators	Women	Men	Total	Women	Men	Total
(1)	(2)	(3)	(4)	(5)	(6)	(7)	(8)
	Demography and Vital Statistics						
1.	Population (in million in 1981 and 2001)	330.0	353.4	683.4	495.7	531.3	1027.0
2.	Decennial Growth (1981 and 2001)*	24.93	24.41	24.66	21.79	20.93	21.34
3.	Sex Ratio (1981 and 2001)**	934	-	-	933	-	-
4.	Life Expectancyat Birth (in years in 1981-85 and 1996-01)	55.7	55.4	-	65.3	62.3	-
5.	Mean Age at Marriage (in years in 1981 and 1991)	18.3	23.3	-	19.5	23.9	-
	Health and Family Welfare						
6.	Birth Rate (per thousand in 1981 and 1999)	-	-	33.9	-	-	26.1
7.	Death Rate (per thousand in 1981 and 1999)	12.7	12.4	12.5	8.3	9.0	8.7
8.	Infant Mortality Rate (per thousand live births in 1988 and 1999)	93.0	96.0	94.5	70.8	69.8	70.0
9.	Child Mortality Rate (per thousand live births under 5 years of age in 1985 and 1997)	40.4	36.6	-	24.5	21.8	-
10.	Maternal Mortality Rate (per one lakh live births in 1980 and 1998)	468	-	-	407	-	-
	Literacy and Education						
11.	Literacy Rates (1981 and 2001)*	29.76	56.38	43.57	54.16	75.85	65.38

(Contd.)

TABLE 1.18 *(Contd.)*

(1)	*(2)*	*(3)*	*(4)*	*(5)*	*(6)*	*(7)*	*(8)*
12.	Gross Enrolment Ratio (1980-81 and 1999-2000)						
	—Classes I-V	64.1	95.8	80.5	85.2	104.1	94.9
	—Class VI-VIII	28.6	54.3	41.9	49.7	67.2	58.8
13.	Drop-out Rate (1980-81 and 1999-2000)*						
	—Class I-V	62.5	56.2	58.7	42.3	38.7	40.3
	—Class VI-VIII	79.4	68.0	72.7	58.0	52.0	54.6
	Work and Employment						
14.	Work Participation Rate (1981 and 2001)*	19.7	52.6	36.7	25.7	51.9	39.3
15.	Organised Sector (No. in million in 1981 and 1999)	2.80 (12.2%)	20.05	22.85	4.83 (17.2%)	23.28	28.11
16.	Public Sector (No. in million in 1981 and 1999)	1.5 (9.7%)	14.0	15.5	2.8 (14.5%)	16.6	19.4
17.	Government (No. in million in 1981 and 1997)	1.2 (11%)	9.7	10.9	1.6 (14.6%)	9.1	10.7
	Decision-Making						
18.	Administration (No. in IAS and IPS in 1987 and 2000)	360 (5.4%)	6262	6622	645	7815	8460
19.	PRIs (No. in thousand in 1995 and 2001)	318 (33.5%)	630	948	725 (26.6%)	1997	2722
20.	Parliament (No. in 1998 and 2001)	59 (7.2%)	761	820	70 (8.5%)	750	820
21.	Central Council of Ministers (No. in 1985 and 2001)	4 (10%)	36	40	8 (10.8%)	66	74

Sources: Census of India, 1991; Census of India, 2001.
Draft: Tenth Plan (2000-2001), p. 237.

CHART 1.1

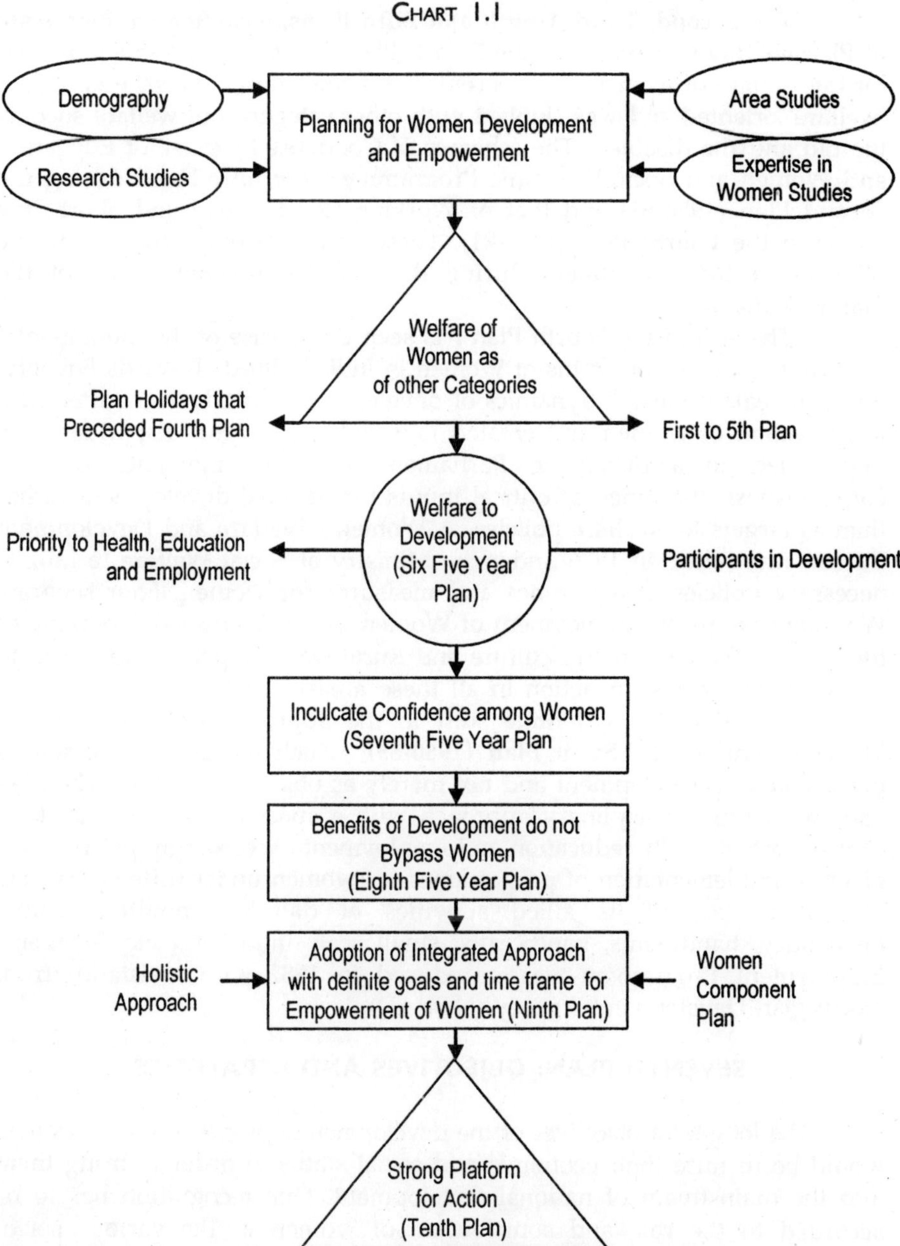

that 'the major burden of organizing activities for the benefit of vast female population has to be borne by the private agencies'. The Central Social Welfare Board (CSWB) was set-up in 1953 to promote voluntary organizations at various levels, especially at the grassroots, to take up welfare-related activities for women.

The **Second, Third, Fourth and Fifth Plans,** including the four years of Plan holiday that preceded the Fourth Plan continued the same approach for the welfare of women. The concept of women's development was mainly 'welfare' oriented and was clubbed with other categories of welfare such as the old and the disabled. The schemes of Condensed Course of Education and Women and Socio-Economic Programme were introduced during the Second Plan (1956-61) and that of Working Girl's Hostel and Short Stay Home in the Fourth Plan (1969-71). These were the only women specific schemes of the Department during the first twenty-eight years of the planning history.

The end of the Fourth Plan has seen the release of the monumental repot of Committee on Status of Women in India entitled 'Towards Equality' which revealed that the dynamics of development has adversely affected a large section of women and created new imbalances and disparities. The Report led to a debate in Parliament and the emergence of new consciousness of women as critical inputs for national development rather than as targets for welfare policies. A Women's Welfare and Development Bureau was set-up in 1976 under the Ministry of Social Welfare to initiate necessary policies, programmes and measures for women. Four separate Working Groups on Employment of Women, Adult Education Programmes for Women, Women in Agriculture and Rural Development were set-up to chalk out strategies for action in all these areas.

These led to a definite shift in the approach from 'welfare' to 'development' in the **Sixth Plan (1980-85)**, which recognized women as participants of development and not merely as objects of welfare. The Plan adopted a multi-disciplinary approach with a special thrust on the three core sectors of health, education and employment. Accordingly priority was given to implementation of programmes for women under different sectors of agriculture and its allied activities of dairying, poultry, animal husbandry, handlooms, handicrafts, small scale industries, etc. Women's Employment Programme was introduced in 1982 with assistance from Norwegian Development Agency (NORAD).

SEVENTH PLAN: OBJECTIVES AND STRATEGIES

The long-term objectives of the developmental programmes for women would be to raise their economic and social status in order to bring them into the mainstream of national development. Due recognition has to be accorded to the role and contribution of women in the various socio-economic, political and cultural activities.

In the Seventh Plan, the basic approach would be to inculcate confidence among women and bring about an awareness of their own potential for development, as also special measures would be initiated for strict enforcement of the Dowry Prohibition Act and also to prevent harassment and atrocities on women. Voluntary agencies and educational institutions would be fully involved in launching organized campaigns to combat these evils. An integrated multi-disciplinary approach would be adopted covering employment, education, health, nutrition application of science and technology and other related aspects that is extend facilities for income-generating activities and to enable women to participate actively in socio-economic development. The educational programmes will be restructured and the school curricula will be modified to higher secondary and higher education courses, formal as well as non-formal. It will be given high priority.

The **Seventh Plan (1985-90)** continued the stress on generation of both skilled and unskilled employment of women through proper education and vocational training. Two new schemes of Support to Training and Employment (STEP) and Awareness Generation Programme for Rural and Poor Women (AGP) were introduced. Three landmark reports, namely, Shram Shakti, the Report of the National Commission on Self-Employed Women and Women in Informal Sector, National Perspective Plan on Women (1988-2000) and SAARC Guidebook on Women in Development were prepared during this period. The Department of Women and Child Development was set-up in 1985 to serve as the nodal point for women and children within the National Machinery.

Alongwith women, major initiatives were taken to focus on girl child for breaking the vicious continuum, of girl child and woman, so that girls can get the much required space for physical and mental development before being asked to take up the responsibilities of wife and mother. Spatial expansion and enrichment of child development services took place through programmes in different sectors. Much emphasis was also given on human development through advocacy, mobilization and community empowerment.

Recognizing the role and contribution of women in development, the **Eighth Plan (1990-95)**, adopted the strategy to ensure that 'benefits' of development from different sectors do not bypass women and special programmes are implemented to complement the general development programmes. Two new schemes, which were introduced during this period, were Mahila Samridhi Yojana and Indira Mahila Yojana. The other major developments during this plan period were setting up of National Commission for Women and National Credit Fund for Women known as Rashtriya Mahila Kosh, and the 73rd and 74th Constitutional Amendments wherein one-third of seats of rural and urban self-governing institutions were reserved for women. The Government declared its commitment to the development of 'every child', which was manifested in the two National Plan of Action adopted in 1992, one for the Children and the other exclusively for the Girl Child.

Special initiatives for the well-being of women during the Eighth Plan (1992-1997)

* Setting up of National Commission for Women in 1992 to safeguard the interests of women.

* Setting up of Rashtriya Mahila Kosh in 1993 to meet the credit needs of poor and assetless women.
* Adoption of the National Nutritional Policy in 1993 to fulfil the constitutional commitment of improving the nutritional status of people in general and in particular that of the children, adolescent girls, expectant and nursing mothers.
* Launching of the schemes of Mahila Samriddhi Yojana in 1993 which sought to empower women by institutionalizing their savings so that they could have greater control over household resources (now being revamped).
* Launching of Indira Mahila Yojana in 1995, advocating an integrated approach for women's empowerment through Self-Help Groups.
* Proposal for setting up of National Resource Centre for Women (in progress).
* Formulation of a draft National Policy for the Empowerment of Women.[4]

THE STRATEGY FOR THE NINTH PLAN[5]

'Empowerment of Women' being one of the primary objectives of the Ninth Plan, every effort will be made to create an enabling environment where women can freely exercise their rights both within and outside home, as equal partners along with men. This will be realised through early finalisation and adoption of the 'National Policy for Empowerment of Women' which laid down definite goals, targets and policy prescriptions along with a well defined Gender Development Index to monitor the impact of its implementation in raising the status of women from time to time.

An integrated approach will be adopted towards empowering women through convergence of existing services, resources, infrastructure and manpower available in both women-specific and women-related sectors with the ultimate objective of achieving the set goal. To this effect, the Ninth Plan directs both the Centre and the States to adopt a special strategy of 'Women's Component Plan' through which, not less than 30 per cent of funds/benefits are earmarked in all the women-related sectors. It also suggests a special vigil to be kept on the flow of the earmarked funds/ benefits through an effective mechanism to ensure that the proposed strategy brings forth a holistic approach towards empowering women.

While organising women into Self-Help Groups marks the beginning of a major process of empowering women, the institutions thus developed would provide a permanent forum for articulating their needs and contributing their perspectives to development. Recognising the fact that women have been socialised only to take a back seat in public life, affirmative action through deliberate strategies will be initiated to provide equal access to and control over factors contributing to such empowerment, particularly in the areas of health, education, information, life-long learning for self-development, vocational skills, employment and income generating opportunities, land and other forms of property including through inheritance, common property, resources, credit, technology and markets, etc. To this effect, the newly elected women members and the women Chairpersons of Panchayats and the Local Bodies will be sensitised through the recently launched special training package to take the lead in ensuring that adequate funds/benefits flow towards the empowerment of women and the girl child.

Approach to the Tenth Plan—Path Ahead (See Chart 1.2)

In the context of having laid down National Policy, approach to the Tenth Plan for empowering women will be very distinct from that of the earlier Plans, as it now stands on a strong Platform for Action with definite goals, targets and a time frame. Further, as the process of empowering women initiated during the Ninth Plan is expected to continue through and beyond the Tenth Plan, there can be no better approach than translating the recently adopted National Policy for Empowerment of Women (2001) into action through—

- Creating an environment, through positive economic and social policies, for the development of women to enable them to realize their full potential;
- Allowing the *de-jure* and *de-facto* enjoyment of all human rights and fundamental freedoms by women on par with men in all spheres—political, economic, social, cultural and civil;
- Providing equal access to participation and decision-making for women in social, political and economic life of the nation;
- Ensuring equal access to women to health care, quality education at all levels, career and vocational guidance, employment, equal remuneration, occupational health and safety, social security and public office, etc.;
- Strengthening legal systems aimed at the elimination of all forms of discrimination against women;
- Changing societal attitudes and community practices by active participation and involvement of both men and women;
- Mainstreaming a gender perspective into the development process;
- Eliminating discrimination and all forms of violence against women and the girl child;
- Building and strengthening partnerships with civil society, particularly women's organization, corporate and private sector agencies;
- The Operational strategy, as prescribed in the Policy, direct all the Central Ministries and State Departments to draw up Bound Action Plans for translating the Policy into a set of concrete actions through a participatory process of consultations with all

CHART 1.2

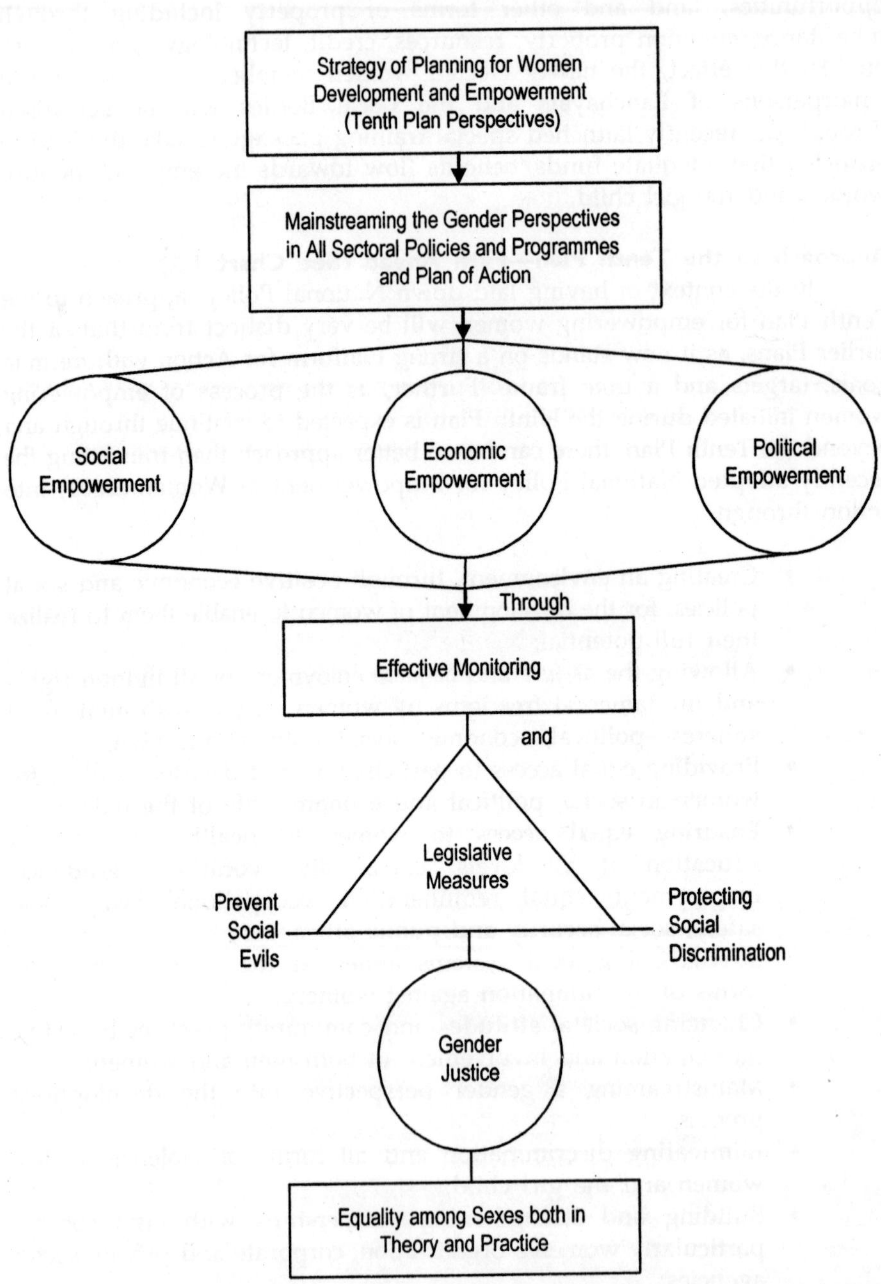

the concerned, both in the governmental and non-governmental sectors. Accordingly, the first step in this direction will be to prepare a National Plan of Action for implementation of the

Policy by the nodal Department of Women and Child Development through identifying its partners; specifying Action Points in all the women-related development sectors; developing an in-built mechanism for effective coordination and monitoring of the implementation of the Policy; besides evaluating/assessing the impact of the implementation of Policy in improving the status of women, based on a Gender Development Index;

- The Plans of Action thus prepared will clearly specify—(i) the measurable goals to be achieved along with the time targets, preferably in consonance with the time frames set by the other women-related national policies; (ii) commitment of resources; (iii) earmarking of the benefits under WCP; (iv) fixing of responsibilities for implementation of the Action Points; and (v) identification of structures and mechanisms to ensure effective review, monitoring, and impact assessment of all the related policies, Plans of Action and programmes in raising the status of women, adolescent girls and girl children on par with their counterparts. As the time target set for achieving the goals in the Policy goes beyond the Tenth Plan, the following measurable/monitorable goals set in the Tenth Plan (Approach Paper) having a direct bearing on the empowerment of women and the girl child, will be adopted in the proposed Action Plans;
- Reduction of poverty ratio by 5 percentage points by 2007 and by 15 percentage point by 2012;
- Proving gainful (high-quality) employment of the addition to the labour force over the Tenth Plan period;
- All children in school by 2003; all children to complete 5 years of schooling by 2007;
- Reduction of gender gaps in literacy and wage rates by at least 50 percent by 2007;
- Reduction in the decadal rate of population growth between 2001 and 2011 to 16.2 percent;
- Increase in Literacy rate to 75 percent within the Plan period;
- Reduction of IMR to 45 per 1000 live births by 2007 and to 28 by 2012;
- Reduction of MMR to 2 per 1000 live births by 2007 and to 1 by 2012; and
- All villages to have sustained access to potable drinking water by 2007.

ELEVENTH PLAN STRESSES ON CURBING VIOLENCE AGAINST WOMEN

Despite improving education levels and consistent economic growth, every form of violence against women including female foeticide, rape, abduction, trafficking, dowry death, domestic violence, and witchhunting, has been increasing. We have 10 million missing girls in India and this number is rising. Dowry deaths rose from 6882 in 2002 to 7026 in 2004. In 2005 highest number of dowry deaths were registered in UP, followed by Bihar, and MP. NFHS-3 shows that more than half of all Indian women believe that husbands can beat wives if they have an appropriate reason and 37% admit to being victims of spousal violence. Data from NCRB reveals little or no change in crime trends in rape and molestation. In 84-89% of the rape cases in the years 2002-04, the victim knew the offenders. In 9% cases, the offender was the father, family member, or close relative, highlighting the prevalence of incestuous and child sexual abuse. Abduction and trafficking for other exploitations accounted for 19.4% and 7.2% cases registered in 2005. Campaigns and stricter laws notwithstanding, 8.3% of registered cases in 2005 were dowry deaths, a fall of 0.3% from 2004.

Despite the high incidence of VAW, reporting is rare and conviction rates for reported cases, abysmally low; conviction rate for cruelty by husband was 19.2% and 25.5% each for dowry and rape.[6]

CONCLUSION

Report on the Status of Women rightly mentions that development in its wider perspective covers all aspects of community life. The accepted goals of national development such as maximum production, full employment, and attainment of economic equality and social justice apply equally to men and women. Their realization in an egalitarian society is not, however, possible, unless special efforts are made to assist the underprivileged groups. Our constitution therefore stresses the urgent need for promoting the educational and economic interests of the weaker sections of the people; and as women are handicapped by social customs and traditions, they need special attention to help them to play their full and proper role in a national life.[7]

"The great occupation of women should be to beautify life; to cultivate, for her own sake and that of those who surround her, all her faculties of mind, soul, and body; all her powers of enjoyment, and powers of giving enjoyment; and to diffuse beauty, elegance, and grace, everywhere. If in addition to this the activity of her nature demands more energetic and definite employment, there is never any lack of it in the world. If she loves, here natural impulse will be to associate her existence with him she loves, and to share his occupations; in which, if he loves her (with that affection of equality which along deserves to be called love) she will naturally take as strong an interest, and be as thoroughly conversant, as the most perfect confidence on his side can make her.[8]

Dr. (Miss) Mira Seth, the then Member, Planning Commission, Govt. of India, delivered the convocation address at the annual convocation of the Banasthali Vidyapeith (Deemed University). She said that the Parliament legislation has been an instruments of giving equality and status to women in our country and this has taken the place of the ancient Vedic, Pauranic, Shastra and Smriti injunctions. Our Parliament has enacted sixteen laws from the Hindu Marriage Act, 1955 to the Commission of Sati (Prevention) Act, 1987 for giving legal sanction to this principle of equality.

In the development processes and the Five Year Plans of our country, they give emphasis to the instrument of education as one of the major tools for empowering women. The focus on educational planning for women has shifted from their traditional role as housewives and mothers to non-traditional roles as producers, partners and partakers in the national development.[9]

Ms. Terjani Vakil, Former Chairman and Managing Director, Export-Import Bank of India, delivered the Convocation address at the Banasthali Vidyapith, Banasthali (Rajasthan). She said, "Keep a space for yourself as a person. Think about what you are, what you want to be, what is your personal *raison de etre* for living. What interests you, what pleases you, do that. Keep a time and space for yourself in your life. For you are an individual, a human being and not just someone's wife, mother, daughter. I would want you to think about this.[10]

Notes and References

1. GOI, Planning Commission, Draft Tenth Five Year Plan, Vol. II, 2002-07, New Delhi, p. 217.
2. ICSSR—Status of Women in India—A Synopsis of the Report of the National Commission, New Delhi, 1975, pp. 84-85.
3. *Ibid.*
4. GOI, Planning Commission, Ninth Five Year Plan, p. 336.
5. *Ibid.*, pp. 321-22.
6. GOI, Planning Commission, Eleventh Plan, 2007-12, p. 190, quoted in National Crime Broad Bureau, 2005.
7. ICSSR, Status of Women in India, p. 71.
8. Johan Sturat Alli, and Lt. T. Mill, Early Essays on Marriage and Divorce, Alice and Rossi (ed.) Essays on Sexual Equality, p. 225.
9. AIU, *University News*, July 22, 1996, pp. 8-19.
10. AIU, *University News*, April 13, 1990, p. 12.

2

Unlimited Potentialities of Women

"Create or Strengthen National Machineries and other governmental bodies advance women."

—*Strategic Objectives. H.I., Platform For Action*

Before we discuss about women development and empowerment, let us examine the potentialities of women. They possess unlimited potential energy in the form of physical, mental and social capacities. Without women, home, society, nation and even human existence would collapse. There is no work on this earth which women can not do. What is required is to tap this potential energy and change them into kinetic energy to make life meaningful for women in particular and humanity in general. Therefore, there is a need to understand women potentialities and develop them which would result in automatic empowerment.

S.R. Bakshi and Kiran Bala feel that working women have to combine their domestic and official obligations so as to ensure, as viable counterpoise, as possible. The imponderables on the home front as well as those at work place could neither be ignored nor wished away. However, each set of obligations has to be fulfilled at respective place.

The double responsibility at home and at work place is in itself a testimony of the capacity and traits of women administrators, which is not to be mistaken for any exaggerated claims for perfection in one case or the other. What is, therefore, more relevant is the fact that despite the social inhibitions and uncharitable evaluations, women have sought to combine their obligations on both the fronts and even a minimum of satisfaction in this context should serve as a beginning in the right direction.

Jyoti Sabherwal rightly feels (*Hindustan Times*, March 12, 1977) that feminine grace, dignity, the quiet rectitude should not be in conflict with feminism. The real strength lies in being able to think, choose and decide for yourself. The empowerment has to be translated into meaningful

CHART 2.1

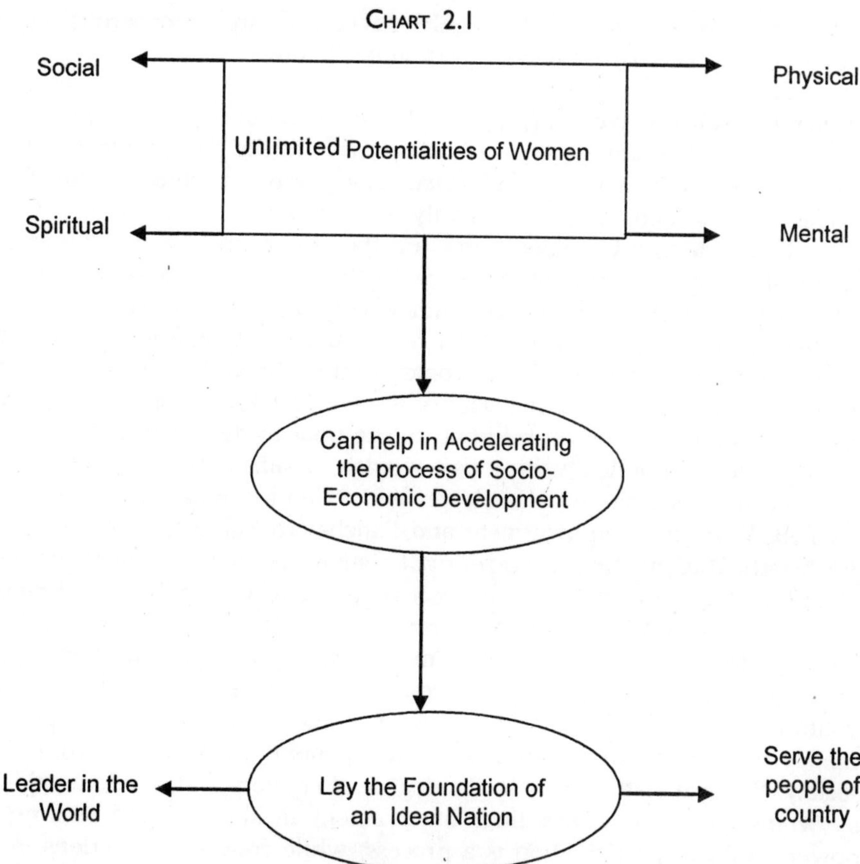

achievements, overcoming obstacles and be coming goal-oriented. To discover the spark within and lighten our lives and not seeking short-cuts for short-term gains. Each struggle is on a monumental scale for a woman achiever and it is of far greater significance that you weather all the storms with your self-esteem intact, without losing sight of what is wrong or right, and then keep moving on, at your own terms.

In the context of adopting human development as the ultimate goal of our developmental efforts, empowerment of women gains priority on the country's development agenda. We are talking about a welfare state and directing our energies towards its realization. We would lay greater stress on some, they would be the welfare of women and children. Women of India have a background of history and tradition behind them, which is inspiring, but they have suffered much from various kinds of suppression and all these have to go so that they can play their full part in the life of the nation.[1]

We cannot hope to solve the increasing international problems of economic and social development and improve the quality of human life while leaving aside half the resources of humanity.

That society would be highly developed and prosperous where women have their rightful place, expounds Manu.

The woman is the pivot around which the family, the society and humanity itself revolves. It is well said that the hands that rock the cradle, rules the world. Women play a significant role in the development of their offspring. Truly, if a man is educated, one person is educated but if the woman is educated, the whole family is educated.

Until men and women work together to secure the vast untapped potential of women, lasting solutions to the world's most serious social, economic and political problems cannot be found. There is some progress after the adoption of the UN charter for gender equality. But it is painfully slow. Nowhere in the world can women claim to have the same rights and opportunities as men. The majority of the world's 1.3 billion absolute poor are women and India's contribution to the pool of deprived and sexually, socially and economically exploited women is substantial.

Ashu Pasricha in a book review, "Gender Related Problems of Women, Women's Empowerment and Panchayati Raj in the *Tribune* dated 9th March, 2003 by Neena Joseph rightly states: A country cannot progress if half of its population is enslaved in the kitchen. India, on attaining independence, was among the first few countries to grant universal franchise to women, on a par with men. It was presumed that here rights was presumed that here rights would automatically translate into the political life of the country. The issue of women's participation in politics cannot be viewed in isolation from the general positiion of women in society. Political status refers to the degree of equality and freedom enjoyed by women in society and their involvement in shaping and sharing of power. Political participation is a process, while contesting elections in its highest form. Despite their vast strength, women occupy a secondary position in the political system. With a few exceptions, they have remained outside the domain of power, governance, decision-making bodies and political authority."

The Status of women varies enormously from one part of the world to another. However, nowhere do women enjoy equal status with men. But in the developing countries like Africa, the Middle East, Asia and Latin America, the Status of women is so low as cannot be imagined by women in the developed countries. Status is a relative term. In sociological expression, it denotes neither rank nor hierarchy but only position *vis-a-vis* others in terms of rights and obligations. In the ultimate analysis, status is "the conjunction of positions a woman occupies . . . as a worker, student, wife, mother . . . the power and prestige attached to these positions and the rights and duties she is expected to exercise." Women's status can then be analysed in terms of their participation in decision-making, access to opportunities in education, training, employment and income. In recent years, there has been an increasing recognition of the interface between women's ability to control their fertility and their exercise and enjoyment of other options in life.

We should not think that we can conceive of women development independently of the socio-economic development of the country. Women development could contribute to the development and modernization of the world. A similar message was conveyed by the UNESCO and it observed that women can play an important part in development. They represent the means through which the changes in attitudes and behaviour necessary for adaptation to the modern world can be achieved. Their responsibility for bringing up new generations means that they must also attend to the education of children and supervise their scholastic progress and critical faculty. As home managers, they have the task of improving the conditions of the family life while as household administrators, they must balance the financial budget.

A UN report also supported this view: "The exclusion of women from many aspects of the development process also has important indirect effects. First, there is the effect on the nature of their influence in the education and socialization of their children, because by and large women will pass on their own experience and attitudes. Secondly, there is the indirect effect on population growth. This is an extremely complex subject. Though it is not easy to isolate the factors affecting fertility, many of the relevant factors can be combined under the heading of Exposure of Women to Modernization."

Swami Vivekananda rightly states: In trying to define the national ideal and suggesting remedies for social evils, Swami Vivekananda's attention was naturally drawn to the plight of women. He wanted their progress, for the progress of a nation depends upon the progress of its women. He wrote about the imperative need of women's progress in the following way:

All nations have attained greatness, by paying proper respect to the women. That country and that nation which do not respect the women have never become great, nor will ever be in future. The principal reason why your race has so much degenerated is that you had no respect for these living images of Sakti. Manu says, "Where women are respected there the gods delight; and where they are not, there all works and efforts come to naught. There is no hope of rise for that family or country where there is no estimation of women, where they live in sadness."

Again he wrote: "Can you better the condition of your women? Then there will be hope for your well-being. Otherwise you remain as backward as you are now. The uplift of the women, the awakening of the masses, must come first, and then only can any real good come about for the country, for India. If the women are raised, then their children will by their noble actions glorify the name of the country—then will culture, knowledge, power and devotion awaken in the country.' But he cautioned that we should not judge their condition through the eyes of others having different standards of morality and outlook on life.

Mahatma Gandhi himself wrote, on women's role in *Harijan,* (February 14, 1940), "My opinion is that, just as fundamentally man and woman are one, their problem must be one in essence. The soul in both is the same. The two live the same life, have the same feelings. Each is a complement of the other. The one cannot live without the other's active help. But somehow or other man has dominated woman from ages past, and so woman has developed an inferiority complex. She has believed in the truth of man's interested teaching that she is inferior to him. But the peers among men have recognized her equal status."

We are sure that new millennium would usher an era where women can enjoy the life in full and in all fields to ensure socio-economic justice.

To awaken people, it is the women who must be awakened. Once she is on the move, the family moves, the villages moves, the nation moves.

"The great occupation of women should be to beautify life; to cultivate, for her own sake and that of those who surround her, all her faculties of mind, soul, and body; all her powers of enjoyment, and powers of giving enjoyment; and to diffuse beauty, elegance, and grace, everywhere. If in addition to this the activity of her nature demands more energetic and definite employment, there is never any lack of it in the world; if she loves, here natural impulse will be to associate her existence with him she loves, and to share his occupations; in which, if he loves her (with that affection of equality which along deserves to be called love), she will naturally take as strong an interest, and be as thoroughly conversant, as the most perfect confidence on his side can make her.[2]

In ancient India, women enjoyed a high place of respect in the society as mentioned in Rigveda and other scriptures. 13 (Rigveda. 2/17/fil; 9/67/10.12) Volumes can be written about the status of our women and their heroic deeds from the Vedic period to the modern times. But later on, because of social, political and economic changes, women lost their status and were relegated to the background. Many evil customs and traditions stepped in, which enslaved the women and tied them to boundaries of the house. The untold miseries and sufferings of women of the 19th century awakened the conscience of mankind. Many reformers like Raja Rammohan Roy, Swami Dayanand, Justice Ranade, Mahatma Gandhi, and other championed the cause of the emancipation of women. The Constitution of India also prohibits any discrimination on grounds of sex. Many laws have also been enacted by the Government of India to protect the rights of women.

Anna Kajumulo Tibaijuka, Executive Director (UNCHS), says: 'Where women are not involved in public decision-making, the quality of services deteriorates. It is time for change from the practice of leaving women to do only the dirty work. We are aware that women have been instrumental in the urban social movements that aim at improving urban poor neighbourhoods. They do this because they want to protect their families' health and create livable communities. These numerous women's initiatives must be recognized. By involving them in governance structures and by addressing the things they care about, in urban policy, planning and management. Women and men have specific and different needs, in areas such as transport, public spaces, the implementation of by-laws and security. These must all be addressed'.[3]

While the impact of various developmental policies, plans and programmes implemented over the last few decades have brought forth a perceptible improvement in the socio-economic status of women, problems like illiteracy, ignorance, discrimination and violence continue to persist even today. The following paragraph give an account of achievements in the selected areas of demography and vital statistics; health and family welfare; literacy and education; work and employment; decision-making; political participation, etc.[4]

There is no doubt that women possess immense potentialities in all fields of socio-economic development. However, the need is to provide opportunities which can promote translating the potential capacities into kinetic energies.

As pointed out in one of the UN Publications, "In every country, whether it is new or long established, whether it is underdeveloped or highly developed, any programme of economic or fiscal development, of improvement in education, health, labour and social conditions and of reform and reconstruction in any of the public services can only succeed if it is supported by machinery and method established under sound principles of public administration and adapted to the circumstances of the country concerned."

The intention of policy-makers and planners to promote Women Development and Empowerment is to be ensured by Organisations entrusted with this work. This requires an ideal structure, material and personnel so that the intentions of policy-makers are translated into action. There is also a need of constant organizational analysis based on method study, Work Measurement and Manpower Planning. In this Book, "Women Development and Empowerment—Administrative Framework" we have engaged our attention on existing framework but also what these should be based on research and analysis so that in the 21st century we can feel proud in achieving our cherished goal of Women Development and Empowerment.

A question arises as to how the developing countries can translate their aims and objectives enshrined in their constitution as well as legislation for Women Development and Empowerment suffering from abject poverty, disease, squalor, hunger, unemployment, low status and other socio-economic ailments. It requires an overhaul of the old administrative structures and creating a new administrative set-up required for socio-economic development of women. Organizations are not mere structures but action systems. Action system is a structured device through which resources are mobilized and transformed by the use of certain skills and technology to produce pre-designed output. The prevailing administrative system dealing with women development and empowerment is a basic aid to the achievement of women welfare objectives. If the design is unsound, the achievement of objectives is likely to fall short of expectations. Administration can provide the means whereby the most effective use can be made of the knowledge and skills of the personnel engaged in different activities. The benefits of modern science and technology can reach the women only if services for women are properly planned and effectively implemented. An increase in the scientific nature of determination is an important factor in raising its efficiency.

The prevailing administrative set-up dealing with women issues in the developing countries is in a state of crisis. Its design and methods are inadequate and outworn. There is a need to design an integrated management system which may cover the planning of work programs, budget preparation, resource programming, reviewing and evaluating results and definitions of programs and aims to promote women development and empowerment. Besides, obsolete methods of work must be improved or replaced. Our experience during the last three decades has demonstrated that the development plans have not been satisfactorily implemented because of inadequate administrative performance resulting from out-dated administrative system entailing organizational defects, lack of co-ordination, complex and cumbersome administrative and financial procedures, etc. These defects and deficiencies need to be corrected in order to bring about a sharp reduction in the administrative obstacles to development of women and to bridge the gap between aspirations and performance.

The concept and role of national machinery was reviewed and redefined at the Beijing Conference. The Platform for Action states that national machinery for the advancement of women is the central policy-coordinating unit within a government. Its main task is to support government wide mainstreaming of a gender-equality perspective in all policy areas. The necessary conditions for an effective functioning of such national machinery include:

(a) Location at the highest possible level in the government, falling under the responsibility of a Cabinet Minister;
(b) The non-government women's movement has made its contribution to the evolutionary process of women's empowerment;
(c) Institutional mechanisms of processes that facilitate, as appropriate, decentralized planning, implementation and monitoring with a view to involving non-governmental organizations and community organizations from the grassroots upwards;
(d) Sufficient resources in terms of budget and professional capacity; and
(e) Opportunity to influence development of all government policies.

A plethora of departments and other agencies exist to promote women empowerment like, Department of Women and Child Development,

National Commission For Women, The Central Social Welfare Board, The National Institute of Public Co-operation and Child Development, Rastriya Mahila Kosh, National Credit Fund for Women, State Departments of Women and Child Development, State Commission for Women, the Lok Sabha Committee on Empowerment of Women, Gender Focal points, Women's Cells Planning Commission of India, UGC, etc.

Many formations exist within large matrix of government structures, such as Committees, Boards and Commission set-up from time to time to focus on a specific area in an intensive manner exist. These are predominately 'non-official' though constituted by and retaining a vital link with the state.

All the defects in the Administrative and Management Systems result from the poor performance of the personnel engaged in the system. The capacity of the Government like all other organizations depends, to a great extent, upon the capability, intelligence, experience, motivation, ethics, ethos, responsiveness, and responsibility of the staff engaged in them. From the top to the bottom, from the centre to the periphery—and in-between—it is the men that make the machinery of administration work. Bacon, philosopher and administrator has rightly said, "It is vain for princes to take counsel concerning matters if they take no counsel likewise concerning persons; for all matters are as dead images, and the life of the execution of the affairs lies in the good choice of persons." Therefore, the first and foremost task of the Government must be to pay attention to the development of personnel so that they can achieve results. Administrators and Managers of all categories and levels cannot fail to be aware of the highly accelerated interest which has been prevalent during the last two decades in improving the tools that are used in the operation of women Organizations. Economic necessity, socio-economic changes, scientific and technological advancement, scarcity of resources and other factors are making the executive comprehend these trends. To get the benefit of this new thinking and advancement in the theory and practice of administrative management the executives must have a basic understanding of the nature of management and the changing principles of Organization to improve performance. Since Women Development and Empowerment is a challenging task, therefore, the personnel appointed to these Organisations should posses—Competence, Capability, capacity to communicate, cultural understanding and missionary zeal and face unfavourable environment.

Andrew Mariadoss Packajraj in his article, "Administration that Delights the People" in MIG, July to Sept. 2000, rightly mentioned that people in India now expect the Governments of India to P-E-R-F-O-R-M. They are disenchanted with hollow promises, speeches, rhetoric's and eloquent repertories. They don't just desire effective and responsive Governments but they demand a Government that meets their aspiration. It is for the Government to be effective and responsive in their (Government's) own interest, otherwise they will be thrown out for falling short of people's expectations.

The three most vital players in the arena are the Elected Ruling Government, the Appointed Administrative Machinery and the Demanding Public. While the ultimate responsibility and answerability/accountability rests with the first component, the actual job of delivering results rests on the administrative machinery. It is, in the ultimate analysis a joint team effort of the three but any weak link can jeopardise the outcome and efforts of any other.

The Platform for Action is an agenda for women's empowerment. It emphasis that women share common concerns that can be addressed only by working together and in partnership with men towards the common goal of gender equality around the world. It respects and values the full diversity of women's situations and conditions and recognizes that some women face particular barriers to their empowerment. The success of the Platform for Action will require a strong commitment on the part of governments, international organizations and institutions at all levels and a sound administrative system. Thus, greater effort is still needed to sensitize policy-makers so that gender impact analysis is incorporated into the development of economic and social policies. Capacity building and tools of ensuring competence and commitment to the goal of mainstreaming gender into all walks of life must be made available at a more rapid pace both within government and civil society.

However, the practice, women potentialities are not recognized and they are not given their due status inspite of realizing the potentialities of women.

Gender equality is an issue of primary importance to the welfare and progress of all nations. It is fundamental to achieving people-centered development. What humanity needs is a world that is free, fair and equal; a world that will have no discrimination, violence, or exploitation, a world where opportunity and prosperity are shared by all. So, why is violence against Women and discrimination so widespread all over the world? It is because discrimination begins in the minds of people, where gender-bias becomes a habit in thought and action. These have over centuries developed deep-rooted cultural traditions which regard women as subservient, the girl-child as a liability, and discrimination as normal. The root of all prejudice is ignorance. Education, greater awareness, public policy and the media can play an important role in eradicating such prejudices. Recent work has brought out very clearly that women's literacy and educated participation of women in decisions within and outside family strongly influence the relative respect and regard for women's well-being.

XIth Five Year Plan, 2002-07 mentions the following to optimize women potentialities.

Gender Justice

Eliminate all forms of gender discrimination and, thus, enable women to enjoy not only *de-jure* but also *de-facto* rights and fundamental freedom on par with men in all spheres, viz. political, economic, social, civil, cultural, etc. through—

- Complete eradication of female foeticide and female infanticide through effective enforcement of both the Indian Penal Code, 1860 and the Pre-Natal Diagnostic Technique (Regulation and Prevention of Misuse) Act, 1994 with most stringent measures of punishment so that a very harsh path is set for the illegal practitioners.
- Adopting measures that take into account the reproductive rights of women to enable them to exercise their reproductive choices.
- Working out strategies, in close collaboration with the Ministry of Labour, to ensure extension of employment opportunities and thus, remove inequalities in employment—both in work and accessibility.
- Initiating intervention macro-economic level to amend existing-legislations to improve women's access to productive assets and resources.
- Ensuring that the value added by women in the informal Sector as workers and producers is recognized through redefinition/re-interpretation of conventional concepts of work and preparation of Satellite and National Accounts.
- Defining the Women's Component Plan (WCP) clearly and identifying the schemes/programmes/projects under each Ministry/Department which should be covered under WCP and ensuring the adoption of women-related mechanisms through which funds/benefits flow to women from these sectors.
- Initiating action for enacting new women-specific legislations; amending the existing women-related legislation, if necessary, based on the review made and recommendations already available to ensure gender justice, besides, reviewing all the subordinate legislations to eliminate all gender discriminatory references.
- Expending action to legislate reservation of not less than 1/3rd seats for women in the Parliament and in the State Legislative Assemblies and thus ensure women in proportion to their numbers reach decision-making bodies so that their voices are heard.
- Arresting the ever-increasing violence against women and the Girl Child including the Adolescent girls on top priority with the strength and support of a well-planned Programme of Action prepared in consultation with all the concerned, especially the enforcement authorities; implementing effectively with the strength of the Law and Order Authorities both at the centre and state levels and assessing the situation.

- Expediting standardization of a Gender Development Index based on which the gender segregated data will be collected at national, state and district levels; compiled/collated and analysed to assess the progress made in improving the status of women at regular intervals with an ultimate objective of achieving equality on par with men.
- Initiating/accelerating the process of societal reorientation towards creating a Gender-Just Society.[5]

CONCLUSION

In the context of adopting human development as the ultimate goal of our developmental efforts, empowerment of women gains priority on the country's development agenda. We are talking about a welfare state and directing our energies towards its realization. We would lay greater stress on some, they would be the welfare of women and children. Women of India have a background of history and tradition behind them, which is inspiring, but they have suffered much from various kinds of suppression and all these have to go so that they can play their full part in the life of the nation.[6]

We cannot hope to solve the increasing international problems of economic and social development and improve the quality of human life while leaving aside half the resources of humanity.

That society would be highly developed and prosperous where women have their rightful place expounds Manu.

The woman is the pivot around which the family, the society and humanity itself revolves. It is well said that the hands that rock the cradle rules the world. Women play a significant role in the development of their offspring. Truly, if a man is educated, one person is educated but if the woman is educated, the whole family is educated.

Notes and References

1. Annual Report, Department of Women and Child Development, 2001-02.
2. John Sturat Mill and H.T. Mill, Early Essays on Marriage and Divorce, Alice and Rossi (ed.) Essays on Sexual Equality, p. 225.
3. *Shelter*, Vol. III, No. 4, Oct. 2000, p. IV.
4. GOI, Planning Commission, Xth Plan, 2007-12, p. 229.
5. GOI, Planning Commission, 2002-07, Xth Five Year Plan, 2007-12, p. 249.
6. Annual Report, Department of Women and Child Development, 2001-02.

3

Women Empowerment

Empowerment as a concept was first brought at the International Women's Conference in 1985 at Nairobi. The conference concluded that empowerment is a redistribution of power and control of resources in favour of women through positive intervention.

The Programme of Action 1992 has comprehensively given the below mentioned parameters of empowerment of women:

- Enhance self-esteem and self-confidence in women.
- Build a positive image of women by recognizing their contribution to the society, polity and economy.
- Develop in them an ability to think critically.
- Foster decision-making and action through collective process.
- Enable women to make informed choices in areas like education, employment and health especially reproductive health.
- Ensure equal participation in the developmental process.
- Provide information, knowledge and skill for economic independence.
- Enhance access to legal literacy and information related to their rights and entitlements in the society with a view to enhance their participation on an equal footing in all areas.

The special attention given to the needs and problems of women to enable them to enjoy and exercise their Constitutional equality of status, along with other specific provisions relating to the hitherto suppressed sections of our society have led many scholars to describe the Indian Constitution as a 'social' document embodying the objectives of a social revolution. There is no doubt that the Constitution contemplates attainment of an entirely new social order by making deliberate departures in norms and institutions of democratic governance from the inherited social, political and economic systems. In doing so the Constitution assigns primacy to law as an instrument of directed social change. It thus demands of the legislature, the executive and the judiciary, continuous vigilance and responsiveness to the relationship between law and social transformation in contemporary India. (See Chart 3.1)

We believe:

1. that equality of women is necessary, not merely on the grounds of social justice, but as a basic condition for social, economic and political development of the nation;
2. that in order to release women from their dependent and unequal status, improvement of their employment opportunities and earning power has to be given the highest priority;
3. that society owes a special responsibility to women because of their child-bearing function. Safe bearing and rearing of children is an obligation that has to be shared by the mother, the father and society;
4. that the contribution made by an active housewife to the running and management of a family should be admitted as economically and socially productive and contributing to national savings and development;
5. that marriage and motherhood should not become a disability in women's fulfilling their full and proper role in the task of national development. Therefore, it is important that society, including women themselves, must accept their responsibility in this field;
6. that disabilities and inequalities imposed on women have to be seen in the total context of a society, where large sections of the population—male and female, adults and children—suffer under the oppression of an exploitative system. It is not possible to remove these inequalities for women only. Any policy or movement for the emancipation and development of women has to form a part of a total movement for removal of inequalities and oppressive social institutions, if the benefits and privileges won by such action are to be shared by the entire women population and not be monopolized by a small minority; and
7. that if our society is to move in the direction of the goals set by the Constitution, then special temporary measures will be necessary, to transform *de-jure* into *de-facto* equality.[1]

The World Summit held during Nov. 25-28, 1996 at Trinidad and Tobago was the First Conference of Ministers Responsible for Women Affairs. 45 Commonwealth Countries participated and very useful decisions were taken regarding the implementation of Commonwealth Plan of Action on gender and development, gender management systems, gender integration into politics and conflict resolution, integration of gender concerns into macro-economic policies and women's human rights. The next meeting was held at Edinburgh in 1997. However, rigorous efforts are being made throughout the world and various schemes/programmes have been launched to minimize the gender bias, and offer ample opportunities to bring women at par with men in respect to education, employment, human rights and decision-making roles, etc. Still status of women varies from country to country and even within a country. It varies with the arbitration in the locality (rural/urban), religion, caste and community. It manifests in terms of level of education, occupation, income, restrictions imposed in their activities and financial independence understand the Indian scenario, history that there were distinct stages of rise and fall of in the status of women.[2]

Empowerment of women being one of the nine primary objectives of the Ninth Plan, every effort will be made to create an enabling environment where women can freely exercise their rights both within and outside home, as equal partners along with men. This will be realized through early finalization and adoption of the 'National Policy for Empowerment of Women' which laid down definite goals, targets and policy prescriptions along with a well defined Gender Development Index to monitor the impact of its implementation in raising the status of women from time to time.

An integrated approach will be adopted towards empowering women through convergence of existing services, resources, infrastructure and manpower available in both women-specific and women-related sectors with the ultimate objective of achieving the set goal. To this effect, the Ninth Plan directs both the Centre and the States to adopt a special strategy of 'Women's Component Plan' through which, not less than 30 per cent of funds/benefits are earmarked in all the women-related sectors. It also suggests a special vigil to be kept on the flow of the earmarked funds/benefits through an effective mechanism to ensure that the proposed strategy brings forth a holistic approach towards empowering women.

While organising women into Self-Help Groups marks the beginning of a major process of empowering women, the institutions thus developed would provide a permanent forum for articulating their needs and contributing their perspectives to development. Recognising the fact that women have been socialised only to take a back seat in public life, affirmative action through deliberate strategies will be initiated to provide equal access to and control over factors contributing to such empowerment, particularly in the areas of health, education, information, life-long learning for self-development, vocational skills, employment and income generating opportunities, land and other forms of property including through inheritance, common property, resources, credit, technology and markets, etc. To this effect, the newly elected women members and the women Chairpersons of Panchayats and the Local Bodies will be sensitised through the recently launched special training package to take the lead in ensuring that adequate funds/benefits flow towards the empowerment of women and the girl child.

COMMITMENTS OF THE NINTH PLAN (1997-2002)

Objective

- Empowering Women as the Agents of Social Change and Development

Strategies

- To create an enabling environment for women to exercise their rights, both within and outside home, as equal partners along with men through early finalisation and adoption of "National Policy for Empowerment of women."
- To expedite action to legislate reservation of not less than 1/3rd seats for women in the Parliament and in the State Legislative Assemblies and thus ensure adequate representation of women in decision-making.
- To adopt an integrated approach towards empowering women through effective convergence of existing services, resources, infrastructure and manpower in both women specific and women-related sectors.
- To adopt a special strategy of "Women's Component Plan" to ensure that not less than 30 percent of funds/benefits flow to women from other developmental sectors.
- To organise women into self-help groups and thus mark the beginning of a major process of empowering women.
- To accord high priority to reproductive child health care.
- To universalise the on-going supplementary feeding programme-Special Nutrition Programme (SNP) and Mid-Day Meals (MDM).
- To ensure easy and equal access to education for women and girls through the commitments of the Special Action Plan of 1998.
- To initiate steps, to eliminate gender bias in all educational programmes.
- To institute plans for free education for girls upto college level, including professional courses.
- To equip women with necessary skills in the modern upcoming trades which could keep them gainfully engaged besides making them economically independent and self-reliant.
- To increase access to credit through setting up of a 'Development Bank for Women Entrepreneurs in small and tiny sectors'.[3]

Women who number 498.7 million according to 2001 census represent 48.2 per cent of country's population of 1,027.01 million. The development of women has always been the central focus in developmental planning, since Independence. Though there have been various shifts in policy approaches in the last 50 years from the concept of welfare in the 70s, to development in the 80s, and now the empowerment in the 90s, the Department of Women and Child Development, since its inception has been implementing special programmes for holistic development and empowerment of women with welfare programme, particularly in the sectors of health, education, rural and urban development, etc. Initiatives undertaken in the area of women's empowerment include:[4]

- Welfare and Support Services
- Employment and Training
- Socio-economic Programme
- Swayamsiddha
- Swa-shakti Project
- Balika Samriddhi Yojna
- Plan of Action to combat Sexual Exploitation of Women and Children
- Declaring 2001 as Women's Empowerment Year
- Instituting National Commission for Women
- Rashtriya Mahila Kosh
- National Institute of Public Cooperation and Child Development
- Central Social Welfare Board
- Food and Nutrition Board
- Information and Mass Education

The Constitution of India has guaranteed equality before law and equal protection of law (Art. 14) and prohibits discriminatory provisions for women and children (Art. 15). It has made provisions to prohibit traffic in human beings and provides for just and human conditions of work along with maternity relief (Art. 23 and Art. 42). It is a constitutional duty of every citizen to renounce practices derogatory to the dignity of women (Art. 51A).

To quote J.P. Singh Indisputably, India is committed to the cause of empowerment of women. However, the journey towards progress is long and arduous. In a world of challenge and competition, both the state and the society have to constantly attune themselves to the changing needs. It is recognized that the development of the country is not possible if women, comprising half of the human resource, as labour force and citizens, stay away from the national development process. Women's participation in the political process of development is of crucial importance from the consideration of both equity and development. India has heralded the new millennium by pronouncing the year 2001 as Women's Empowerment Year. In terms of political empowerment, nearly seven lakh women occupy positions as members and chairpersons of grassroots democratic institutions in India, following the reservation clause in 73rd and 74th Amendment providing one-third seats at district, taluk, village and municipal level for women. This is for the first time in our history that an opportunity has been provided for such substantial entry of women in public life and large numbers have come forward to tackle the challenge of leadership at all levels of Panchayats. In fact, right from the days of freedom struggle the Indian women have been consistently encouraged to take part in the active politics. But due to the vitiated political milieu, resulting from increasing politicization and criminalisation of politics, the level of political participation of women has been adversely affected despite the fact that there has been a marked increase in the level of literacy and political awareness of women.[5]

It is recognized that the goals of poverty alleviation are difficult to achieve without the full and active participation of women, who constitute a large section of the workforce in the country. Women's empowerment is critical to the process of development of the community and, therefore, bringing them into the mainstream of development has been a major concern of the Government.

Towards this end and in order to empower women, an enabling environment, with requisite policies and programmes, institutional mechanisms at various levels and adequate financial resources has been created. The Ministry of Rural Development has special components for women in its programmes and funds are earmarked as 'Women's Component' to ensure flow of adequate resources for their development.[6]

The 73rd and 74th Amendments to the Constitution passed by the Parliament in 1992 and ratified in 1993 provide for 33 per cent reservation among elected representatives to the local governments. This has been hailed as a watershed achievement in empowerment of women, as over one million rural women have joined village panchayat posts as sarpanch or adhyaksha or members of community administration.

Policy for the Empowerment of Women

In order to address the concerns of women in society, the Government of India has established the Department of Women and Child Development within the Ministry of Human Resource Development. A National Policy for the Empowerment of Women, 2001, provides the framework for addressing women's issues. The objectives of the policy are as follows:

- Creating an environment through positive economic and social policies for full development of women to enable them to realize their full potential.
- The *de-jure* and *de-facto* enjoyment of all human rights and fundamental freedom by women on equal basis with men in all spheres—political, economic, social, cultural and civil.
- Equal access to participation and decision-making of women in social, political and economic life of the nation.
- Equal access to women to health care, quality education at all levels, career and vocational guidance, employment, equal remuneration, occupational health and safety, social security and public office, etc.

- Strengthening legal systems aimed at elimination of all forms of discrimination against women.
- Changing societal attitudes and community practices by active participation and involvement of both men and women.
- Mainstreaming a gender perspective in the development process.
- Elimination of discrimination and all forms of violence against women and the girl child.
- Building and strengthening partnerships with civil society, particularly women's organizations.

Poornima Advani in her Preface to Year of Endeavour, 2002 rightly states that the last century has been witness to several revolutions, economic and political, with various 'isms' e.g. socialism, capitalism, fascism, etc. wrestling for primacy. They sought to redefine the relations between classes and masses, and between man and man. But the social revolution which promises to transform society even more fundamentally has just begun. This is the movement for women's rights, which affects every home, every factory and every office. Concerning, as it does, half the population of the globe, that is, all womankind, this issue will be centre stage in the political discourse of the coming decades world-wide.

The winds of change have been blowing furously here at home also. The Constitutional mandate of equality for all citizens, the myriad law and rulings designed to protect this equality and the numerous schemes introduced by the Government to strengthen women's status have erected a frame-work for protecting and promoting the rights and conditions of women in our country.

However, true equality and dignity are still a far cry for women. Social degradation, economic inequality and criminal wrongs are commonly head of even today. There is thus a huge shadow that falls between the promise and the reality.

POLICIES AND PROGRAMMES: A REVIEW (See Chart 3.1)

Development of women has been receiving attention of the government right from the very First Plan (1951-56). But, the same has been treated as a subject of 'welfare' and clubbed together with the welfare of the disadvantaged groups like destitute, disabled, aged, etc. the Central Social Welfare Board (CSWB), set-up in 1953, acts an Apex Body at national level promote voluntary action at various levels, especially at the grassroots, to take up welfare-related activities for women and children. The Second to Fifth Plans (1956-79) continued to reflect the very same welfare approach, besides giving priority to women's education, and launching measures to improve maternal and child health services, supplementary feeding for children and expectant and nursing mothers.

The shift in the approach from 'welfare' to 'development' of women could take place only in the Sixth Plan (1980-85). Accordingly, the Sixth

CHART 3.1

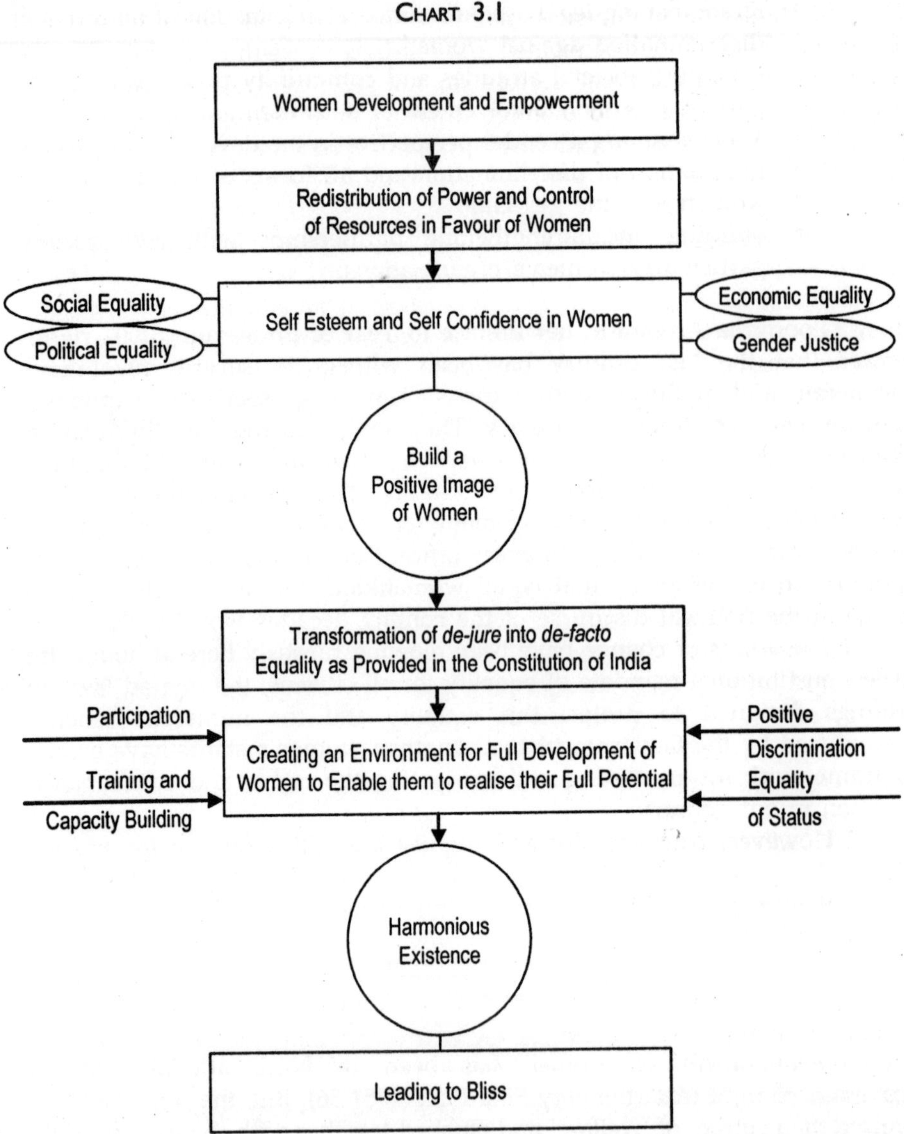

Plan adopted a multi-disciplinary approach with a special thrust on the three core sectors of health, education and employment. In the Seventh Plan (1985-90), the developmental programmes continued with the major objective of raising their economic and social status and bringing them into the mainstream of national development. A significant step in this direction was to identity/promote the 'Beneficiary-Oriented Schemes' (BOS) in various developmental sectors which extended direct benefits to women. The thrust on generation of both skilled and unskilled employment through proper education and vocational training continued. The Eighth Plan (1992-

97), with human development as its major focus, played a very important role in the development of women. It promised to ensure that benefits of development from different sectors do not by-pass women, implement special programmes and to monitor the flow of benefits to women from other development sectors and enable women to function as equal partners and participants in the development process.

The Ninth Plan (1997-2002) made two significant changes in the conceptual strategy of planning for women. Firstly, 'Empowerment of Women' became one of the nine primary objectives of the Ninth Plan. To this effect, the Approach of the Plan was to create an enabling environment where women could freely exercise their rights both within and outside home, as equal parterns along with men. Secondly, the Plan attempted 'convergence of existing service' available in both women-specific and women-related sectors. To this effect, it directed both the center and the states to adopt a special strategy of 'Women's Component Plan' (WCP) through which not less than 30 per cent of funds/benefits flow to women from all the general development sectors. It also suggested that a special vigil be kept on the flow of the earmarked funds/benefits through an effective mechanism to ensure that the proposed strategy brings forth a holistic approach towards empowering women.

To ensure that other general developmental sectors do not by-pass women and benefits from these sectors continue to flow to them, a special mechanism of monitoring the 27 BOS for women was put into action in 1986, at the instance of the Prime Minister's Office (PMO). The same continues to be an effective instrument till today.

SUGGESTIONS TO STRENGTHEN WOMEN EMPOWERMENT

Women empowerment is not something which can be handed over to women. This is a process which involves sincerity, earnestness and capacity and capability on the part of both men and women. It is a challenging task in village India as even today, if a woman is to travel to her parents house or go somewhere, she must be accompanied by some male members of the family. She cannot take an independent decision. She feels even subordinate to her son. Let us discuss ways and means to improve the process of women empowerment.

1. Low Status: Need of Upgradation

Most of the women in a family feel inferior to male members of the family. From olden times, women act as workers and do not take part in decision-making. This attitude needs change to make women as part and parcel of the family by carving out an important place for her. Swami Vivekananda repeatedly stressed the need for cultivating the faith in one self: "The ideal of faith in ourselves is of the greatest help to us. If faith in ourselves had been more extensively taught and practised. I am sure a very large portion of the evils and miseries that we have would have vanished."

Throughout the history of mankind, if any motive power has been more potent than another in the lives of all great men and women, it is that of faith in themselves. Born with the consciousness, that they were to be great they come great. Prof. V.C. Kulandaiswamy, Former Vice-Chancellor, Indira Gandhi National Open University, New Delhi, delivered the convocation address at the Eleventh Convocation of the Avinashilingam Institute for Home Science and Higher Education for Women (Deemed University), Coimbatore. He said, "Women's studies should (therefore) concentrate on the nature of opportunities that now emerge for women to prepare themselves for playing an equal role—not necessarily identical role—with men in the affairs of the society. The research studies should consider the areas of disability, the handicaps, the impediments and the prejudices that women face and devise ways of educating and enabling men and women to remove them."[7]

2. Low Morale: Need of Creating Positive Attitude

At present women possess low morale which is a depressing situation where she does not get a sense of belongingness. We must develop positive attitude in her by enlightening her about her creative potential for contributing to the overall development of self, family and society. Dr. (Miss) A.S. Desai, Chairperson, University Grants Commission, delivered the Convocation Address at the annual convocation on the S.N.D.T. Women's University, Mumbai. She said, "While education for women is a necessary condition for social development, it has to be accompanied by increasing levels of awareness with respect to the place of women in a patriarchal society, the means to change their position and role, as also to assure that women's rights are seen as an important and major component of human rights.

All this leads us to consider the importance of empowerment of women achieved through both education and greater social awareness. No one, ever in history, has achieved rights without a struggle. Women have to unite across caste, class, ethnicity and religion, if change has to be brought. Political empowerment is now made possible for women at the local levels through the 73rd and 74th Amendments to the Constitution. It has brought a million women opportunity to participate in decision-making and policies at the village, block and district levels as also in the urban municipal corporations. Educated women have a major social obligation to participate in this great experiment, uniquely launched in our country by reserving one-third of the seats at this level. Expanding women's education will serve no purpose if women do not participate in policy and decision-making.[8]

3. Dependence upon Men since Childhood: Need of Independence from Early Stages

In Indian villages, girls remain dependent upon father, brother or cousin and this very feeling continue in their married life. We must give capacity building training to girls in schools to be independent. It does not mean breaking the linkages of family rather it leads to strengthening the bond on an equal platform.

4. Change of Attitude of Men towards Capability of Women

Men have built an impression through observation that women are inferior and they cannot face emerging situations. This attitude has to be changed through positive examples from our country and abroad. Pictures of women doing all types of work need to be screened and shown to both men and women. Though, attitude is changing but it is slow and needs to be accelerated. Face life and its upheavals around you. Be active and tirelessly dynamic. Each exertion undertaken is a shooting spark of "life" from the well of Existence in you. Fearlessly work with a clear vision, plan and selflessly execute it. Fear not sweat! Hesitate not to face disappointments. Live life, so long as you are alive. Grow through work. Evolve in work. Expand while striving. Make your own life thus rich and sweet. You can. You must. The highest and noblest type of an individual working in the world is known as the "man of achievements" (Yogi).

Such men work, neither for the sake of wages, nor for success; they are not after mere sensual pleasures, nor do they aspire to reform the world; they delicately perform their obligatory duties finding peace and fulfilment in their very activity. Their fulfilment consists of doing their duties to the best of their ability without claiming any rights and they are totally unmindful of whether the society commends or condemns their actions.

Sri K. Anbazhgan, Minister of Education, Govt. of Tamil Nadu, delivered the Convocation Address at the eighth convocation of Avinashilingam Institute for Home Science and Higher Education for Women (Deemed University). He said, "Women's empowerment is a complex issue having many societal ramifications. It cannot be solved by women alone. Men also should understand the need for women's empowerment and support their cause. Women should learn to articulate their needs and rights in clear terms and work for them, without at the same time upsetting the domestic harmony and family life. They have to work tirelessly in their march towards their empowerment and a life with an identity of their own."

Women's empowerment is a complex issue having many societal ramifications. It cannot be solved by women alone. Men also should understand the need for women's empowerment and support their cause. Women should learn to articulate their needs and rights in clear terms and work for them, without at the same time upsetting the domestic harmony and family life. They have to work tirelessly in their march towards their empowerment and a life with an identity of their own. The great poet Bharathidasan had laid down categorically that until women became independent, the independence of the nation is meaningless. In the literature, we find several attempts to uphold the dignity of womanhood. Hence women should use their education to recognize their status in life and to improve by taking up and exercising their rights by themselves. Education is a means of liberation for everyone. But it is more so for women.[9]

5. Women Elected Representatives of PRIs give way to their men Folk: Need of taking Independent Decisions

Women representatives in PRIs must be trained in the art and science of decision-making so that they are not influenced by extraneous factors. They should discuss among other women and take their opinion. They must develop leadership qualities. K.D. Gangrade in his Article, "Gandhi and Empowerment of Women—Miles to Go", Smt. Savita Singh (International Centre of Gandhian Studies and Research, Gandhi Samiti and Darshan Samiti, New Delhi, "The 74th and 73rd Constitutional Amendments on Panchayati Raj and Nagarpalika with 33 per cent reservation for women has created political space for women. But in most cases they exercise "proxy" power on behalf of men. In reality women have never been able to get more than ten-percent seats in Parliament or other bodies of decision-making. It is hoped that 81st Constitutional Amendment when passed will give 33 per cent reservation of seats in Parliament and State legislatures. This will go a long way to have their say. We should be ashamed of ourselves that after more than half a century of freedom we have neither been able to clothe our women nor able to provide them something as basic as secure and adequate number of toilets and shelter even in the capital city of Delhi."

6. Lack of Interest and Enthusiasm: Need of Enthusiasm

Women lack interest in PRI on account of luke warm attitude to PRIs by state and Union Government. To make life worthwhile and fruitful, they must generate enthusiasm within themselves. Generation of enthusiasm will take place when they discover for themselves a goal and attach ourselves to the Altar with a spirit of dedication, reverence and love. Once they have surrendered themselves to it, the ideal itself will provide them with the inspiration and strength. Then nothing can hinder the progress of women's march towards that Goal and the ideal. The love for the ideal will overcome and vanquish all the hurdles from the ideal, and if it comes to that, life itself will be cast-off with a smile, a dedication at that Altar. That was how Bhagat Singh could walk to the gallows with a smile on his face. What is important is that one should choose the right ideal an ideal worthwhile even it comes to sacrificing one's own life in the endeavour. The ideal should be inspiring, it should arouse the spring of activity in us. Thus, the discovering of the ideal is the secret of generating in ourselves, dynamism and vitality in its fullness. Dr. Ela R. Bhatt, Founder, Self-Employed Women's Association (SEWA).

Ahmedabad delivered convocation address at the Ninth Convocation of Sri Padmavati Mahila Visvavidyalayam, Tirupati on Monday, the 8th March, 1999 (Women's Day). She said, "Over a period of time, we realized that the right to vote was not enough for the poor and women. They wanted a voice and visibility. It took still more years for us to realize that this was not possible without access to and ownership of economic resources by these poor women. Coming out of their state exploitation by men, society, and the State, the poor women wanted to enjoy what I now call second Freedom: Doosri Azadi." Exerpts.[10]

7. No Forum to Exchange Ideas: Need for All Women Forum

Elected representatives of three tiers should meet once in three months. At present elected representatives rarely meet at one platform to form opinion upon different activities being carried out at various levels. There is a need to have a quarterly meeting of all the elected representatives to exchange their view points. In this way, the would be more participate while deliberating on important issues.

8. Women MLAs and MPs do not take Interest in them

Need for all Women Forum—by their own examples Women MLAs and MP's should visit frequently the elected representatives of PRIs to solve the problems faced by women members.

9. Women do not Struggle for Employment

Need to acquire empowerment Sarojini Vardappan in her Article, "The Challenge of the 21st Century and Role of Indian Women"—"The emphasis now is empowerment, Empowerment is now active process. Power is not a commodity to be transacted. . . . Power cannot be given away as alms. Power has to be acquired, once acquired it needs to be exercised, sustained and preserved. Women have to empower themselves. It is a multi-dimensional process which should enable individuals or group and individuals to realise their full identity and power in all spheres of life. It consists of greater access to knowledge and resources, greater autonomy in decision-making to enable them to have greater ability to plan their lives or have greater control over the circumstances that influence their lives and freedom from shackles imposed on them by customs, belief and practice. Discrimination of women from womb to tomb is well known, age long traditions and worn out customs are handicaps, women have to struggle on their way up."

One of India's greatest poet, Rabindranath Tagore, a pain and inequity of the situation more than half a century ago, thus:

"O Lord Why have you not given
woman the right to conqu'er her destiny?
Why does she have to wait head bowed,
By the roadside,
Waiting with tired patience, I
Hoping for a miracle in the morrow

10. Mere Legislations do not keep "Women": Need of Action

Every new legislation has only worsened the position of women. And now her right to property granted by law in a recent judgement by the Supreme Court poses a new threat to her life.

These developments only reinforce the belief that laws alone do not lead to social transformation, unless followed by resolute action and societal awareness of the wrong from time immemorial. And as the eminent jurist V.R. Krishna Iyer rightly says, "The Constitutional provisions are weapons, not victories. Law has to be activated." In short, the struggle for justice—social, economic and political remains to be fought and won. In this scenario, all talk of women Empowerment is nothing more than empty jargon. The situation demands a revolution of consciousness in the minds of women—in the ways they think about themselves. Women must realize that gender deprivation is inconsistent with their basic human rights. They must realize that they have Constitutional rights to quality health care, economic security, access to education, employment opportunities, equity and political power.

11. Group Discussions are not Sufficient: Need of Positive Mass Media

Arun K. Gupta, Nisha Jain in their article, "Gender, Mass Media and Social Change: A case study of T.V. Commercials" in *Universal News* (August 11, 1997) observe that T.V. commercial also place heavy emphasis on the sexuality of women. In fact, the modernized version of commercials has resulted in a greater emphasis on woman's body and beauty. In the process, woman is reduced to her sexual personality's whatever else maybe the basis of projection of women, the sexual stereotyping of women continues.

A strong awareness requires to be inculcated among leaders of industry, business and corporate sectors, advertising executives and media directors and personnel to exhibit realistic but emancipated attitude with respect to women. Such an outlook should be in tune with the requirement of increasing consciousness among both men and women about women. As commercials have mass appeal, these can and should be used for generating gender friendly consciousness and for reducing bias against women.

Report on the Status of Women rightly mentions that development in its wider perspective covers all aspects of community life. The accepted goals of national development such as maximum production, full employment, and attainment of economic equality and social justice apply equally to men and women. Their realization in an egalitarian society is not, however, possible, unless special efforts are made to assist the underprivileged groups. Our constitution therefore stresses the urgent need for promoting the educational and economic interests of the weaker sections of the people; and as women are handicapped by social customs and traditions, they need special attention to help them to play their full and proper role in a national life.[11]

"The great occupation of women should be to beautify life; to cultivate, for her own sake and that of those who surround her, all her faculties of mind, soul, and body; all her powers of enjoyment, and powers of giving enjoyment; and to diffuse beauty, elegance, and grace, everywhere. If in addition to this the activity of her nature demands more energetic and definite employment, there is never any lack of it in the world; If she loves, here natural impulse will be to associate her existence with him she loves, and to share his occupations; in which, if he loves her (with that affection of equality which along deserves to be called love) she will naturally take as strong an interest, and be as thoroughly conversant, as the most perfect confidence on his side can make her.[12]

Dr. (Miss) Mira Seth, the then Member, Planning Commission, Govt. of India, delivered the convocation address at the annual convocation of the Banasthali Vidyapeeth (Deemed University). She said that the Parliament legislation has been an instruments of giving equality and status to women in our country and this has taken the place of the ancient Vedic, Pauranic, Shastra and Smriti injunctions. Our Parliament has enacted sixteen laws from the Hindu Marriage Act, 1955 to the Commission of Sati (Prevention) Act, 1987 for giving legal sanction to this principle of equality.

In the development processes and the Five Year Plans of our country, they give emphasis to the instrument of education as one of the major tools for empowering women. The focus on educational planning for women has shifted from their traditional role as housewives and mothers to non-traditional roles as producers, partners and partakers in the national development.[13]

Ms. Terjani Vakil, Former Chairman and Managing Director, Export-Import Bank of India, delivered the Convocation address at the Banasthali Vidyapith, Banasthali (Rajasthan). She said, "Keep a space for yourself as a person. Think about what you are, what you want to be, what is your personal *raison de etre* for living. What interests you, what pleases you, do that. Keep a time and space for yourself in your life. For you are an individual, a human being and not just someone's wife, mother, daughter. I would want you to think about this.[14]

Indian National Council for Women suggested the following to bridge the gap between theory and practice:

- Empowerment should be viewed as a two-fold process. Constructive activities to reorganize women's role system have to be accompanied by effective interventions leading to the community internalizing the idea of women's empowerment for its better future.
- Providing economic and political strength to women through collective activities, should be given the necessary focus. Clubbing of women's issues should be avoided.
- The need for women to have social space like "Sakhi Sabha", "Mahila Mandal", etc. within the community set-up through

Panchayat Samities should be given due recognition. Formalization of women NGOs network to play a catalytic role in the social transformation should be given due attention. Development of leadership among women for advancement of the community is also necessary.

- Communication within the women's organizations and the community at large has to be fostered.[15]

NATIONAL POLICY FOR EMPOWERMENT OF WOMEN

One of the landmark achievements of the year 2001 was the approval of the first ever National Policy for the Empowerment of Women. The main objective of this Policy is to bring about the advancement, development and empowerment of women and to eliminate all forms of discrimination against women and to ensure their active participation in all spheres of life and activities.

The policy prescribes affirmative action in areas such as Legal System, Decision-making Structure, Mainstreaming of Gender Perspective in Development Process, Economic Empowerment through increased access to resources like micro-credit, better resource allocation through Women's component Plan, Gender Budget exercises and development of Gender Development Indices and Social Empowerment of Women through, *inter-alia*, universalisation of education, adoption of holistic approach to women's health, etc. The policy commits to making compulsory the registration of marriages and to eliminate child marriage by 2010. The Policy takes into account the new developments initiated by the process of economic reforms and the impact of globalization and liberalization on women, particularly in the informal sector. The policy further prescribes that the provisions of various legislation including personal laws, which are discriminatory against women shall be reviewed and amended with the support and initiatives of concerned communities. Review of women-oriented legislations will be completed by 2003.

The Policy envisages setting up of a Council at the National level to oversee the implementation of the Policy. The National Council will be headed by the Prime Minister. Similar Councils will also be set-up at the State levels to be headed by the concerned Chief Ministers. All Central and State Ministries/Departments would be required to draw up Action.

The Department of Women and Child Development, which was designated as the Nodal machinery for the development and empowerment of women, is playing crucial role in the formulation and monitoring of women's component Plan which was devised as an operational strategy in the Ninth Plan to ensure that not less than 30 percent of funds/benefits earmarked for women in all the women-related sectors.

The Department has advised all the concerned Ministries/ Departments for inclusion of an identifiable Women Component Plan in their programmes right from the planning process and implementation and monitoring of their programmes to ensure that the benefits reach the women. The Department has further requested all the Ministries/ Departments to set-up Advisory Committees for women in each sector to help in the preparation, monitoring and implementation of Women's Component Plan, set-up a women's cell and to include a Chapter on Women's Component Plan in their Annual Report.

On the instruction of Prime Minister's Office (PMO), the Department has also been monitoring 27 Beneficiaries Oriented Schemes or Women implemented by Central Government. It has been decided to extend the scope of the monitoring to include the entire gamut of the women's Component Plan.

The review of the disabilities and constraints on women, which tern from socio-cultural institutions, indicates that the majority of "women are still very far from enjoying the rights and opportunities guaranteed to them by the Constitution. Society has not yet succeeded in among the required norms or institutions to enable women to fulfil the multiple roles that they are expected to play in India today. On the other hand, the increasing incidence of practices like dowry indicate a further lowering of the status of women. They also indicate a process of regression from some of the norms developed during the Freedom Movement. We have been perturbed by the findings of the content analysis of periodicals in the regional languages, that concern for women and their problems, which received an impetus during the Freedom Movement, has suffered a decline in the last two decades. The social laws that sought to mitigate the problems of women in their family life have remained unknown to a large mass of women in this country, who are as ignorant of their legal rights today as they were before independence.

Changes in social attitudes and institutions cannot be brought about very rapidly. It is, however, necessary to accelerate this process of change by deliberate and planned efforts. Responsibility for this acceleration has to be shared by the State and the community, particularly that section of the community which believes in the equality of women. We, therefore, urge that community organizations, particularly women's organizations, should mobilize public opinion and strengthen social efforts against oppressive institutions like polygamy, dowry, ostentatious expenditure on weddings and "child marriage, and mount a campaign for the dissemination of information about the legal rights of women to increase their awareness. This is a joint responsibility, which has to be shared by community organizations, legislators, who have helped to frame these laws and the Government which is responsible for implementing them.

Women of India have a background of history and tradition behind them, which is inspiring, but they have suffered much from various kinds of suppression and all these have to go so that they can play their full part in the life of the nation.[16]

COMMITMENTS OF THE TENTH PLAN TO EMPOWER WOMEN

The Approach

To continue with the major strategy of 'Empowering Women' as Agents of Social Change and Development.

Strategies

To adopt a Sector-specific 3-Fold Strategy for empowering women, based on the prescriptions of the National Policy for Empowerment of Women. They include:

- *Social Empowerment*—to create an enabling environment through various affirmative developmental policies and programmes for development of women besides providing them easy and equal access to all the basic minimum services so as to enable them to realize their full potentials;
- *Economic Empowerment*—to ensure provision of training, employment and income-generation activities with both 'forward' and 'backward' linkages with the ultimate objective of making all potential women economically independent and self-reliant; and
- *Gender Justice*—to eliminate all forms of gender discrimination and thus, allow women to enjoy not only the *de-jure* but *de-facto* rights and fundamental freedom on par within all spheres, viz. political, economic, social, civil, cultural, etc.

SOCIAL EMPOWERMENT

Create an enabling environment through adopting various affirmative development policies and programmes for development of women, besides providing them easy and equal access to all the basic minimum services so as to enable them to realize their full potential through—

- Providing easy and equal access to ensure basic minimum service of primary health care and family welfare with a special focus on the under-served and under-privileged segments of population through universalizing Reproductive and Child Health (RCH) services.
- Achieving the goals set by the National Population Policy (2000) with regard to reducing Infant Mortality Rate (IMR) to 30 per thousand and Maternal Mortality Rate (MMR) to 100 per lakh live births by 2010.
- Supplementing health care and nutrition services through the Pardhan Mantri Gramodaya Yojana (PMGY) to fill the critical gaps in the existing primary health care infrastructure and nutrition services.

- Taking both macro and micro-nutrient deficiencies through nutrition supplementary feeding and nutrition education and nutrition awareness, etc.
- consolidating the progress made under female education and carrying it forward for achieving the set goal of 'Education for Women's Equality' as advocated by the National Policy on Education, 1986 (revised in 1992).
- Providing easy and equal access to and free education for women and girls at all levels and in the field of technical and vocational education and training in up-coming and job-oriented trades.
- Increasing enrolment/retention rates and reducing drop-out rates by expanding the support service through mid-day meals, hostels and incentives like free supply of uniforms, textbook, transport charges, etc.
- Extending the existing network of regional vocational training centres to all the states and Women's Industrial Training Institutes and Women's Wings with General Industrial Training Institutes with residential facilities in all districts and sub-districts and provision of training in marketable trades.
- Encouraging the media to project positive images of women and the Girl Child: change the mind-set of the people and thus promote the balanced portrayals of women and men.
- Gender sensitizing both the administrative and enforcement machinery and ensuring that the right and interests of women are taken care of, besides involving them in planning, implementation and monitoring of processes.

ECONOMIC EMPOWERMENT

Ensure provision of training, employment and income generation activities with both 'forward' and 'backward' linkages with the ultimate objective of making all women economically independent and self-reliant through—

- Organising women into Self-Help Group under various poverty alleviation programmes, viz. Swarnajayanti Gram Swarozgar Yojana (SGSY), Swaran Jayanti Shahari Rozgar Yojana (SJSRY), Rashtriya Mahila Kosh (RMK), Support of Training and Employment Programme (STEP), Training-*cum*-Production Centers for Women (NORAD), etc. and offering them a range of economic option along with necessary support measures to enhance their capabilities and earning capacities with an ultimate objective of making them economically independent and self-reliant.
- Ensuring that women in the informal Sector who account for

more than 90 per cent are given special attention with regard to improve their working conditions as the same continued to be very precarious without even minimum or rqual wages, leave aside other legislative safeguards.

- Making concerted efforts to ensure that the benefits of training an extension in agriculture and its allied activities of horticulture, small animal husbandry, poultry, fisheries, etc. reach women in proportion to their numbers; and also issue of Joint Pattas for husband and wife under the Social Forestry and Joint Forest Management Programmes.
- Ensuring that the employers fulfil their legal obligations towards their women workers in extending child care facilities, maternity benefits, special leave, protection from occupational hazards, allowing formation of women workers, associations/ unions, legal protection/aid, etc.
- Re-training/upgrading the skills of women displaced from traditional sectors due to advancement of technology so that they can take up hobs in the new and expanding areas of employment and formulating appropriate policies and programmes to promote alternative opportunities for wage/self-employment in traditional sectors like khadi and village industries, handicraft handlooms, sericulture, small scale and cottage industries.
- Initiating affirmative action to ensure at least 30 per cent of reservation for women in services in the Public Sector as their representation in 1999 was only 14.5 per cent, along with required provisions for upward mobility.
- Increasing access to credit for women either through the establishment of new micro-credit mechanisms or micro-financial institutions catering to women or strengthening existing arrangements in these areas along with an expansion of the limited coverage of RMK.

The Eleventh Plan, 2007-12 suggests the challenges for gender equity and the roadmap for the Eleventh Five Year Plan can be clubbed under a five-fold agenda—

(i) Ensuring economic empowerment.
(ii) Engineering social empowerment.
(iii) Enabling political empowerment.
(iv) Effective implementation of women-related legislations.
(v) Creating institutional mechanisms for gender mainstreaming and strengthening delivery mechanisms.

The gender perspectives incorporated in the plan are the outcome of extensive consultations with different stakeholders, including a Group of

Feminist Economists. In the Eleventh Plan, for the first time, women are recognized not just as equal citizens but as agents of economic and social growth. The approach to gender equality is based on the recognition that intervention in favour of women must be multi-pronged and they are: (i) provide women with basic entitlements, (ii) address the reality of globalization and its impact on women by prioritizing economic empowerment, (iii) ensure an environment free from all forms of violence against women (VAW—physical, economic, social, psychological, etc., (iv) ensure the participation and adequate representation of women at the highest policy levels, particularly in Parliament and State Assemblies, and (v) strengthen existing institutional mechanisms and create new ones for gender mainstream and effective policy-implementation.

CONCLUSION

The Government of India has declared the year 2001 as women's Empowerment Year with the three-fold objectives of:

(i) creating a nation-wide awareness about the problems and issues affecting women and their importance for national development;

(ii) initiating and accelerating action to improve access to and control of resources by women; and

(iii) creating an enabling environment to enhance the self-confidence and autonomy of women so that they can take their rightful place in the mainstream of the nation's social, political and economic life.

Women empowerment should ensure harmonious existence. Dr. Farncis Soundaraj, Principal, Kodaikanal Christian College, Kodaikanal, delivered the Convocation Address at the annual convocation of the Fatima College (Autonomous), Maduari. He said, "Education has empowered women: they compete better, perform more efficiently and secure values and traditions more carefully than their male counterparts. Are these not reasons and justifications enough for educated women to shake-off pessimism and rise up to meet the challenges which non else but they alone can meet?"

God created human race male and female. He made neither of them superior to the other; on the other hand, he created them for a harmonious existence together. Therefore, the challenges that lie ahead of you cannot be met unless they are approached with a sense of humility and with a sense of togetherness with men. While some of them can be met exclusively by women, they can achieve more by pooling the resources of all.

NOTES AND REFERENCES

1. GOI, Deptt. of Social Welfare, Ministry of Education and Social Welfare, Towards Equality, Report on the Committee on the Status of Women in India, 1974, pp. 3-8.
2. Beena Shah, Women and Empowerment in India—The Educational Dimension in *University News*, August 31, 2000.
3. GOI, Planning Commission, Ninth Five Year Plan, 1997-2002, Vol. II, p. 322.
4. India, 2002, Ministry of Information and Broadcasting, GOI, New Delhi, p. 230.
5. J.P. Singh, Indian Democracy and Empowermnt of Women, In *IJPA*, Oct.-Dec., 2000.
6. GOI, Ministry of Rural Development, Annual Report, 1999-2000, p. 66.
7. *University News*, Dec. 6, 1999, p. 27.
8. *University News*, April 6, 1999.
9. *University News*, January 13, 1997.
10. *University News*, January 26, 1999.
11. ICCSR, Status of Women in India, *op. cit.*, p. 116.
12. John Stuart Mill and H.T. Mill, Early Essays on Marriage and Divorce, Alice and Rossi (ed.) Essays on Sexual Equality, p. 225.
13. AIU, *University News*, July 22, pp. 18-19.
14. AIU, *University News*, April 13, 1990, p. 12.
15. NCW, 1990-2000, New Delhi, p. 135.
16. GOI, Deptt. of Social Welfare, Ministry of Education and Social Welfare, Towards Equality, Report of the Committee on the Status of Women in India, New Delhi, Dec. 1974, p. 101.

4

Economic Empowerment: Work and Employment

Shanta Kohli Chandra in an article, "Women and Empowerment" in Indian Journal of Public Administration, "Fifty Years of Indian Administration: Retrospect and Prospects" rightly observes: Empowerment in its simplest form means the manifestation of redistribution of power that challenges patriarchal ideology and the male dominance. It is both a process and the result of the process. It is transformation of the structures or institutions that reinforces and perpetuates gender discrimination. It is a process that enables women to gain access to, and control of, material as well as informational resources. The concept of women's empowerment, throughout the world, has its roots in women's movement. It is since the mid-1980s that this term became popular in the field of development, especially in reference to women. In India, it is the Sixth Five Year Plan (1980-85) which can be taken as a landmark for the cause of women. It is here that the concept of 'women and development' was introduced for the first time. It was realised that no more piecemeal strategies but an integrated approach would deliver the desired goods. The realistic and regenerative developmental efforts in the direction of progress, in terms of economic independence for women and educational advancement of them is what would answer the basic questions raised for empowering women.

Women because of pre-occupation with home related activities do not find time to devote fully for their skill development and employment. Indian women is more busy in her household work than men folk. Eleventh Five Year Plan has stated that entrenched patriarchal norms and customs mean that women's work goes unnoticed and is unpaid for. The double burden of work placed on her (unrecognized household work and low pay in recognized work) coupled with social norms that prevent her from getting the requisite educational and technical skills result in low female work participation rate, either real or statistical. Female workforce participation rate in India was 28% (2004) as compared to other developing nations like Sri Lanka (30%), Bangladesh (37%), and South Africa (38%). As per NSSO, however, (Table 4.1) work participation rate for female in rural areas has increased from 28.7% in 2000-01 to 32.7% in 2004-05, whereas in urban areas it has increased from 14% in 2000-01 to 16.6% in 2004-05. The work participation rate remains lower for women than for men both in rural and urban areas.[1] (See Chart 4.1)

A sectoral breakdown of women workers reveals that 32.9% are cultivators, 38.9% agricultural labourers (as against 20.9% men) and 6.5% workers in the household industry. Much of the increase in employment among women has been in the form of self-employment; 48% of urban and 64% of rural women workers describe themselves as 'self-employed'. The Tenth Plan has, however, seen a welcome increase in the share of regular employment among female workers in urban India.

As in the case of education, women's employment characterization differs across communities the Sachar Committee Report shows that work participation rate among Muslim women is 25%, and as low as 18% in

CHART 4.1

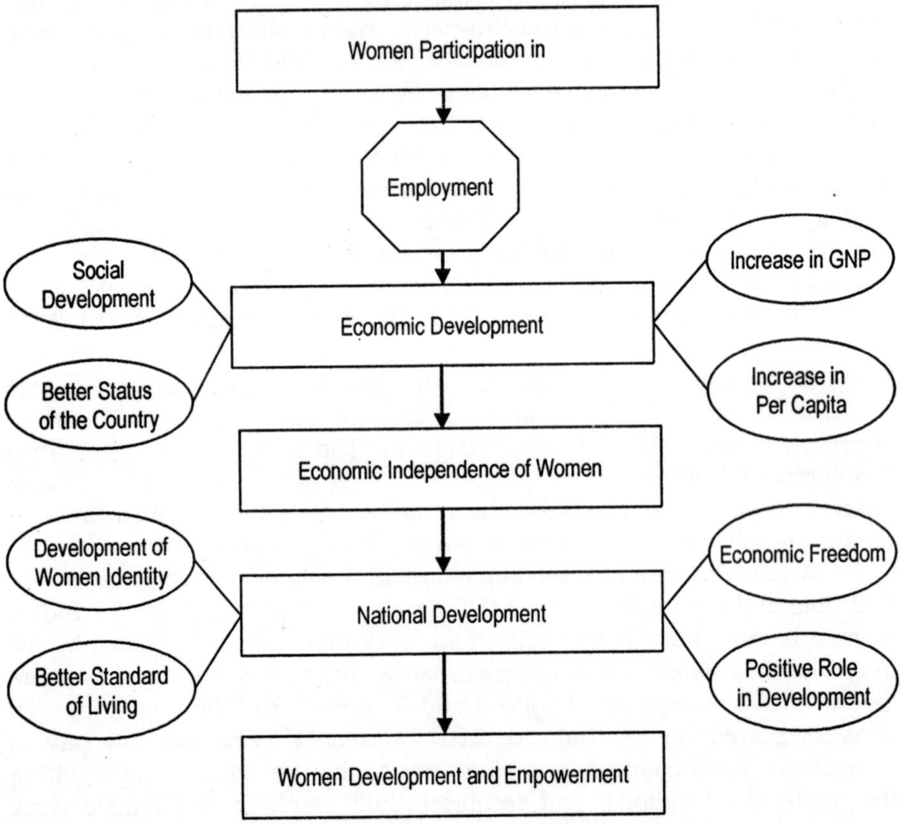

Women Participation in
Employment
Social Development
Better Status of the Country
Economic Development
Increase in GNP
Increase in Per Capita
Economic Independence of Women
Development of Women Identity
Better Standard of Living
National Development
Economic Freedom
Positive Role in Development
Women Development and Empowerment

TABLE 4.1

Work Participation Rates by Sex (1972 to 2005)

(in %)

Year	Rural		Urban	
	Female	Male	Female	Male
1972-73	31.8	54.5	13.4	50.1
1987-88	32.3	53.9	15.2	50.6
1996-97	29.1	55.0	13.1	52.1
2000-01	28.7	54.4	14.0	53.1
2004-05	32.7	54.6	16.6	54.9

Source: NSSO.

urban areas. A larger proportion (73%) of Muslim women is self-employed compared to 55% Hindu women, a much smaller proportion of SC/ST women are self-employed; 45% of SC/ST women are casual workers compared to around 20% Muslim and 15% of upper caste Hindu women.

Another worrying fact is that despite a slight increase in employment, the average earning for rural women has declined between 1999-2000 and 2004-05. This decline is more pronounced among poorer women, that is, illiterate women and women who have dropped out of primary, secondary, or higher secondary (see Table 4.2). The average wage for men has, on the other hand, shown an increase across all categories, leading to a widening of the wage disparity ratio (ratio of female wage/male wage) from 0.89 in 1999-2000 to 0.59 in 2004-05 for rural and 0.83 in 1999-2000 and 0.75 in 2004-05 in urban areas, for all categories.

Another distorting factor is the low wages to women. Though most of the women are less qualified but even for the same qualifications less wages are given in Table 4.2.

TABLE 4.2

Average Wage/Salary Earning (Rs. Per Day) Received by Regular Wage/Salaried Employees of Age 15-59 Years for Different Education Levels

Category	Rural Males		Rural Females		Urban Males		Urban Females	
	1999-2000	2004-05	1999-2000	2004-05	1999-2000	2004-05	1999-2000	2004-05
Not Literate	71.2	72.5	40.3	35.7	87.6	98.8	51.8	48.7
Literate upto primary	91.6	98.6	161.5	97.8	105.1	111.4	64.4	64.8
Sec/H.Sec	148.2	158.0	126.1	100.2	168.2	182.6	145.7	150.4
Dip./Cert.	-	214.4	-	200.4	-	274.9	-	237.0
Graduate and others	220.9	270.0	159.9	172.7	281.6	366.8	234.7	269.2
All	127.3	144.9	113.3	85.5	169.7	203.3	140.3	153.2

Source: NSSO 55th and 61st.

Government Sector

Women's representation in government sector has improved from 11% in 1981 to 18.5% in 2004 (Table 4.3). At the grass roots level, women are playing a more active role in Panchayati Raj bodies and their representation in Panchyats has gone up from 33.5% in 1995 to 37.8% in 2005. Women's presence in Parliament has, however, only increased slightly; from 6.1% in 1989 to 9.1% in 2004. The issue of reservation of seats for women in Parliament remains unresolved. In 2004, only six Ministers of State and one Cabinet Minister were women.[2]

TABLE 4.3

Women in the Government Sector

Year	Central Govt.			State Govt.			Local bodies			Total (In million)		
	Female	Total	Female %	Female	Total	Female %	Female	Total	Female %	Female	Total	Female %
1981	0.14	3.19	4.3	0.65	5.67	11.4	0.41	2.04	20.4	1.2	10.91	11
2004	0.25	3.03	8.25	1.46	7.22	20.22	0.58	2.13	27.23	12.38	12.38	18.5

Source: Directorate General of Employment and Training, Ministry of Labour, New Delhi.

Economic survey 2001-02 has also discussed about women in the work force as:

Women constitute a significant part of the work force in the country. Amongst rural women workers, a majority are employed in agriculture as labourers and cultivators. In the urban areas, women workers are primarily employed in the unorganised sectors such as household industries, petty trades and services, buildings and construction, etc. As on March 31, 1999, women constituted about 17.2 per cent of the organized sector (both public and private) employment.

The distribution of women employees across industries reveals that community, social and personnel services sectors employed 55.6 per cent of women workers followed by manufacturing (21.4 per cent) agriculture and allied occupations (9.8 per cent) and finance, insurance, real estate and business (4.9 percent).

The distribution of female work participation by status of employment indicates that there is a pronounced declining trend in the importance of the self-employed category in both rural and urban areas and an overall increase in the casualisation of the women work force from 31.4 per cent in 1972-73 to 40.9 per cent in 1997 in rural India with a marginal decline to 39.6 per cent in 1999-2000. In urban India there is a reversal of this trend with an increase in work participation rates of females under regular employment category and a decline in casualisation.

Looking to the requirements for providing a supportive legal framework, the Equal Remuneration Act, 1976 provides for payment of equal remuneration to men and women for work of a similar nature. The Supreme court in its order dated 13.8.97 has laid down guidelines for the prevention of sexual harassment of women employees at the workplace. In February 1998, an amendment in the Central Civil Services (Conduct) Rules, 1964 has been carried out to give effect to the guidelines. The Ministry of Labour has also amended the Industrial Employment (Standing Orders) Act, 1964 to make the Supreme court guidelines applicable to private employees. Improvement in the quality of women's employment depends upon increased access to education and skill development training. The Women's Vocational Training Programme was launched by Ministry of Labour in 1974. A separate Women's Cell has also been formed for the purpose and has now developed into the Women's Occupational Training Directorate. Under this directorate, the institutional network includes a National Vocational Training Institute at Noida and 10 regional Vocational Training Institutes in different parts of the country. There are about 765 Institutes [231 Women Industrial Training Institutes and 543 Women Wings in General Industrial Training Institutes (ITI)]/Private ITI with about 46,750 training seats for providing vocational training facilities for women at craftsman level. Statutory provisions have also been made in existing labour laws for organizing child care centres for the benefit of women workers.[3]

In the Economic Survey, 2002-03 it is observed that the Female Work Participation Rate (FWRR) was very low at 22.3 in 1991 against 51.6 for males. The provisional results of the Census 2001 has shown a moderate rise of FWPR to 25.6 percent. In 2001, the gender gap in work participation ranged between 41-43 for A & N islands, Chandigarh and Delhi and was maximum at 48 for Daman and Diu. The gender gap was the minimum for Manipur.[4] (Table 4.4)

Decision-making[5]

(i) Administrative

The representation of women in the decision-making levels through the Premier Services viz., the Indian Administrative Service (IAS) and Indian Police Service (IPS), which stood at only 5.4 per cent in 2000 (Table 4.5). However, the figure is still very low, requiring not only affirmative action but also special interventions to help raise the number of women at various decision-making levels.

(ii) Political

The 73rd and 74th Constitutional Amendments in 1993 have brought forth a definite impact on the participation of women, in terms of absolute numbers, in grassroot democratic institutions, viz. Panchayati Raj institutions (PRIs) and Local Bodies (Table 4.6). In fact, these amendments have helped women not only in their effective participation but also in decision-making in the grassroot democracy of the 475 Zila Parishads in the country, 158 are being chaired by women. At the Block Level, out of 51,000 members of Block Samitis, 17,000 are women. In addition, nearly one-third of the Mayors of the Municipalities are women. In the elections

TABLE 4.4

Gender Differences in Group Participation—2001

Rank	States	Gender Gap
1.	Daman and Diu	48
2.	Delhi	43
3.	Chandigarh	42
4.	Andaman and Nicobar Islands	41
5.	Lakshadweep	36
6.	West Bengal	36
7.	Pondicherry	36
8.	Kerala	35
9.	Punjab	35
10.	Goa	33
11.	Uttar Pradesh	31
12.	Tripura	30
13.	Bihar	29
14.	Assam	29
15.	Jammu and Kashmir	28
16.	Orissa	28
17.	Gujarat	28
18.	Tamil Nadu	27
19.	Karnataka	25
20.	Haryana	23
21.	Dadra and Nagar Haveli	23
22.	Jharkhand	21
23.	Andhra Pradesh	22
24.	Maharashtra	20
25.	Uttaranchal	19
26.	Sikkim	19
27.	Madhya Pradesh	19
28.	Rajasthan	17
29.	Arunachal Pradesh	15
30.	Meghalaya	13
31.	Chhatisgarh	13
32.	Himachal Pradesh	11
33.	Nagaland	9
34.	Mizoram	9
35.	Manipur	8
	India	26

Source: Census 2001 and Annual Report of D/O Women and Child Development, 2001-02.

TABLE 4.5

Representation of Women in Premier Services (1987-2000)

Service	1987		1997		2000	
	Women	Total	Women	Total	Women	Total
IAS	339 (7.5)	4,204	512 (10.2)	4,991	535 (10.4)	5,159
IPS	21 (0.9)	2,418	67 (2.2)	3,045	110 (3.3)	3,301
Total	360 (5.4)	6,622	579 (7.2)	8,036	645 (7.6)	8,460

Note: Figures within parentheses indicates percentage to total.
Source: Department of Personnel and Training, GOI, New Delhi.

TABLE 4.6

Women in Pachayati Raj Institutions (1995-2001)

Year	Women	Men	Total
1995#	318 (33.5)	630	948
2001@	725 (26.6)	1,997	2,722

Note: Figures within parentheses indicate percentage to total.
Data refers to 9 states—Gujarat, Haryana, Karnataka, Kerala, Madhya Paradesh, Punjab, Rajasthan, Tripura and West Bengal.
@ For whole of India. (As on 18.10.2001).
Source: Ministry of Rural Development, GOI, New Delhi.

to PRIs held between 1993 and 1997, women have achieved participation even beyond the mandatory requirement of $33\frac{1}{3}$ per cent of the total seats in states like Karnataka (43.45 per cent), Kerala (36.4 per cent) and West Bengal (35.4 per cent). However, the all India figures for women show that their representation in 2001 is still low.

Although the number of women in Parliament has increased from 59 in 1998 to 70 in 2001, their share continues to be very low representing only 8.5 per cent (Table 4.7) of the total Members in Parliament in 2001.

The number of women in the Central Council of Ministers continues to remain extremely low, but with a marginal increase of 0.8 per cent between 1985 and 2001 (Table 4.8). Of these 2 are of Cabinet rank and 6 are of the rank of Minister of State, and of these, 2 are holding Independent Charge. These trends point out very clearly to the need for affirmative action besides addressing these issues in a systematic and expeditious way so that women's concerns gain political prominence and a fairly representative

TABLE 4.7

Representation of Women in Parliament (1998-2001)

Year	*Females*	*Males*	*Total*
1998	59 (7.2)	761	820
1999	67 (8.5)	723	790
2001	70 (8.5)	750	820

Note: Figures within parentheses indicate percentage to total.
Source: 1. Election Commission of India.
2. National Informatics Centre, Parliament House, New Delhi.

TABLE 4.8

Representation of Women in the Central Council of Ministers (1985 and 2001)

Year	*Females*	*Males*	*Total*
1985	4 (10.0)	36	40
2001	8 (10.8)	66	74

Note: Figures within parentheses indicate percentage to total.
Source: National Informatics Centre, Parliament House, New Delhi.

number of women are in position not only at grassroot level, but also at the state and national levels.

To sum up, Table 4.9 presents the status of women including that of the girl child along with the progress made by them over a period of two developmental decades (1981-2001) as reflected in the 21 Selected Gender Development Indicators.

A quick review of the progress made by women (Table 4.9) has not only focused light on the gains but also brought forth to surface certain critical areas of concern relating to women requiring.[6]

Seema Singh in her Article, 'Gender Based Labour Market Segmentation', some theoretical foundation in Anita Banerji, Raj Kumarsen (ed.) Women and Economic Development states 'Women labour constitutes a significant portion of the total labour force'. However, labour market does not play fair to them. Their labour does not receive expected attention and sometimes, becomes marginalized in the process of development. Generally, they have no equal access to the labour market. They are predominantly employed in the labour intensive unskilled jobs with less security of tenure and lower wages, while their male counterparts have access to the capital

TABLE 4.9

The 21 Selected Gender Development Indicators: 1981 to 2001

Sr. No.	Indicators	Women	Men	Total	Women	Men	Total
(1)	(2)	(3)	(4)	(5)	(6)	(7)	(8)
Demography and Vital Statistics							
1.	Population (in million in 1981-2001)	330.0	353.4	683.4	495.7	531.3	1027
2.	Decennial Growth (1981 and 2001)*	24.93	24.41	24.66	21.79	20.93	21.34
3.	Sex Ratio (1981 and 2001)**	934	-	-	933	-	-
4.	Life Expectancy at Birth in years in (1981-85 and 1996-01)	55.7	55.4	-	65.3	62.3	-
5.	Mean Age of Marriage in years in (1981 and 1991)	18.3	23.3	-	19.5	23.9	-
Health and Family Welfare							
6.	Birth Rate (per thousand in 1981 and 1999)	—	-	33.9	-	-	26.1
7.	Death Rate (per thousand in 1981 and 1999)	12.7	12.4	12.5	8.3	9.0	8.7
8.	Infant Mortality Rate (per thousand live births in 1988 and 1999)	93.0	96.0	94.5	70.8	69.8	70.0
9.	Child Mortality Rate (per thousand live births under 5 years of age in 1985 and 1997)	40.4	36.6	-	24.5	21.8	-
10.	Maternal Mortality Rate (per one lakh live births in 1980 and 1998)	468	-	-	407	-	-
	Literacy and Education						
11.	Literacy Rates (1981 and 2001)*	29.76	56.38	43.57	54.16	75.85	65.38
12.	Gross Enrolment Ratio (1980-81 and 1999-2000)						
	—Classes I-V	64.1	95.8	80.5	85.2	104.1	94.9
	—Classes VI-VII	28.6	54.3	41.9	49.7	67.2	58.8
13.	Drop-out Rate (1980-81 and 1999-2000)						
	—Classes I-V	62.5	56.2	58.7	42.3	38.7	40.3
	—Classes VI-VIII	79.4	68.0	72.7	58.0	52.0	54.6

(Contd.)

TABLE 4.9 (*Contd.*)

(1)	*(2)*	*(3)*	*(4)*	*(5)*	*(6)*	*(7)*	*(8)*
Work and Employment							
14.	Work participation Rate (1981 and 2001)*	19.7	52.6	36.7	25.7	51.9	39.3
15.	Organised Sector (No. in million in 1981 and 1999)	2.80 (12.2%)	20.05	22.85	4.83 (17.2%)	23.28	28.11
16.	Public Sector (No. in million in 1981 and 1999)	1.5 (9.7%)	14.0	15.5	2.8 (14.5%)	16.6	19.4
17.	Government (No. in million in 1981 and 1997)	1.2 (11%)	9.7	10.9	1.6 (14.6%)	9.1	10.7
Decision-Making							
18.	Administration (No. in IAS and IPS in 1987 and 2000)	360 (5.4%)	6262	6622	645 (7.6%)	7815	8460
19.	PRIs (No. in thousand in 1995 and 2001)	318... (33.5%)	630...	948...	725 (26.6%)	1997	2722
20.	Parliament (No. in 1998 and 2001)	594 (7.2%)	761	820	70 (8.5%)	750	820
21.	Central Council of Ministers (No. in 1985 and 2001)	4 (10%)	36	40	8 (10.8%)	66	74

* Figures in per cent; ** Females per 1,000 males; *** Refers to 1995 in respect of some states, namely, Gujarat, Haryana, Karnataka, Kerala, Madhya Pradesh, Punjab, Rajasthan, Tripura and West Bengal.

Note: (i) Figures in prentheses indicate the percentage to the total and year of the data in respective columns. Athough, efforts were made to keep a common 'base and common comparable year', but the same could not be kept up because of the limitations in the availability of data and other practical problems; (ii) The years given in the parentheses refers to the year of the data in columns 3, 4 and 5 and 6, 7 and 8 respectively.

Source: Official Documents.

1. Census of India, 1991, Census of India, 2001: Provisional Population Totals; and SRS Bulletins for respective years, Registrar General and Census Cimmissioner, GOI, New Delhi; 2. Selected Educational Statistics for respective years, Dept of Education Ministry of HRD, New Delhi; 3. Annual Report, 1999-2000, Depts. of Elementary and Literacy and Secondary and Higher Education, Ministry of HRD, New Delhi; 4. Employment Exchange Statistics, DGE&T, Ministry of Labour, New Delhi, 5. Dept. of Personnel and Training, New Delhi; 6. Ministry of Rural Development, New Delhi; 7. Election Commission of India, New Delhi; 8. National Informatics Centre, Parliament House, New Delhi.

intensive jobs with greater stability, higher wages and better career prospects (Boserup, 1970). In advanced industrial countries, where there has been a dramatic rise in female participation rate, there has been no corresponding decrease in occupational segregation. There are simply more women doing the same kind of jobs (Rodgers, G., 1991, Rodgers and Rodgers, 1989). In developing countries, the situation is even worse. Not only the participation rates of women is low, but their concentration in much more pronounced in unorganised, unskilled and low paid occupation.

The World Bank country study on "Gender and Poverty in India" presents the problems faced by poor women against a background of depressing statistics which show how Indian women continue to be denied access to productive assets, in the form of financial credits, markets or land ownership and human capital such as education and skill training which would enhance their abilities as economic agents. It is now well accepted that the poorest families are most dependent on women's earnings and that a lowering of economic status increases the importance of the women's contribution to the family income. Yet despite these facts which suggest that women could play a crucial role in alleviating the poverty of the country's sixty million households living below the poverty line, the government invests far less in women workers in terms of education, health and productive assets compared to male workers. At present barely six percent of the economically active women are in the formal sector. Majority of the women workers are in the informal sector and any plan to improve women's economic condition will have to focus in this area.

The status of women is directly connected with their economic position which in turn depends on opportunities for participation in economic activities. The economic status of women is now accepted as an indicator of a society's stage of development. Participation of women in the work force has also been found to be an important element in the adoption of the small family norm, essential for the achievement of the twin goals of economic development and population planning. It is of the utmost importance therefore that the country make full and effective use of its human resources by providing economic empowerment to women who constitute 50% of it. The committee feel that besides basic education, women should be given adequate opportunities for vocational training to enable them to undertake various types of work and thus raise the living standard of their families.[7]

The long-term objectives of the developmental programmes for women would be to raise their economic and social status in order to bring them into the main-stream of national development. Due recognition has to be accorded to the role and contribution of women in the various socio-economic, political and cultural activities.

In the Seventh Plan, the basic approach would be to inculcate confidence among women and bring about an awareness of their own potential for development, as also of their rights and privileges. The various mass communication media would be utilised extensively in this task. Special measures would be initiated for strict enforcement of the Dowry Prohibition Act and also to prevent harassment and atrocities of women. Voluntary agencies and educational institutions would be fully involved in launching organised companies to combat these evils. An integrated multi-disciplinary approach would be adopted covering employment, education, health, nutrition, application of science and technology and other related aspects in areas of interest to women. Efforts would be made to extend facilities for income-generating activities and to enable women to participate actively in socio-economic development. The educational programmes will be restructured and the school curricula will be modified to eliminate gender bias. Enrolment of girls in elementary, higher secondary and higher education courses, formal as well as non-formal, will be given high priority.

First Five Year Plan rightly states:

> "Maximum production, full employment, the attainment of economic equality and social justice constitute the accepted objective of planning.... plan for development must place balanced emphasis on all these."[8]
>
> "Development touches all aspects of Community life and has to be viewed comprehensively. Economic planning thus extends out into extra economic spheres—educational, social and cultural."[9]

Participation of women in economic activity is prevalent in all countries and their role in the process of economic growth and development has been recognised the world over. Women perform productive role in two ways—one as productive worker in outside market and secondly, as unpaid worker in her household. Inspite of various measures undertaken by the Indian Government women have lagged behind men in different spheres in terms of employment in the organised sectors, etc.

Women constitute almost half of the total population of the world economy but their participation in the gainful employment is very poor. They, according to an I.L.O. estimate, work for about 67% of the world's total work hours and get only 10% of the world income. The share in world property comes out to be even less than 1% of the world property. This glaring economic disparity is simply because of an accident of birth and not because of any inability or incompetence of the women. The problem of violence against women is not new. Women in Indian society have been victims of humiliation, torture and exploitation for long and a few decades back, their condition was pitiable and worst.

Despite five decades of the grant of constitutional equality in India, statistics have over the years revealed that while there is acceptable visible manifestation of gender equality at the voter level, gender invisibility with in the power structure shows case for concern. The thirty-three percent reservation for women at all tiers of Panchayat has made a significant beginning. The Parliamentary bill for 33 percent reservation of seats for women in the Lok Sabha and Assemblies has been pending as the 81st Amendment. The provision for providing reservation is to be seen as a unifying instrument which would enable the women to join the mainstream and usher in an egalitarian society. Various political parties in the country which are considered the main vehicle to increase women's mobilisation and are important tools of political empowerment reflect the established values of a male dominated society.

'Freedom depends on economic conditions even more than political. If a woman is not economically free and self-earning, she will have to depend on her husband or someone else, and dependents are never free.' These were the ideas of Pandit Jawaharlal Nehru, first Prime Minister of India, which vividly highlight the importance of economic independence of women.

Nancy Reagan, wife of former US President, has rightly quoted, "A woman is like a teabag—you can't tell how strong she is until you put her in hot water." And it is perhaps in the world of entrepreneurship that the recognition and value of women's contribution is the most vital to the making of a better tomorrow.

An ILO report in 1980 states that 'Women are 50% of the world's population, do the two-third of world's work hours, receive 10 percent of world's income area and own less than one percent of world property. All because of an accident of birth'.

Swami Vivekanand, stressing the need for the girl education said, "I ask you earnestly to open girls' school in every village. If women are educated. . . culture, knowledge, power and devotion awaken in the land. That nation which does not respect women, has never become great, nor will even in future. . .. The principle reason why our race has so much degenerated in that we have no respect for these living images of shakti."

The status of any given section of population in a society is intimately connected with its economic position, which (itself) depends on rights, roles and opportunities for participation in economic activities. The economic status of women is now accepted as an indicator of a society's stage of development. This does not, however, mean that all development results in improving women's economic status. Patterns of women's activity are greatly affected by social attitudes and institutions, which stem from the social ideology concerning basic components of status in any given period. These may differ according to the stage of economic development.

"The emancipation of women and their equality with men are impossible and must remain so as long as women are excluded from socially productive work and restricted to house work, which is private."[10]

"Today the sole occupation of a woman amongst us is supposed to be to bear children, to look after her husband and otherwise to drudge for the household ..... not only is the woman condemned to domestic slavery, but when she goes out as a labourer to earn wages, though she works harder than man she is paid less.[11]

"Discrimination against women is incompatible with human dignity and the welfare of the family and of society, prevents their participation on equal terms with men in the political, social, economic and cultural life of their countries and is an obstacle to the full development of the potentialities of women in the service of their countries and humanity."[12]

"To maintain the proper quantitative balance between various economic activities was one of the principal functions of the economic system, which, it was felt, should operate to give equal freedom of choice to men and women. The orientation of society as a whole regarding the desirability that women should play an equal part in the country's development was taken as very important precondition for the advancement not only of the women but of the country as well.[13]

"This concept of women as a sort of balancing force in the family or national economy has a whole series of practical implications which have the net effect of making it difficult for women to become integrated as a permanent part of the work force and to rendering them particularly susceptible to unscrupulous or discriminatory treatment in the employment market."[14]

Rani Jethmalani in her article, "Empowerment, Law and Dowry Deaths (ed.), Kali's Yug, New Delhi, (Har Anand Publication), 1995 rightly states, "The lack of economic opportunities for women socialised through a lifestyle of dependence leads to a kind of emotional indecurity. India's women psyche to believe in the patriarchial processes which control the female gender."

This concept of women as a sort of balancing force in the family or national economy has a whole series of practical implications which have the net effect of making it difficult for women to become integrated as a permanent part of the work force and of rendering them particularly susceptible to unscrupulous or discriminatory treatment in the employment market.

"In countries which are marked by labour surpluses, the need for providing employment for women when many men are available for work raises questions which cannot admit of categorical answers. It is in these developing countries that incomes by and large are low and the family requires the assistance of an additional earner. Where social conventions do not weigh oppressively against bringing women into paid employment, the family income can best be supplemented by a draft on the female population in the working age group."[15]

National Action Plan for Women States:

> The Constitution guarantees equality of opportunity in matters relating to employment and directs the State to secure equal rights to an adequate means of livelihood, equal pay for equal work and just and humane conditions of work. The impact of transition to a modern economy has resulted in the exclusion of an increasing number of women from active participation in the productive process and only a limited recognition of their contribution and ability to

contribute. The factors which have caused such an exclusion need to be examined and corrective action and supportive measures initiated to ensure equal opportunity in the economic process "which would enable women to play their full and proper role in building up the nation."

Fuller economic participation has to be understood then, in the context of human rights and social justice, utilization of human resources, bridging economic disparities and providing the impetus for social and economic change towards an equality of "status".

The problems constraining participation of women as wage employees may be broadly listed as follows:

(i) Limited overall opportunities available for wage employment.
(ii) Attitudes towards employment and working women, whether by women themselves, by men or society at large.
(iii) Prejudices of employers in terms of women's employment.
(iv) Inadequate education/training opportunities for women and attitudes to such education/training.
(v) Lack of easily available information and guidance on career choices, i.e. vocational counselling.
(vi) Inability to combine work with other household and child rearing responsibilities.
(vii) Lack of situational support: whether at home in terms of household work, availability of organised creaches, etc., freedom from incessant child bearing, etc.

The Action Plan besides finding solutions to the problems affecting participation of women will have to actively promote participation of women so as to bring about improvement in the economic and social status of women and a positive change in the attitude towards working women. In this context analysis of the existing situation at a national level through an examination of published data indicate that the following guidelines will be meaningful:

(i) Increase participation of women in occupations where women can be more than or as "productive" as men. "Productive" both in terms of job/skill requirements and of women's ability to manage a job alongwith household chores and fulfil her child rearing responsibilities. The occupations indicated are largely those requiring either certain levels of professionals/vocational/technical training and skills requiring manual dexterity in handling the work or non-formal education. The major occupations in which women are employed in significant numbers are nurses, other medical and health technicians, teachers, stenographers, typists, card punching operators, maids, sweepresses and such other service workers; plantation, forestry and mining labour, spinning weaving, tobacoo production. Some of these are occupation where women are perceived as being more/equally productive; in some employment is a result of economic incidence.

(ii) Encourage participation of women in occupation where women can be equally productive as men but where participation has been negligible. At the national level, some/such occupations indicated by the 1 per cent sample of the 1971 Census data are salesman. (Sales agents), Shop assistants and Demonstrators; Agents and Salesman—Insurance.

(iii) Encourage participation in certain types of occupation where such increased participation will provide the impetus for change in women's status. This relates, particularly, to rural women educated and trained in rural institutions and seeking employment in rural areas. These are in subject fields, such as, Veterinary Science/Medicine, Commerce and Agriculture. As per the Census, G-Series table, there are such professionally trained women who are unemployed.

Impact of Globalization and Eleventh Plan strategy[17]

Liberalization has led to a paradigm shift in the country's economy. While this has provided many increase in opportunities; it has also posed challenges. We have moved towards technology dominated sectors. Many traditional livelihood that have high employment potential like handlooms and other home-based non-agro enterprises that are women-dominated have become unviable. Unequal access for women to schooling, land, credit facilities, alternate employment, skill training, and technology has led to the crowding of women in the lowly paid jobs of most sectors. The Eleventh Plan will examine the impact of globalization of women in the unorganized sector, lack of skill-training, technology, and marketing support, etc. While seeking to provide relief to deprived and women-dominated sectors, such as agriculture and small enterprises, the plan will also work towards mainstreaming women in new and emerging areas of the economy through necessary skill training, vocational training, and technology education. It will work towards a social security policy that mitigates the negative impact of globalization on women.[16]

Let us discuss about Haryana one India:

Women in developed countries, in general, are economically more active and they enjoy more comforts and have better status than their counterparts in LDCs. But at the same time we find that women's role is related not only to the level of development but also demographic, social and other factors which vary from culture to culture and from country to country. Though the right to equality and equal pay for equal jobs have been guaranteed by legislation in many countries, the traditional attitude of sex bias still continues and women are not only ill paid but also ill treated.

Though women today have more education, more job mobility, and prefer less number of children than their mothers, yet in every country, developed or developing, they are expected to fulfil their traditional roles as mothers and wives. So various economic and social measures are needed to enhance their roles.

It is now more or less universally recognized that the problem of optimising the roles of men and women in future is more than only economic in character. All kinds of discriminations originated from physical relative superiority of men over women and this feature is found to be manifested in a very ugly manner even in highly civilized societies today. The accumulated vested interests growing out of the initial wrongs have now crossed the limits of tolerance and this called for actions on the part of authorities throughout the world. But as the root of the problem lies in the human psychology, economic and other steps will be able to remove temporarily only some amount of discriminations. But permanent and optimum solutions cannot be obtained unless the development strategies are changed for the suggested alternative to consider the productivity (in both economic and non-economic senses) of human being in the wider perspective of quality of life and not in the narrow economic sense only. A substitution of the modern economic approach of unlimited wants and scarce resources by limited resources and limited wants at least to certain extent through consumption and production planning in the LDCs specially can put once again economic growth and economic development in a complementary relationship. As men's and women's roles are only sub-sets of this socio-economic set, an optimisation of their role is probably feasible in such a situation. The process of increasing capabilities can be smooth, fast and lasting leading to a perfect complementary relationship between men and women in the economy of future which, as our experience and commonsense show, is slow, temporary and inadequate under the present set-up.

ENSURING ECONOMIC EMPOWERMENT: EMPLOYMENT WOMEN IN THE UNORGANIZED SECTOR

The Eleventh Plan recognizes that women in the unorganized sector need social security covering issues of leave, wages, work conditions, pension, housing, childcare, health benefits, maternity benefits, safety and occupational health and complaints committee for sexual harassment. While it is difficult to tackle some of these issues immediately due to the nature of unorganized enterprises, steps will be taken to ensure safety, childcare facilities, toilets, etc. for women. The Plan will ensure increased availability of micro-credit to women in the unorganized sector.

Women in Agriculture

The Challenge in the Eleventh Plan is to improve the availability of agricultural inputs, credit, marketing facilities, technology, and skill training for the increasing number of women farmers. Resources pooling and group investment, financial and infrastructural support will be provided. Women in agriculture will be on the top of the Eleventh Plan agenda and a two-pronged strategy will be adopted; (i) ensuring effective and independent land rights for women, and (ii) strengthening women's agricultural capacities.

A specific scheme will be devised by MoWCD for identifying and helping women in States where agrarian crisis have ravaged families. Women's vulnerabilities resulting from farmer suicides due to crop failure and inability to pay loans will be addressed.

Land

Land rights not only empower women economically but strengthen their ability to challenge social and political inequities. The Eleventh Plan will carry out a range of initiatives to enhance women's land access. The group approach to women's ownership of land and productive assets will be explored and appropriate linkages will be made with the SHG movement. In case of displacement, a gender sensitive rehabilitation policy that includes equitable allocation of land of women will be devised. The Eleventh Plan will also ensure the rights of poor, landless, and tribal women over forest land, commons, and other resources.[17]

CONCLUSION

The above mentioned facts and analysis reveals a high degree of differences between theory and practice. Women are discriminated in employment at every level. Excuses are found to keep women workers out. Government has to play a positive role for economic empowerment of women without which the word empowerment has no meaning. Economic independence is the first criteria of empowerment of women.

NOTES AND REFERENCES

1. GOI, Planning Commission, Eleventh Five Year Plan, 2002-12, p. 188.
2. *Ibid.*, pp. 188-89.
3. GOI, Economic Survey, 2001-02, pp. 245-46.
4. GOI, Economic Survey, 2002-03, pp. 221-22.
5. GOI, Planning Commission, Xth Plan, pp. 235-36.
6. *Ibid.*
7. Lok Sabha Secretariat Committee on Women Empowerment (2001-02) Seventh Report, Thirteenth Lok Sabha, Training Programme for Women, Ministry of Labour and HRD, p. 1.
8. GOI, Planning Commission, First Five Year Plan, p. 28.
9. GOI, Planning Commission, Second Five Year Plan.
10. Karl Marx and F. Engles, *Selected Works*, Vol. II, p. 310.
11. M.K. Gandhi, *Young India*, 1918, 263.
12. Declaration on the Elimination of Discrimination Against Women, (UN) 1967,
13. *Ibid.*
14. International Labour Conference, 48th Session, Women Workers in a Changing World, 1963, p. 19.
15. Report of the National Commission Labour, Govt. of India, p. 179.
16. GOI, Planning Commission, XIth Five Year Plan, 2007-12, pp. 190-191.
17. *Ibid.*

5

Empowerment through Health

Thus, there can be no two opinions that health is basic to national progress and in terms of resources for economic development. Nothing could be of greater significance than the health of the people. To quote Herophilas, C., 300 B.C.

"When health is absent
Wisdom cannot reveal itself
Art cannot manifest
Strength cannot fight,
Wealth becomes useless
And Intelligence cannot be applied."

As such, good health must be a primary objective of every development programme. It is a precursor to improving the quality of life for a major portion of mankind.

Now, let us discuss the special need of women's health in the overall process of health development. A world health organization report rightly submits:

Health conditions in one phase of a woman's life affect other phases of her life as well as the health and well-being of future generations. This concept guided the Technical Discussions on Women, Health and Development at the 45th World Health Assembly in 1992. Since then WHO has advocated strongly for a lifespan approach to women's health—from conception to old age. It has also called for multicultural action for women's health, particularly in the areas of raising female literacy, creating opportunities for income generation, increasing the participation of women in national development, and in short, empowering women to make decisions on matters that impact their health.[1]

There is a growing realization that investing in women's health is investing in the health of families, communities and societies, in other words—investing in health for all.

"Gender" is used to describe those characteristics of men and women which are socially constructed and therefore can change, in contrast to those that are biologically determined and therefore cannot change. Gender is thus a dynamic concept which looks at the social divisions and the interrelations between men and women.

A "gender approach to health" is based on an analysis of how differences and disparities between women and men determine their differential exposure to risk, their access to technology and health care, their rights and responsibilities, and their control over their own lives.[2]

A Report on the status of women in India reports that health of women is directly related to their status and hence status need to be improved as already dealt with in Chapter 1 and Chapter 2. To quote the report:

Health is both an important factor in the achievement of status as well as an indicator of social status, particularly for women, whose health is conditioned to a great extent by social attitudes. The health status of women includes their mental and social condition as affected by prevailing norms and attitudes of society in addition to their biological and physiological problems. Societies delineate women's roles partly according to their biological and physiological problems. Societies delineate women's roles partly according to their biological functions and partly from prevailing attitudes regarding their physical and mental capacity. These social attitudes also influence the provision and use of preventive and curative health care, including maternal care. The health care facilities offered by a community in the form of medical particularly maternity services for women, is a significant index of the emphasis that community places on the health of its women. Some studies in both the developed and developing countries have shown a definite link between low status of women and deficiencies in the knowledge and utilisation of preventive health services.[3]

Committee on Empowerment of women rightly observes the need of Gender specific approach to health:

There is a growing recognisation that since women also suffer from other disabilities and morbidities, some of which are again very gender specific, there is need to examine the adequacy of our strategies in ensuring that they are appropriately covered. The scanty data available has shown that women in reproductive age groups of 18-45 years, constituting a bulk of the working population, suffer from TB, Malaria, UTI, STDs, Cancer, Leprosy, etc. Women working in cities are also subject to stressful conditions and are seen to suffer from mental health problem as well as heart ailments, blood pressure and other stress induced diseases. Likewise, the National Commission for Women had also brought out the special needs of women working in agriculture and informal sectors where they are exposed to chemicals and pesticides. Besides the longevity of life has resulted in a higher burden of diseases among the older aged women. The women in this age group suffer medical disorders such as Alzheimer's and arthritis, etc.

The various Disease Control Programmes are being implemented without any specific allocation for women. However, it is felt that the sensitisation to women's health is the need of the hour. Certain areas on women's health may require specific interventions especially those disabilities and morbidities which are very gender specific such as cervical and breast cancer. Main constraints are: inadequate funding and inadequate development of gender perspective in programme formulation.[4]

National perspective Plan for Women, 1988, spell out the following activities for better health to girls and women:

(i) Change our attitudes to provide prompt and adequate medical care for girls.
(ii) Prepare girls for better motherhood.
(iii) Reduce infant and child mortality of girls.
(iv) Reduce maternal mortality.
(v) Ensure adequate maternal health care—pre-natal, natal and post-natal.
(vi) Ensure proper knowledge and services for family planning.
(vii) Provision of basic health and nutrition services for girls and women.
(viii) Raise the level of literacy and education among women.[5]

Beijing UN International Conference emphasized a life span perspective for health of women.

A lifespan approach addresses the health issues of women—at conception and birth, in infancy and childhood, during adolescence, throughout the reproductive years, into old age—within the context of their biological and social vulnerabilities and their status in society. It also takes into account both the specific as well as the cumulative effects of poor health and nutrition.

A lifespan approach to women's health takes into account both the specific as well as the cumulative effects of poor health and nutrition. There is increasing evidence that health problems that begin in childhood and adolescence affect the health status of women during their reproductive years and beyond, as well as the health of their newborns. Discrimination against the girl child as seen in some countries of the Region can also significantly retard her growth and development.[6]

Ninth Five Year Plan stresses holistic approach to health of women. The Ninth Plan recognises the special health needs of women and the girl child and the importance of enhancing easy access to primary health care. There are many indicators to point out that the neglect of health needs of women especially that of the pregnant women, adolescent girls and girl-babies, is responsible for the present high rates of IMR/CMR/MMR.

Therefore, a holistic approach with Reproductive Child Health (RCH) measures will be adopted in improving the health status of women by focussing on their age-specific needs.[7]

We may discuss the areas in which women health services need be promoted.

In this context committee on Empowerment has also suggested the following observations which are of great significance.

Since the vast majority of women live in rural areas, where there are hardly any medical facilities available, women become victims of various diseases due to mal-nutrition, lack of clean and safe drinking water, unhygienic conditions, etc. The government ought to integrate various programmes and take a holistic approach to immunization, nutrition, health care, drinking water, cleanliness, health infrastructure, trained personnel, etc. so as to improve the health of the rural women. As 33 per cent women are now in panchayats and other local bodies they can be utilized for improving the condition of women all over the country. The Committee desire that the government should coordinate with various concerned Departments in this regard to draw up appropriate programmes and schemes along these lines.

The demand and supply of health facilities is highly skewed. There is urgent need to improve the conditions of the Government hospitals by making available doctors, para-medical staff, requisite medicines and necessary medical equipments. Not only is there need for more doctors and nurses but the norms for doctor-patient ratio and nurse-patient ratio needs to be reviewed and appropriate steps taken to provide medical staff as per those norms. It is known fact that the emergency wards of Government hospitals in major cities are managed by junior doctors while the senior doctors have to be called, if need arises. The Government should take appropriate steps to ensure the presence of senior doctors round the clock in each discipline in the emergency wards of major hospitals.[8]

PROVISION OF HEALTH SERVICES (Chart 5.1)

1. Adequate Health Facilities

Health facilities are undoubtedly inadequate, especially in rural areas. The women services have four components: care of general medical problems; care of gynaecological problems; obstetric care and family problems. The purpose is to provide planned maternal and child health services to ensure that expectant and nursing mothers maintain good health, have a normal delivery and bear healthy children. It is a service planned for the promotion and restoration of health of mothers and children and provision of safe confinement. The following suggestions may be considered to improve the health services for women:

(a) Since a major part of our population stay in villages, where dais play a significant role, we should accelerate the training

CHART 5.1

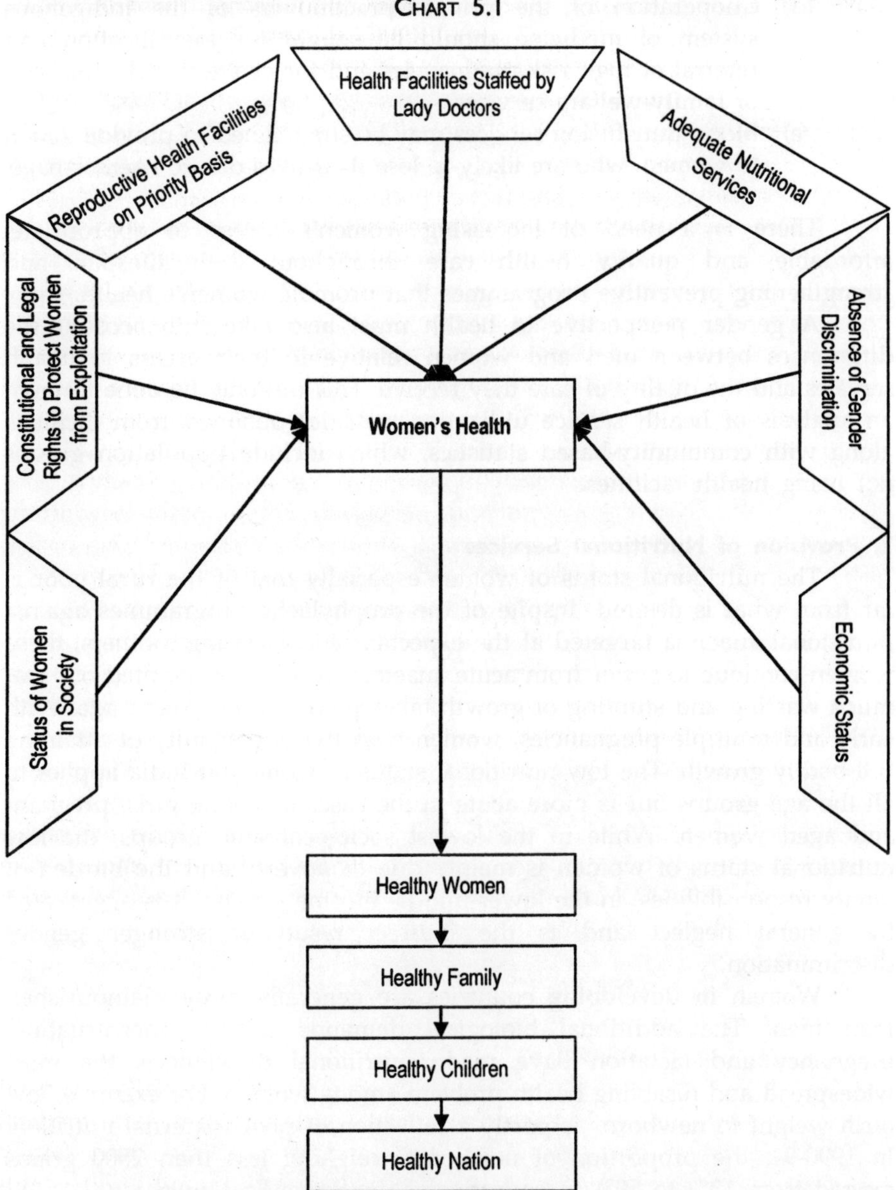

programme for them. This would reduce greatly the maternal and infant mortality rates.

(b) Arrangements may be made for special identifiable services for women in all types of institutions, especially in the PHCs.

(c) At present, one PHC is provided for 30,000 population. It is suggested that one PHC be provided for not more than 25,000 population.

(d) Cooperation of the private practitioners of the indigenous system of medicine should be sought for identification and referral of high risk pregnancies and for delivery and expansion of family-welfare services.
(e) Blood transfusion services may be streamlined to provide .blood to women, who are likely to lose their lives due to haemorrhage.

There is a need of increasing women's access to appropriate, affordable and quality health care throughout their lifespan and strengthening preventive programmes that promote women's health.

A gender perspective to health must also take into account the differences between men and women relative to their access to health services and the quality of care they receive. This can only be done through an analysis of health service utilization statistics obtained from facilities along with community-based statistics, which include population groups not using health facilities.

2. Provision of Nutritional Services

The nutritional status of women especially that of the rural poor is far from what is desired. Inspite of the prophylactic programmes against nutritional anaemia targeted at the expectant and lactating mothers, these women continue to suffer from acute anaemia. It has been pointed out that much wasting and stunting of growth takes place during young age. With early and multiple pregnancies, women miss the opportunity of attaining full bodily growth. The low nutritional status of women in India applies to all the age groups but is more acute in the cases of young girls, pregnant and aged women. While in the lowest socio-economic groups, the low nutritional status of women is mainly due to poverty and the burden of family responsibilities, in the lower middle income groups, it is aggravated by general neglect and is the indirect result of stronger gender discrimination.

Women in developing countries are generally more malnourished than men. The additional biological demands due to menstruation, pregnancy and lactation have made nutritional deficiencies the most widespread and disabling health problem among women. For example, low birth weight in newborns is partly a reflection of poor maternal nutrition. In 1990-94, the proportion of newborns weighing less than 2500 grams ranged from 13% to 50% in countries of the South-East Asia.

Iron deficiency anaemia is more common in women than in men. About 55% of pregnant women and 44% of all women suffer from anaemia in developing countries. At ages between 15-44 years, the burden of iron deficiency anaemia in developing countries in 1990 in terms of thousands of DALYs per year was 4898 for men and 7135 for women. Anaemia lowers the physical work capacity of women and their ability to cope with various infections. It also has serious repercussions on their reproductive health, with maternal mortality being significantly higher in anaemic women.[9]

The most serious problem afflicting women is lack of adequate nutrition. Girls and women generally get the leftovers because of the social customs, poverty and their poor social status. A pleasant and healthy diet, not necessarily an expensive one, is one of the most satisfying and stimulating activities of family life. It contributes to the physical, the mental and social well-being of all the members of the family. Man does not always instinctively choose the right nutrition for maintaining his health. He is influenced in his food habits by religion, culture, social status, traditions and beliefs.

Nature abounds in good nutritious foods within reach of the economically under-privileged families. A balanced diet does not mean an expensive diet. With proper education, families with limited financial resources can take better care of their nutritional needs. It is, therefore, essential for the health department and voluntary organisations to impart this type of education as this can go a long way in promoting the health and well-being of family members. Health institutions do not provide, at present, any special nutritional services. There is a need to plan well-equipped and staffed nutrition clinics attached to all hospitals and PHCs. There may be arrangements to educate the women about the nutritive value of locally available foods and also teach methods of cooking that would retain food value. The properties of medical herbs and medicines and traditional cures can be analysed and popularized among mothers.

The Prime Minister, in his Independence Day speech on 15th August, 2001 announced the setting up of a National Nutrition Mission. Under this Mission, subsidized food grains would be made available to adolescent girls and expectant and nursing mothers, belonging to below-poverty-line families.

A two-tier structure is envisaged for the Mission. The National Nutrition Mission would be headed by the Prime Minister and its Executive Committee would be under the Human Resource Development Minister.[10]

3. Planning and Development of Health Personnel for Women's Health

We have already discussed the various aspects of health manpower planning. We may suggest here some methods which can help in making more women health personnel available to cater to the health needs of women:

(a) More reservation of seats for women in medical colleges till a sufficient number of qualified lady doctors are available.
(b) More women may be encouraged to undergo training in ISM through the reservation in service as well.
(c) In order to encourage self-employment among women doctors, financial assistance may be provided to set-up clinics, etc.
(d) Community Health Workers' Scheme must include at least fifty per cent women to deal effectively with the women health problems.

4. Planning Adequate Facilities for Reproductive Health

The greatest burden of reproductive health problems, however, falls on women. It is they who face the risks from complications of pregnancy and childbirth, from unwanted pregnancies and from unsafe abortions. Over one-third of all healthy life lost in adult women in the developing world is due to reproductive health problems, as compared to only 12% in men. And yet large number of women remain ill-informed about basic facts related to their reproductive health.[11]

Women must be encouraged to adopt family planning in rural areas. Women start their reproductive life when they are barely out of adolescence and may have four or five children by the time they are thirty. This adversely affects their health and well-being.

Women in the rural and urban areas have hardly any say in family planning. It is men who decide matters, but among the educated women, some mutual understanding is evident. The education of women, population change and overall development are closely inter-related. Women have a crucial role to play in all these areas still uncovered. A study of the inter-relationship between the status of women and family planning was conducted in accordance with the Economic and Social Council Resolution. The report affirmed:

(a) The right to decide freely and responsibly on the number and spacing of their children is a fundamental right of individuals which facilitates the exercise of other human rights especially by women;
(b) Adequate information, education and services enabling individuals to exercise this right are essential pre-requisites for the promotion of the status of women, and for ensuring their complete integration in social and economic development at all levels; and
(c) Family planning which should constitute an integrated and essential part of development plan and programmes, in countries suffering from over-population can only succeed in concert with other measures which also improve the status of women."

The establishment of a close doctor-patient relationship is an absolutely essential requirement for the success of the programme. Careful follow-up by doctors of vasectomy and tubectomy cases is as necessary as the operation itself, for the psychological rehabilitation of the patient, as well as for the assurance of potential acceptors.

A maternal death is defined as the death of a woman while pregnant or within 42 days of the termination of pregnancy, irrespective of the duration and site of the pregnancy, from any cause related to or aggravated by the pregnancy or its management but not from accidental or incidental causes.

Most maternal deaths are preventable. The medical interventions necessary to prevent them are trained assistance at delivery, a well established primary health care infrastructure with a good referral system, and referral facilities (e.g. at district level) for managing complications. Most women do not receive the services of a skilled attendant (midwife, nurse or doctor) at the time of delivery.

For example, the report of a three-year study covering a population of 686,000 in a rural area of India showed that "delay in seeking care and too many and inappropriate referrals through lower levels of the health system not capable of dealing with the problem, significantly increased the risk of dying. Similarly, residence in the village proper (which has better transport facilities) as compared to the hamlets had a protective effect. A trained attendant at delivery, presence of an ANM (Auxiliary Nurse Midwife) in the village, an educated husband (the usual decision-maker) and the social custom of migrating to the natal home for delivery all had a protective effect."[12]

5. Planning Women Education for Family Health

Healthy families make healthy people. The family is the primary unit of healthy care, a front line in the sequence of education, prevention, diagnosis, treatment and rehabilitation of its constituents. "Health begins at Home" was the theme chosen for World Health Day (1973) on 25th Anniversary of WHO in recognition of the important role of the family in promoting and protecting the health of its members. Women occupy an important place in shaping the lives of its family members. The mother is still the best teacher on life and health. The education imparted by her remains with children as long as they live. Government should provide health education to women as notions of health and hygiene given at home to children would help them to be good citizens. Women, if properly educated, can really help in the socio-economic development of the country. This would release the potential energy of the women and help in channelizing it for the welfare of the family and ultimately national development.

6. Planning for HIV/AIDS and STDs, Infertility and Gynaecological Disorders

Acquired immune deficiency syndrome (AIDS), unknown even 15 years ago, has now become a major challenge to public health. It is important to educate women about STDs and HIV infection. It is even more important to empower them to say "NO" to unsafe-sex. STDs in women are not easily identified or cured because over 50% of STDs in women are a symptomatic, diagnosis is difficult, and women's access to services for STD treatment is poor. STDs in pregnant women cause complications such as seplis, spontaneous abortion, premature birth, still-birth and congential infection. Almost two-thirds of cases of infertility among women and 35% of cases of *post-partum* morbidity are attributable to STDs.

Worldwide, the disease burden of STDs in women is more than five times that in men.[13]

During the Ninth Plan, attempts are being made to provide for screening for syphilis, gonorrhea and HIV infection at PHC/CHC level wherever possible. Utilising the microscope and laboratory technician available at PHCs vaginal/cervical smears in women with symptoms of RTI are to be screened for identifying organisms responsible and appropriate treatment provided.

Infertility

It is estimated that between 5 to 10% of couples are infertile. While provision of contraceptive advice and care to all couples in reproductive age group is important, it is equally essential that couples who do not have children have access to essential clinical examination, investigation, management and counselling. The focus at the CHC level will be to identify infertile couples and undertake clinical examination to detect the obvious causes of infertility, carry out preliminary investigations such as sperm count, diagnostic curettage and tubal potency testing. Depending upon the findings, the couples may then be referred to centres with appropriate facilities for diagnosis and management. By carrying out simple diagnostic procedures available at the primary health care institutions it is possible to reduce the number of couples requiring referral. Initial screening at primary health care level and subsequent referral is a cost-effective method for management of infertility both for the health care system and those requiring such services.

Gynaecological Disorders

Women suffers from a variety of common gynaecological problems including menstrual dysfunctions at peri-menarchal and peri-menopausal age. Facilities for diagnosis of these are at the moment available at district hospitals or tertiary care centres. During the Ninth Plan period the CHCs, with a gynaecologist, have started providing requisite diagnostic and curative services. Yet another major problem in women is prolapse uterus of varying degrees. The PHCs and CHCs refer women requiring surgery to district hospitals or tertiary care centres.

Cancer Cervix is one of the most common malignancies in India and accounts for over a third of all malignancies in women. Cancer Cervix can readily be diagnosed at the PHCs and CHCs. Early diagnosis of Stage I and Stage II and referral to places where radiography is available will result in rapid decline in mortality due to cancer cervix in the country in the near future.

7. Environment and Work Related Health Problems

Health problems that are work-related or those arising out of averse environment conamons, cover a board range or Illnesses disabilities. Such problems arise out of injuries, infections, exposure to dust, chemicals and gases, from psychological stresses, and from the harmful effects of a degrading environment.

Women often work long hours, increasing their exposure to illness and injuries. A large proportion of women are engaged in agricultural work. This can expose them to worm infestations, which aggravate anaemia, to injuries, snake bites and insecticide poisoning on as well as to disorders resulting from extreme climatic conditions. Exposure to pesticides and chemical fertilizers can also result in abortion and stillbirth. The health department must provide facilities against such risks.[14]

8. Violence against Women

Many women face violence throughout their lives, like rape and domestic violence. Although national statistics on violence against women are not readily available, the problem is serious.

Domestic violence is relatively common. Available evidence suggests that thousands of cases of domestic violence are reported directly to police stations each year like dowry deaths are regularly reported by the media. However, domestic violence is often regarded as a private family matter and many cases may therefore go unreported. Fear and shame also contribute to the non-reporting of domestic violence.

9. Increasing General and Functional Literary for Good Health

Education is the most potent factor for changing women's position in society. We must correct the imbalances by encouraging the education of girls. We can use the adult education or non-formal education system. What can be the future of a country where general illiteracy, especially among women, is very high? Besides, the women have also to handle the new generation, i.e. the child who is the future hope.

All this would remain a dream unless women are themselves enlightened. Education is the key factor in elevating the status of women. It equips them to contribute in different fields more meaningfully. Dr. (Mrs.) P.K. Devi, Professor of Gynaecology, in PGI, Chandigarh, has rightly stated on the basis of her critical examination of the various states of the Indian Union, that "Literacy, especially of women seems to be a significant factor in differences in the mortality and morbidity rates between various Indian states and infant mortality rates coincide with a very low female literacy rate."

In India, planners, statesmen, educationists and administrators have come to realise that the pace of development cannot accelerate unless women are also properly qualified. So to improve the education of women quantitatively and qualitatively, the following steps are submitted for consideration:

(a) Expansion of the facilities of women education including adult and vocational education tremendously so that the literacy in respect of this group may be increased.

(b) Removal of disparity between rural and urban literacy by (i) provision of good institutions in villages to avoid the attraction for cities; (ii) to bring awareness towards hygiene among women through community development programmes; (iii) preference in employment to rural people; (iv) setting up of professional and other training institutions in the villages; (v) setting up of rural-based industries in village; (vi) training of women in modern methods of agriculture; (vii) encouraging the formation of mahila mandals to exchange information on various problems facing the nation; and (viii) setting up of model villages.

(c) The contents of women education may be somewhat different from men as women have to devote a lot of their time in homes as well. Jobs in the country are limited and hence the women education (general) can create more frustration rather than prove an asset. Hence along with general education, some course like Home Science, Agriculture, Music, etc. may also be imparted.

(d) Involvement of women at the policy-making, planning and implementation of all the programmes aimed at national reconstruction, e.g. Family Planning, Rural Planning, Rural Development, etc. This would give the impetus to women education.

(e) The share of the women in the Government jobs is very limited at present as the men presume without any justification that women cannot be effective in good administration. The State must employ more and more women if eligible and even, I would suggest that preference may be given till they are properly represented. Strangely, when one sees the University results, the girls are surpassing the boys but the same is not true in Government jobs. More and more women may also be assigned gazetted jobs of responsibility. Women may be encouraged even to take up part-time jobs.

(f) Women may be imparted education in the fields like management, marketing, etc. so that they can actively participate in cooperative organisations. They can make the cooperative movement a success.

(g) Incentive like mid-day meals, scholarships, free school uniforms, free books and study material, stipends, awards, etc., should be extended to all gjrls in the rural areas and urban slums.

(h) Scheme to activate the reduction of drop-outs may be planned.

It may be concluded that women education can help in nation-building. Napoleon once said, "Give me good mothers, I will give you a good nation."

Illiteracy is a great obstruction in the path of development and education is the backbone of democracy. The Director-General of UNESCO has described illiteracy as "the most monstrous of all the many instances of wasted human potential which still at the present time keeps more than one-third of the human race in a state of hopelessness-below the level of modern civilisation." Therefore, in order to translate the essence of the Preamble and the Directive Principles of the State Policy enshrined in the Constitution of India into practical life, it is imperative for us to increase the literacy rate in general and of women in particular.

10. Collecting Accurate Data for Improving Health Status of Women

A lot of difficulty has been experienced with regard to data pertaining to the status of women. Lack of data in quantity and quality would impede effective planning. The action plan suggested that there is a need to augment the information available in the field of health, family planning and nutrition through the following research studies:

1. The data available at present regarding maternal morbidity and mortality are based on hospital statistics and hence are of limited value. The system of registration of vital events is also incomplete. It is suggested that periodic special surveys be undertaken to study the pattern and causes of mortality and morbidity among women and female children. The studies should cover different communities and different regions. Such studies would also provide information on the relative value of age-structure, parity and other "High Risk" factors in the delivery of maternity services.
2. Practical service-oriented field studies should be undertaken to assess the felt needs of the community and their attitudes towards the services offered, with a view to providing guidelines for framing health policy decision relating to the delivery of maternal care and family planning services.
3. Studies be conducted on the inter-relationship between pattern of family formation, nutrition, health and causes and incidence of sterility.
4. Studies of attitudes, beliefs and practice of traditional birth attendants (dais) should be made to improve upon the training programme now designed for them and to obtain their greater participation in maternity and family planning services.
5. The base-line data will have to be established first against which the impact of this plan of action would be measured.

The World Plan of Action has also emphasised that "A scientific and reliable data base should be established and suitable economic and social indicators urgently developed which are sensitive to the particular situation and needs of women as an integral part of the national and inter-national programme of statistics."[15]

11. Planning Women's Participation in their own Welfare

Women should themselves exert pressure to get the due benefits for their welfare. They should unite to form voluntary organizations to help themselves and ultimately the nation. It was rightly stated in the National Plan of action for women that:

> "Women voluntary organisations are best suited for motivation in the field of health, family planning and nutrition. There is therefore, every need for creating a conducive climate, so that they can render the needed service effectively."[16]

The women's voluntary organisation in the form of Mother's Club in the Republic of Korea has been quite useful in raising the status of women. By mid-1997, nearly 70,000 such clubs had been organised. The clubs provide opportunities for village women to get together to talk about health, education of children and improvement of environment. The club helps in family planning, vaccination and treatment of emergency cases. The mother's clubs are a genuinely grass-root community network, which owes little to outside administrators or planners. l.C. Abacde, in his article on "Women Power in Korea" observes that mother's clubs are helping to change age-old social attitudes towards women. He says: "The growth of women's clubs in Korea has coincided with considerable changes in social attitudes towards women. The trend is towards greater recognition between husband and wife, and more open discussion of family planning matters. It seems clear that the enhanced status of women and the growth of mother's clubs have gone hand-in-hand and are contributing significantly to the development of rural communities in Korea."[17]

Such clubs should be set-up in other countries as well. These would help mobilise voluntary resources lying idle and if not used can be a source of destruction. In the developing countries like India, voluntary organisations are urban-based and serve the urban area. These organisations must create a strong base by setting up such clubs and diffuse information to them to be passed on to the members of the community. This would bring about a socio-economic revolution and contribute substantially to modernisation and development.

The planners, policy-makers and administrators responsible for the improvement of the status of women should not be satisfied only with effective planning and policy-making, but should think of the vehicle or administrative structure through which plans and policies are to be implemented. Myron Weiner has rightly pointed out:

> "India's forte is one of the crisis management. Instincts of leadership are to cope, rather than innovate, and to work within an existing framework not only of institutions but of ideas as well."[18]

Thus, with the help of well designed administrative machinery using modern management methods we should try to put the policy into action.

In this implementation process, women themselves will have to be the most forceful agents for change and active participants in the development effort, wherever they have the opportunity to play a dynamic role. The contemporary social situation of women in India should not be frustrating and disheartening but should be rather challenging and it is the men and women of India, particularly the women who have to face the challenge. It has been demonstrated by the women in the field that they are as capable and efficient as men in carrying out various kinds of work and have even much more endurance for hardships than is commonly believed. All of us who are associated with the development of the country in any capacity, must renew our dedication to the cause of women which would eventually lead to national development and modernisation.

The National Health Policy, 2001 (Draft) promises to ensure increased access to women to basic health care and commits highest priority to the funding of the identified programmes relating to women's health. During the Ninth Plan period, several new initiatives were taken as part of the Reproductive and Child Health (RCH) Programme (1997), in order to make it broad-based and client-friendly. All the interventions of the erstwhile programme of Child Survival and Safe Motherhood (CSSM) became part of RCH. During this period, the focus shifted from the individualised vertical interventions to a more holistic integrated life-cycle approach with more attention to reproductive health care. This includes access to essential obstetric care during the entire period of pregnancy, provision of emergency obstetric care as close to the community as possible, improving and expanding early and safe abortion services and provision for treatment of Reproductive Tract Infections/Sexually Transmitted Infections (AT//STI) cases at the sub-district level.

Under the Universal Immunisation Programme, launched in 1985-86, which became part of the RCH Programme in 1997, the coverage of Tetanus Toxoid Vaccination of pregnant women increased from 40 per cent in 1985-86 to 76.4 per cent in 1996-97 and to 83.4 per cent in 2000-01. The scheme of Training of *Dais* was initiated in (2000-01 in 142 districts in 17 states. An extensive network of 2,935 Community Health Centres (CHCs), 22,975 Primary Health Centres (PHCs) and 11,37,271 village level Sub-Centres was put into operation by the end of the Ninth Plan. The Ninth Plan also envisaged to promote institutional deliveries, both in urban and rural areas. A comparison of National Family Health Survey (NFHS) I and II shows that the institutional deliveries has risen from 26 per cent in 1992-93 to 34 per cent in 1998-99. As a result of the above initiatives, the Crude Birth Rate fell from 29.5 to 26.1 and the Crude Death Rate from 9.8 to 8.7 between 1991 and 1999.

The National Nutrition Policy (1993) advocates a comprehensive inter-sectoral strategy for alleviating all the multi-faceted problems of under malnutrition and its related deficiencies and diseases so as to achieve an optimal state of nutrition for all sections of society but with a special priority for women, mothers and children who are vulnerable as well as 'at-risk'. Of the two major problems of macro and micro-nutritional deficiencies that the women, mothers and children suffer from, while the former are manifested through chronic energy deficiency (CED), the latter are reflected in Vitamin A, Iron and Iodine deficiencies. The strategies adopted in the Ninth Plan include—screening of all pregnant women and lactating mothers for CED; identifying women with weight below 40 kg and providing adequate ante-natal, intra-partum and neo-natal care under the RCH programme and ensuring they receive food supplementation through the Integrated Child Development Services (ICDS) Scheme. The ICDS, launched in 1975, provides supplementary feeding to bridge the nutritional gaps that exist in respect of children below 6 years and expectant and nursing mothers.

Besides this, since 2000-01, the Government of India has been providing Additional Central Assistance to the states under the nutrition component of Pradhan Mantri Gramodaya Yojana (PMGY) in an effort to prevent the onset of under-nutrition in the age-group 6-24 months. Supplementary nutrition is also provided to 105 million school-going children under the National Programme of Nutritional Support to Primary Education (also popularly known as Mid-Day Meals Programme).[19]

Inspite of these singular policies, programmes and achievements, there are certain critical areas, which call for immediate attention, as following:

- Inadequacy of institutional mechanisms for the advancement of women.
- Persistent and institutionalised discrimination against the girl child.
- Feminisation of poverty.
- Gender blindness in macro-economic policies.
- Invisibility of women's contribution to the economy and environmental sustenance.
- Poor participation by women in decision-making structures and processes.
- Gender gaps in literacy, education and health.
- Growing trend of violence against women.
- Barriers encountered by women in accessing legal entitlements.
- Gender-biased societal norms.
- Negative portrayals and perpetuation of gender stereotypes by mass media.

Prevailing ill-health among women is a major concern. These are being addressed through several programmes, such as nutrition, RH, MCH and WHD. Inspite of realisation that it is women who die in the process of reproduction, who pay the highest toll for untreated sexually transmitted disease, who bear the largest brunt of poverty, and yet who are conditioned to remain silent. Accordingly, investment in women's health has been one of the actions identified in the Declaration for Health Development in the South-East Asia Region in the 21st Century. It has been recognised in the Declaration that since women's health is integral to development, a multi-sectoral approach would be needed through the development of partnerships with other relevant sectors.[20]

There is a need of increasing women's access to appropriate, affordable and quality health care throughout their lifespan and strengthening preventive programmes that promote women's health. Investing in women's health has strong synergistic effects on other dimensions.

PROBLEMS AND SUGGESTIONS

The Members of the National Commission For Women briefed the Committee about the various problems being faced by women with regard to Health and Family Welfare and spelt out certain areas to which the commission had restricted its activities. These were stated to be as under:

- (i) Need to look at health for women in a holistic and integrated way including physical, mental and social health.
- (ii) Lack of primary health care facilities, viz. primary health centres and sub-centres to cater to women at the district and block level.
- (iii) Inaccessibility of health care facilities by women in remote areas like hilly and tribal regions and need for mobile health clinics.
- (iv) Inadequate budget allocation for women's health and need for specific allocation in the budget allocation for women's health especially in hospital treatment.
- (v) Ignorance about beneficial aspects of other alternate systems of medicine (Ayurveda, Homoeopathy, etc.) for health and family welfare and need to rejuvenate the Ayurveda and other Indian systems of Medicine.
- (vi) Malnutrition among women and lack of gender specific data in this regard.
- (vii) Female foeticide and infanticide leading to a falling female-male ratio.
- (viii) Misuse of pre-natal diagnostic techniques for promoting sex-related abortion.
- (ix) Unmet need for contraceptives both for birth control and prevention of AIDS.
- (x) Lack of proper survey in the field of family welfare and gender specification.
- (xi) Increasing prevalence of Sexually Transmitted Diseases and HIV/AIDS among sex workers.
- (xii) High rate of prevalence of Urinary Tract Infection (UTI) among women.

The Members shared with the commission their views and experience on the lack of basic health facilities specially among the rural women and sex workers and the problems being faced by them. They asked the members of the commission to concentrate in this direction with the help of NGOs, etc. so as to highlight their problems and impress upon the State and Central government to act speedily for their welfare. Members wanted that more Hospitals are opened in rural and semi-rural areas, making it compulsory for all doctors to serve in rural areas for a specified period and ensuring that sufficient numbers of lady doctors posted there.

We may conclude in the words of Pt. Jawaharlal Nehru: "To awaken people; it is the women who must be educated. Once she is on the move, the family moves, the village moves, the nation moves."

RECOMMENDATIONS OF XIth PLAN[21]

During the Eleventh Five Year Plan, for improving maternal health, spcial attention will be focused on the following areas:

- Ensuring universal provision of comprehensive ANC.
- Providing widespread screening for anaemia and high-risk conditions.
- Ensuring comprehensives training programme for skilled birth attendants.
- Ensuring the services of skilled birth attendant at child birth, both for home deliveries and in institutional settings.
- Providing SBA training to dais who are ubiguitous in every nook and corner of the country.
- Enhancing availability of facilities for institutional deliveries and effective EmOC.
- Providing 24-hours Delivery Service at PHC's and CHCs.
- Training of health personnel at PHCs and CHCs to perform emergency obstetrical procedures, especially c-sections.
- Providing additional ANMs and Public Health and Staff Nurses in certain SCs, PHCs and CHCs.
- Providing EmOC in all CHCs in a phased manner (CHCs will have well equipped operation threatre, access to safe banked blood, qualified obstetricians, paediatricians, and anaesthetists).
- Operationalizing FRUs through supply of drugs in the form of Emergency Obsteric drugs kits.
- Providing special attention to roads linking habitations to CHCs.
- Providing Referral Transport.
- Orienting ASHAs to post-partum care and linking her remunerations to health checks of both the mother and newborns.
- Providing Safe Abortion Services.

- Preventing, detecting, and effectively managing common lower RTI through the existing primary health care infrastructure.

Gender Responsive Health Care

The GOI has taken several policy measure to reduce gender bias. The practice of gender budgeting in Health will be made mandatory in all programmes of the Centre and the States. The performance of different programmes will be judged on the basis of gender disaggregated data.

To reduce maternal mortality, several initiatives have been taken to make the maternal health programme broad based and client friendly. The major interventions include providing additional ANMs and Staff Nurses in certain health care facilities; referral transport; 24-hours delivery service at PHCs and CHCs essential and emergency obstetric care; and optimal operationalization of FRUs. All these interventions will have to actually be done on a large sacle during the Eleventh Five Year Plan. The goal is to reduce MMR to 100 per 1,00,000 live births by 2012.

Sex Ratio

The Eleventh Five Year Plan target is to raise the sex ratio for age group 0-5 to 935 by 2011-12 and subsequently to 950 by 2016-17. State specific goald has also been suggested. Other steps for integrating the issue of prenatal sex selection in the initiatives and programmes include the following:

- Increasing community awareness through ASHAs. (See Chart 5.2)
- Including these issues in training modules and programmes and in IEC.
- Adding sex selection information in medical curriculum.
- Including indicators on improvements in sex ratios and birth registrations as monitoring targets.
- Ensuring convergence with other ministries such as Women and Child Development (WCD), Panchayati Raj, and Youth Affairs.

During the Eleventh Five Year Plan, the following additional strategies will be adopted.

- Develop clear targets of natural sex ratio at birth (SRB) which is 105 males per 100 females and give financial benefits to states that have improved SRB. From 2007 onwards, the Annual Health Survey will include estimates of SRB at the district level. The states will be asked as monitor the SRB of the institutional deliveries, by parity, for each facilities as well as for the districts. Improvements in SRB will be considered one of the indicators for arriving at decisions on plan assistance to States.
- Improve availability of data plus its access and quality on SRB. The option of PHC level enumeration will be considered to monitor the SRB on a routine basis.

CHART 5.2

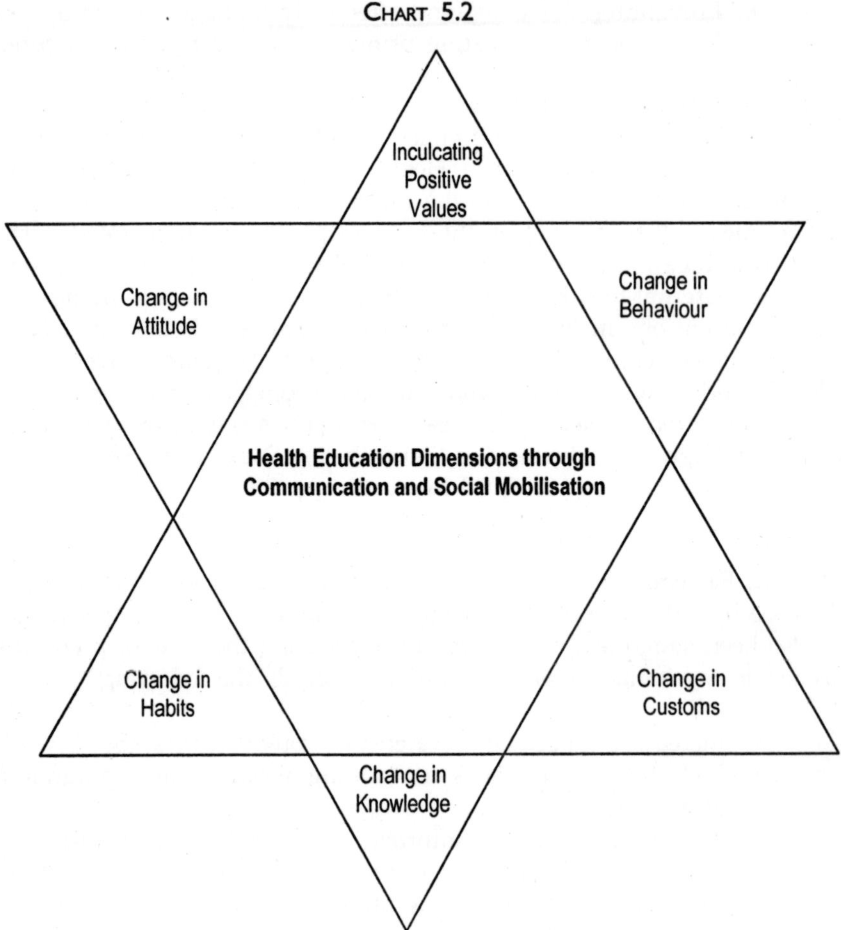

- Provide financial support for capacity building, awareness generation and strict enforcement of PC and PNDT Act.
- Amend the PC and PNDT Act to provide for the independence of the Appropriate Authorities at the district level.
- A National Research and Resource Centre in Health for women will be developed under NRHM.

CONCLUSION

Discrimination against women and girls impinges upon their right to health manifests itself in the form of worsening health and nuturition indices. Thus, India continues to grapple with unacceptably high MMR, IMR, and increasing rats of anaemic, malnutrition, HIV/AIDS among women. According to NFHS-3, incidence of anaemia has risen from 49.7% to 57.9% in pregnant women and from 51.8% to 56.2% in ever-married women within a period of seven years (1988-99 to 2005-06). This has raised anaemia among children by 5 percentage points (to 79.2%) and is also partially responsible for the high MMR. Maternal mortality has a direct correlation with lack of accessibility to health care facilities. Paucity of resources and age-old discriminatory practices deny large number of women access to good nutiriton and care before, during, and after child birth, thus increasing their mortality. Only 22% of mothers consume Iron Folic Acid (IFA) tablets for 90 days or more, and less than half of them receive three ANC visits. As many as 51.7% birth takes place without assistance from any health personnel. Practices such as female foeticide also affect women's health, as they are forced to go through multiple pregnancies and abortions. As a result, although MMR has fallen from 398 in 1998 to 301 in 2001-03 (SR) we are far from meeting the Tenth Plan target of reducing MMR to 200 per 1,00,000 lives briths. States like UP (707), Uttaranachal (517), Assam (409), and MP (498) have very high MMRs.[22]

While the mean age of marriage of women has increased from 15.5 years in 1961 to 19.5 in 1997, 44.5% women are still married off by the age of 18.

Certain states such as Jharkhand (61.2%), Bihar (60.3%), and Rajasthan (57.1) have a much higher percentage of undergate marriage among girls. Among other things, this results in early pregnancies and takes its toll on the health of the women as well as the child.

Women also disproportionately lack access to health services. Inaccessibility of health centres and poverty prevent them from getting timely medical aid. Absence of toilets and drinking water adversely impacts their health. NFHS-3 data reveals that only 27.9% households in rural areas and 70% in urban areas have access to piped water. Further, only 25.9% household in rural areas have access to toilets.

Inadequacies of clean cooking fuels adversely impacts women and children's work burden, health, and nutrition. Till date 92% of rural domestic energy comes from unprocessed biofuels (firewood, crop waste, cattle dung), and 85% of rural cooking fuel is gathered from forests, village commons and fields. Women and girls spend a great deal of time gathering fuel, adversely affecting their productivity and education. Use of firewood and inferior fuels such as weeds or crop wastes leads to smoke-related ailments including respiratory diseases, cancer, and cataracts resulting in blindness.

Then there are sexually transmitted diseases (STDs). NACO estimates that one in three persons living with HIV in India is a woman. The National Council for Applied Economic Research survey shows that women account for more than 70% of the caregivers, 21% of who are themselves HIV positive. Disowned by family and disinherited from property, they are unable to access drugs to prevent mother-to-child-transmission. Nearly 60% of HIV-positive widows are less than 30 years of age and live with their natal families; 91% of them receive no financial support from their marital homes. Thus not only are women more vulnerable to getting infected, but when they are found positive they face much greater discrimination than their male counterparts.[23]

Notes and References

1. WHO: SEARO: Regional Health Report, 1998, Focus on Women, New Delhi; 1998, p. 1.
2. *Ibid.*, p. 2.
3. Government of India, Department of Social Welfare, Ministry of Education and Social Welfare, Towards Equality, Report of the Committee on the Status of Women in India, December, 1974, New Delhi, p. 310.
4. Lok Sabha Secretariat, Committee on Empowerment of Women (2001-02), Fourth Report, Thirteenth Lok Sabha, Health and Family Welfare Programmes for Women, New Delhi, Aug. 2001, pp. 13-16.
5. Department of Social Welfare, GOI, Blue Print of Action. Points and National Plan of Action for Women, New Delhi, 1988.
6. WHO: SEARO, Regional Health Report, 1998, Focus on Women, New Delhi, 1998, p. 7.
7. GOI, Planning Commission, Ninth Five Year Plan, 1997-2002, Vol. II, New Delhi, p. 322.
8. Lok Sabha Secretariat, Committee on Empowerment of Women (2001-02), Fourth Report, 13th Lok Sabha, p. 21.
9. WHO: SEARO Regional Health Report, 1998, Focus on Women, New Delhi, 1998, p. 8.
10. GOI, Economic Survey, 2002-03, p. 233.
11. Regional Health Report, 1998, *op. cit.*, p. 610.
12. WHO, SEARO: Regional Health Report, 1998, Focus on Women, New Delhi, 1998, p. 13.
13. *Ibid.*, pp. 21-23.
14. *Ibid*, p. 26.
15. World Plan of Action, Para 166.
16. National Plan of Action for Women, p. 71.
17. WHO: World Health, May 1979, p. 19.
18. ICSSSR: Programme of Women's Studies, New Delhi; 1977, p. 10.
19. GOI, Planning Commission, Xth Five Year Draft Plan, 2002-07, pp. 217-23.
20. WHO: SEARO: Highlights of the World of WHO in the South-East Asia Region, I July 1997-30 June, 1998, New Delhi, SEARO, 1998, p. 37.
21. GOI, Planning Commission, XIth Five Year Plan, 2007-12.
22. India, Registrar General and Census Commissioner (2004), Primary Census abstract, "Total Population—Census of India, 2001", New Delhi, p. iii.
23. GOI, Planning Commission, XI'th Five Year Plan, pp. 87-88.

6

Empowerment through Education

Education has been of central significance to the development of human society. It can be the beginning, not only of individual knowledge, information and awareness, but also of a holistic strategy for development and change.[1] Late Prime Minister Jawahar Lal Nehru rightly remarked: "Some people seem to think that education is not so important as putting up a factory. I may sacrifice any number of factories, but I will not sacrifice human beings and their education because it is the human beings who set-up factories and produce the things we want." UNESCO has described illiteracy as "the most monstrous of all the many instances of wasted human potential—which still at the present time keeps more than one-third of the human race in a state of Hopelessness, below the level of modern civilization." It is imperative to increase the literacy rate to bring about all round development. Education helps an individual to develop his potential to the full, to increase his productivity and to become a useful and productivity member of society. Education is holistic in concept and is multi-dimensional. (See Chart 6.1)

Education is a critical input in human resource development and is 'essential for the country's economic growth. Though the major indicators of socio-economic development viz., the growth rate of the economy, birth rate, death rate, infant mortality rate (IMR) and literacy rate, are all inter-connected, the literacy rate has been the major determinant of the rise or fall in the other indicators. There is enough evidence even in India to show that a high literacy rate, especially in the case of women, correlates with low birth rate, low IMR and increase in the rate of life expectancy. The recognition of this fact has treated awareness on the need to focus upon literacy and elementary education programme, not simply as a matter of social justice but more to foster economic growth, social well-being and social stability.[2]

CHART 6.1

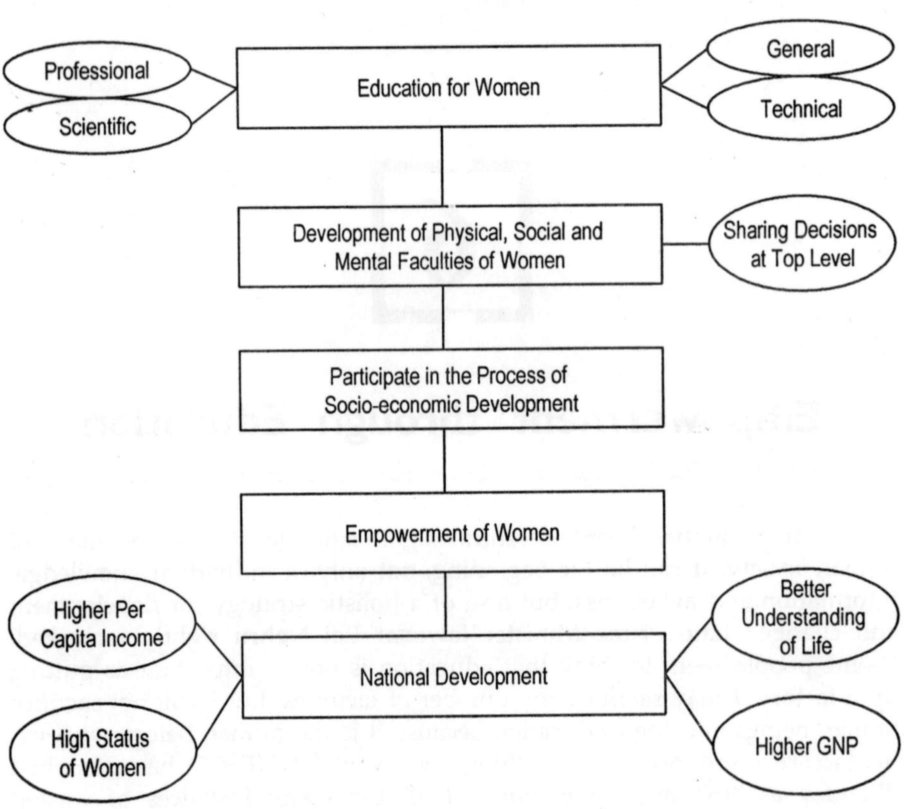

"The general purpose and objective of women's education cannot, of course, be different from the purpose and objective of men's education . . . At the secondary and even at the university stage women's education should have a vocational or occupational bias.[3]

"In a democratic society where all citizens have to discharge their civic and social obligations, differences which may lead to variation in the standards of intellectual development achieved by boys and girls cannot be envisaged."[4]

"In the progressive society of tomorrow, life should be a joint venture for men and women. Men should share the responsibility of parenthood and home-making with women and women in their turn should share the social and economic responsibilities of men."[5]

"Women and men education should have many elements in common, but should not in general be identical in all respects, as is usually the case today. A woman should learn something of problems that are certain to come up in all marriages, and in the relations of parents and children, and how they may be met. Her education should make her familiar with problems of home management and skilled in meeting them, so that she may take her place in a home with the same interest and the same sense of competence that a well trained man has in working at his calling."[6]

"The educational system must produce young men and women of character and ability committed to national service and development. Only then will education be able to play its vital role in promoting national progress, creating a sense of common citizenship and culture and strengthening national integration."[7]

Education was a state subject till 1976 and then was placed in the Concurrent List by the 42nd Constitutional Amendment. Placing education in the Concurrent List means a dominant role for the Central Government viz.:

(i) to determine the policies, priorities and programmes relating to education,
(ii) to provide effective leadership to the States,
(iii) to provide funds for educational development in the States,
(iv) to take steps for minimizing regional imbalances in educational development and for equalization of educational opportunities in different States,
(v) to take steps for promoting national integration through education, and
(vi) to carry out uniform educational reforms in the country.

The following Table 6.1 indicates the literacy rate in India and male and female literacy rates in the country from 1951:

TABLE 6.1

Male and Female Gap in Literacy

Census year	*Persons*	*Males*	*Females*	*Male-female gap in literacy rate*
1951	18.33	27.16	8.86	18.30
1961	28.30	40.40	15.35	25.05
1971	24.35	45.96	21.97	23.98
1981	43.57	56.38	29.76	26.62
1991	52.21	64.13	39.29	24.84
2001	65.38	75.85	54.16	21.70

Source: Census of India.

It is evident from the above table that the gap in male-female literacy rates of 18.30 percentage points in 1951, increased to 26.62 in 1981, but has improved since then. In 1991 this gap was reduced to 24.84 and in 2001 it has further gone down to 21.70 percentage points. These declines according to the Department of Elementary Education and Literacy are bound to be slow initially as a result of the continuing past legacy of a large number of adult illiterate women, but will show accelerated trends in the coming decade.

The following Table 6.2 indicates the number of literates and illiterates in the population aged 7 years and above, and their change from 1991 to 2001. It is seen from Table 6.2 that out of the 203 million added to the literate population during 1991-2001, 107 million were males and 95 million were females. On the other hand, during this period the contribution to the total decrease of 31 million among illiterates is dominated by males (21 million) as compared to the females (10 million).

TABLE 6.2

Number of Males and Females

Literates	*Persons*	*Males*	*Females*
1991	358,402,626	228,983,34	129,419,492
2000	562,010,743	336,969,695	225,041,048
Increase in 2001 over 1991	203,608,117	107,986,561	95,621,556
Illiterates			
1991	328,167,288	128,099,211	200,068,077
2001	296,208,952	106,654,066	189,554,886
Increase in 2001 over 1991	-31,958,336	-21,445,145	-105,131,991

Source: Census of India

It is seen from the above table that the literacy rate for the country as a whole in 2001 works out to 65.38 per cent for the population aged 7 years and above. The corresponding figures for male and female literacy are 75.85 and 54.16 per cent respectively. Thus, three-fourths of the male and more than half of the female population aged 7 years and above are literate in the country today. Although female literacy has improved to 54.16% in 2001 from 39.29% in 1991, it is still far behind the male literacy rate of 75.85%. In fact, no State or Union Territory has an equal or greater literacy rate for women. Further, female . literacy rate is very low in Jharkhand, (39.38%), Arunachal Pradesh (44.24%), Bihar (33.57%), Uttar Pradesh (42.97%), Rajasthan (44.34%), and Jammu and Kashmir (41.82%).[7]

ENROLMENT TRENDS

Enrolment at the primary level (Grades I to V) increased from 19.16 million in 1950-51 to 113.8 million in 2000-01. In comparison, the growth in enrolment at the upper primary level (grades VI to VIII) has been much more impressive, although it is still not adequate to attain the

Constitutional goal of universal enrolment of children up to the age of 14. From 3.12 million in 1950-51, enrolment at the upper primary level increased to 42.06 million in 1999-2000, indicating a 13.5 times increase as against six times at the primary level. The percentage share of girls in total enrolment, both at the primary and upper primary levels, has increased consistently between 1950-51 (28.1 per cent) and 1999-2000.

Shockingly, of the 900 million illiterates in the world, almost one-third belong to India. In other words, Indians constitute the largest number of uneducated people in the world. It is a paradoxical situation in which the gains made in the realm of education since independence have been overshadowed by the presence of a huge population of illiterates, especially in rural India, and more so among girls. Admittedly, the massive increase in the population in the last 50 years has been one of the major reasons for the imbalance in the literacy-population ratio. But, this can hardly be a ground for absolving the nation of its responsibility for the failure in providing primary education to all children.

Inter-State disparities also exist in regard to the female literacy rate. The Committee feel that special measures should be taken in those States, where female literacy rate is very low as compared to the all India average. These States are: Jharkhand (39.98%), Arunachal Pradesh (44.24%), Bihar (33.57%), Uttar Pradesh (42.97), Rajasthan (44.34%) and Jammu and Kashmir (41.82%). The Government need to study the situation in these States with a view to identifying the precise reasons for the low female rates there, so that necessary steps could be taken in consultation and coordination with the respective State Governments, apart from vigorously implementing the Schemes/Programmes already in operation.

The Department of Elementary Education and Literacy have asserted that consistent efforts have been made to improve the participation of girls in the field of education in the last 50 years. According to them, the Gross Enrolment Ratio (GER) for girls has gone up from 24.8 per cent in 1950-51 at the primary level to 81.8 per cent in 1996-97. The Committee find that while the GER for girls at the primary stage in the country, as a whole and in most States, has improved, it is low as compared to GER for boys. A study of the progressive enrolment of girls and boys at primary and middle school levels points to a massive gender gap. Further, there are a few States/UTs where the (GER) is considerably low in respect of girl students. These are Bihar (54.6%), Jammu and Kashmir (53.1%), Uttar Pradesh (59.9%) and Chhatisgarh (62.1%). Similarly, the drop-out rate in respect of girls is very high in some of the States such as Bihar (63.44%), West Bengal (55.59%), Tripura (56.65%), Sikkim (55.4%), Rajasthan (57.2%), Mizoram (56.95) and Meghalaya (62.46%).

The Committee are concerned over the lower Gross Enrolment Ratio and higher drop-out rates among girls especially as compared to those in respect of boys. Low enrolment ratio and high dropout rates lead to children especially girls, lapsing into illiteracy, rendering futile, the efforts and investments made in improving literacy. The main reason for this situation in rural areas is that girls are engaged in household works such as fuel and fodder collection, fetching of water and care of siblings. The other reasons could be parent's lack of interest, poverty, absence of single sex schools, unsafe travel and lack of facilities in schools such as women teachers, separate toilets, etc.

The Committee strongly feel that there is urgent need to remove the fronstraints that lead parents to keep their daughters out of school. And once girls are in school, it must be ensured they are prepared for life, by developing curricula, textbooks and teaching attitudes that emphasise the life skills they will need. But the first step is for society to recognize that educating girls are not an option, but a necessity. This calls for a massive programme of awareness generation in the educationally backward areas of the country.

The Committee are of the firm opinion that the achievement of universalisation of elementary education is essential as it is an index of the general, social and economic development of the country. Primary education plays an important role in laying the proper foundation of the cultural, emotional, intellectual, moral, physical, social and spiritual developments of the children. The economic and social returns for education of women are, on the whole, greater than those of men. Education empowers girls by building up their confidence and enabling them to take firm decisions about their lives. By educating women we can reduce poverty, improve productivity, ease population pressure and offer the children a better future.

The Committee are informed that various schemes/programmes such as the National Literacy Mission, Mahila Samakhya, Operation Blackboard, Non-formal Education, Lok Jumbish and District Primary Education Programme, have been initiated/undertaken for improvement of girls' education. These schemes are stated to have made enormous progress in terms of increase in number of schools, teachers and students in elementary education. The progress achieved in the female literacy rate during the last decade has been attributed to a great extent to the implementation of these schemes. The Sarva Shiksha Abhiyan (SSA) is stated to be another new holistic and integrated approach for universalising elementary education. Based on the experience of programmes for girls' education and women's empowerment, the proposed Sarva Shiksha Abhiyan, which is in mission mode, adopts many of the successful initiatives. The Sarva Shiksha Abhiyan has the objective of bringing every child in the 6-14 age group to school/back to school to an Education Guarantee Scheme Centre by 2003. It also aims at providing 5 years of primary schooling for all by 2007 and 8 years of elementary schooling by 2010. Mainstreaming of gender in all the proposed interventions through the District Elementary Education Plan (DEEP) is central to the proposed Sarva Shiksha Abhiyan. The Committee hope that vigorous efforts would be made under the aforesaid schemes/ programmes to ensure that the constitutional obligation of providing free and compulsory education for all children upto the age of 14 years becomes a reality.

The Committee or Empowerment of Women (2001-02), Sixth Report, Thirteen Lok Sabha desires that the following measures be taken on priority basis to achieve the objective of education for all and especially for girls:

(i) Universal enrolment of all children.

(ii) Provision of primary school, within one kilometer of walking distance.

(iii) Facility of non-formal education for school drop-outs, working children and girls who cannot attend schools.

(iv) Reduction of drop-out rates especially of girls.

(v) Achievement of minimum levels of learning by all children at the primary level, and introduction of this concept at the upper primary stage on a large scale.

(vi) Increased allocation of funds for various schemes/programmes initiated for girls' education and optimum utilization of allotted funds.

(vii) Taking up of intensive awareness generation activities for bringing about change in societal attitude towards girls' education.

(viii) Orientation of educational policies to take care of specific needs and requirements of girls and women, particularly in their socio-economic context.

(ix) Orientation of policies in other sectors for providing support and facilitating access to services like pure drinking water, fuel, fodder and creches, thus freeing them from the drudgery of households chores, to help girls attend to their education.

(x) Gearing up of economic policies to improve employment of women and their earning capabilities so that they can relive.

(xi) Exploring the possibilities/potential of imparting distance education, through to reach backward areas—SC/ST/Rural women/nomadic tribes/slum-dwellers of urban centres.

The Committee further recommend that to increase retention and reduce drop-outs, the following measures may be taken by the Department in consultation with the State Governments:

(i) School should be made an attractive place, learning an enjoyable experience and teaching child centred and activity-oriented, with text books made colourful and attractive from the child's point of view.

(ii) Early childhood education or pre-school education focuses on providing a learning environment for children under the age of six years. This fosters the natural process of initiating children into self-motivated education in which they learn as they play.

Apart from enabling the all round development of children through child-centred play activities, this ensures that young girls are freed of their responsibility of sibling care enabling them to go to schools and thus contributing to universalisation of primary education. The Committee, therefore, emphasise the need for pre-school education as a significant input for providing a sound foundation for the growth and development of a child, especially from poor families. Government should pay special attention to this aspect.

(iii) The teachers should be motivated, dedicated and fully tramed. NCERT should launch a pilot programme in close collaboration with State Councils of Education, Research and Training for the training of teachers. There should be provision for substitute full time teachers in all schools including Kendriya Vidyalayas when regular teachers go on long leave so that students do not suffer.

(iv) Instead of raw wheat/rice, cooked meals should be served to children.

(v) Free text-books, uniforms and teaching/learning materials may be provided at the start of the academic session especially in rural areas for girls.

(vi) Proper toilets and drinking water facilities should be made available particularly in the girls and co-educational schools.

(vii) The children of the nomadic tribes, shifting cultivators, and construction workers are the most vulnerable group of school drop-outs. Therefore, special attention must be paid to the target groups.

(viii) Vigorous steps are needed to associate, the elected representatives of the Panchayati Raj Institutions in the Literacy Programmes. The women elected to local bodies should be actively involved in such programme and be provided sufficient protection while they act as supervisors of the educational institutions.

(ix) The Anganwadi Workers should also be involved to play an active role and should be the focal point for a number of activities and support services for the literacy programmes especially for girls.

(x) Basic education programmes such as Lok Jumbish and District Primary Education Programme have built in decentralisation as part of their management structures. The Committee desire that the local community, parents, women and local bodies should be associated in education through participation in the decentralised management structures like Village Education Committees, Parent-Teacher Associations, etc.[8]

STATUS OF WOMEN IN EDUCATION

Women in education possess immense potentialities as they have entered in this profession in a big way. However, their number at top levels is very less as compared to their intellectual attainments. Let us explain with the example of Vice-chancellors in the Universities. These positions are mostly occupied by male members with low qualifications as compared to female members. This has resulted in demoralization of women in the education system. In a Seminar at National Institute of Education Planning and Administration, it was unanimously decided that search panels for Vice-Chancellors should include one woman educationist. The policy-makers have always obliged male candidates as compared to female. It is high time that women should be selected, nominated to top positions to make their place in higher education. They possess more qualities of head and heart in providing leadership in higher education. From childhood, girl child is made a small manager of the house to support her mother. She works systematically and can change the deteriorating institutions into institutions of excellence.

Swami Vivekananda states that "the ideal of all education, all training, should result in man/woman making. But, instead of that, we are always trying to polish up the outside. What use is polishing up the outside when there is no inside? The end and aim of all training is to make the man/woman grow. The man who influences, who throws his magic, as it were, upon his fellow-beings, is a dynamo of power, and when that man is ready, he can do anything and everything he likes; that personality put upon anything will make it work.

Training is defined as:

(a) an action process,
(b) by which capabilities of the personnel can be improved,
(c) to meet the needs in terms of their knowledge, skills and attitudes required in performing tasks and functions, and
(d) within relatively short period of time.

The objective of the training is to provide an individual with the knowledge of the environment or ecology under which he is to function; the knowledge of administrative management to achieve optimum performance and cultivation of necessary attitudes.

The objectives of imparting knowledge through training are:

(i) Development of rational thinking,
(ii) Development of objective thinking,
(iii) Development of social understanding,
(iv) Development of aesthetic responsiveness,
(v) Development of practical abilities, and
(vi) Development and placement of memory in action.

Swami Ashoka Nanda wants the leader to gain wisdom. To quote him: that wisdom beyond which there is no further knowledge to be gained, in Sanskrit it is called vidya or jnana-terms that indicate not intellectual knowledge but final knowledge. This final knowledge is really the exact meaning of the Sanskrit word Vedanta; Veda means "knowledge," and anta means "final" or "end."

Kanwalpreet in her article, "Leading the leadership race" in *The Tribune* dated November 10, 2002 opines that successful leaders are like ants who never wave even if a lot is placed as an obstacle in their way. They have a knack of springing up after every failure. When Michealangelo was asked as to why he spends so much time in trying to perfect every piece of art, he replied, "Trifles make up perfection and perfection is no trifle." Dr. Rashmi Diwan, in her article, "Self-Development must for Transformational Leadership" feels that Transformational leadership would call for drastic changes in the behaviour of self before it could be applied to the organization. Good managers can be transformed into successful leaders but through real world leadership training.

Swami Chinmayananda says that a life organized for the discovery of the potentialities already exists within ourselves, and the ordering of our behaviour so as to nurture and nourish them, is a life well spent. Herein our success depends upon the amount of transformation we can successfully bring about in our personality and character. The vital question is not how many talents each one of us has, but how much of our existing talents are we capable of exploring, developing and exploiting. An individual may have many talents, and yet, he can be a miserable failure in life. That person is successful who makes a practical use of at least one great talent that he possesses. Our present and future welfare thus mainly depends upon ourselves. Let us never look outside ourselves for help. Let us not fall into the delusion that the influence of others would enable us to do better or accomplish more. All our success entirely depends upon ourselves. Let us realize these fundamentals. We must.

UGC and its autonomous body National Assessment and Accredition Council have chalked out programmes for sensitizing women in the art and science of leadership role in higher education. Prof. V.N. Rajasekhran Pillai, Former Director NAAC feels that the scope of training programmes on women managers' capacity building as a post-accreditation activity of NAAC. The women identified during the process of assessment and accredition are listed for capacity building and training. Dr. Armati Desai, the Former Chairperson of UGC mentioned that the purpose of training women is to sensitise for assuming leadership roles in higher education.

UGC had initiated the project of developing base material for training in the Indian context in line with the manuals developed by the Commonwealth Secretariat, London. The aim of the series of training workshops is to address the invisibility of women in managerial positions in higher education and enable women to understand and deal with such barriers in reaching leadership positions in colleges and Universities in the higher education system.

Based upon discussion with women who are already leaders and potential leaders, we mention the following suggestions to enhance the share of women's leadership in higher education:

(I) Policy Guidelines to Nominate Outstanding Women as Vice-Chancellors

This training-*cum*-capacity building programme can be a success only if the women are sure that they are going to be encouraged and not discouraged. A Chief Minister of a State while considering the outstanding bio-data of a woman remarked, "can these women manage Universities which have become complex institutions." If it was so, how could women become Chief Ministers, Ministers without any training and majority of them doing excellent work. This training to women in education leadership should not spread the message that the women lack in leadership. It may not be out of context to mention that women are second to none. Alongwith the training programme, policy-makers like Chief Ministers, Chancellors, UGC authorities, Ministry of Human Resource Development should also be apprised that women should not be ignored while appointing people on key bodies in the Universities. Even nomination to the University decision-making bodies by the Chancellors are done mostly of men, while women are only marginal. This training programme would be depressing in the long-run, until and unless, more and more women are encouraged to occupy positions of leadership in educational system.

(2) Training should be Practical Based on Case Studies

NAAC should prepare case studies in the same area of leadership for women Vice-Chancellors and men Vice-Chancellors. This would provide both positive and negative points particularly faced on account of being a woman. It has been seen that the universities and colleges headed by women run better and in a positive direction. Whatever the failures, we may analyse them and include these problems in the curriculum of training. Women who have worked for 20-25 years in a college or a University are well aware of the University system, what is needed is to build confidence or faith in them.

(3) Developing Faith and Confidence among Potential Women Leaders

Faith is one of the forces by which men and women live and the total absence of it means collapse. Unlimited energy is latent in every woman but because of her restricted imagination, it results into inaction. Self-confidence will activate the spirit of enthusiasm and lead women along the path of achieving great things in life.

Swami Vivekananda repeatedly stressed the need for cultivating the faith in one self: "the ideal of faith in ourselves is of the greatest help to us. If faith in ourselves had been more extensively taught and practised, I am sure a very large portion of the evils and miseries that we have would have vanished. Throughout the history of mankind, if any motive power has been more potent than another in the lives of all great men and women, it is that of faith in themselves. Born with the consciousness that they were to be great, they became great. Let a man or woman go down as low as possible; there must come a time when out of sheer desperation he will take an upward curve and will learn to have faith in himself or herself. But it is better for us that we should know from the very first experience. Why should we have all bitter experiences in order to gain faith in ourselves? We can see that all the difference between man and man or woman to woman is owning to the existence or non-existence of faith in himself or herself. Faith in ourselves will do everything.

Behind every achievement that we see in this world today, is the unseen hand of the human will. The material comforts, scientific achievements are all the products crystallized out of the human will and determination. The human will-power has conquered Nature, and made her a slave for the welfare of mankind, and in the process, has, even created things which were not even available in the world before. Behind all the technological progress are the determined efforts of hundreds of dedicated men and women, who faced all the challenges to make their dreams come true.

Many of us, what we see today as solid facts of life and proof of man's achievements were only mere ideas yesterday in the minds of a few men of great will power. Those ideas would not have become realities, had they not put the will and determination to their ideas into practice. Our scriptures too have given us examples of men of great will, like Viswamitra who could even create a new world outfit out of sheer will power. All men of achievement had the blessing of tremendous will power in their makeup, and History is full of names of such men and women of achievement.

(4) Specific Action Plan and Strategy

The training for women in leadership in higher education should consist of the following measures to make an all round improvement:

(a) Arresting obsolescence, both individual and organisational (preventive);
(b) Bridging pre-active insufficiencies of knowledge and professional skills (curative);
(c) Shaping adjustments with socio-technological, environmental changes (adaptive);
(d) Developing new outlook, an ethological version of quality excellence and accomplishment (promotive); and
(e) Making a total woman with new cultural attributes (transformative).

The value of work is judged, not by its quantum but by the quality and texture thereof. The quality of action depends upon the deals which guide and inspire an individual working in the world. The tier and nobler the ideas, the greater will be the beauty of his actions and efficiency. All mighty men and women of superhuman achievements have, inspired by such ideals, done wonderfully great and noble work in he, world and fruits of their actions are enjoyed by generations which follow them.

In the present world, man or woman is found wanting in definite ideas for canalising his or her activities. He or she works with a selfish attitude and has no goal or vision in life to inspire him or her to take better and brighter actions. He/she experiences monotony in any work undertaken by him/her, whether one be a clerk in the secretariat or a manager of an organisation. He/she is fatigued no sooner than he/she reaches his/her office and commences his/her work; and by evening he/she has hardly any energy left to reach his/her home. In such a state of affairs, his/her work becomes worthless and he/she becomes a burden upon the society.

The secret of success, therefore, lies in overcoming such mental dissipation by choosing a definite and noble ideal or goal in life, working relentlessly and with dedication, concentrating thereupon for Its achievement. Such activities, undertaken in a spirit of surrender and selflessness, lend constant inspiration and inward solace, a charm and a cheer to life and lead us to efficiency and success.

(5) Emphasis on Positive Work Culture which is Lacking in our Educational System

The first factor necessary for success is work. An individual has to work even though he or she would like to have success without work. There is only one place where success comes before work, and that is in the dictionary. So work is a must for success. We see many people working laboriously. Still, they do not seem to accomplish anything. This is because there is no efficiency in their work. Efficiency is the second factor required for success. The skill or knack of working or performing an action in such a way that it will bear the desired fruit is called efficiency. The third factor required is knowledge, to perform work, knowledge is a must. Knowledge means:

(1) knowledge of our desired goal;
(2) knowledge of the means to attain the goal; and
(3) knowledge of the performer who is going to adopt the means and strive for the goal.

This knowledge is called proficiency. A person who has knowledge but no efficiency cannot be successful. The difference can be seen in the material progress of India as compared to other countries such as the United States or Japan. In India, more emphasis is given to theoretical knowledge. Indian universities impart a lot of information, but practical knowledge is overlooked, while in America more emphasis is given to the practical aspect and work is done efficiently. Therefore, even though so many students are graduating from universities in India with outstanding degrees, what is the condition of India materially? We are speaking only from the material point of view at the moment. India's prosperity cannot be compared to the prosperity of the United States, Canada or Japan because India has neglected the practical aspect.

When a person works with inspiration, he never gets tired or exhausted. When man works only for himself, there is perspiration; but when he works for a noble goal, there is inspiration. In cases where a person cannot dedicate one's actions to the cause, even if he works for some ideal or goal he will derive tremendous strength from his chosen altar of dedication. The nobler the goal, the greater will be the strength one gains. This is the beauty of love and dedication, which brings efficiency in life.

Work ethic embraces work responsibility, work conscience, ethical work conduct. If one has the satisfaction that he is contributing his very best to his organization and is not just earning the bread, then this would be the true feeling of work ethics. Work ethic demands that one works for attaining organizational objectives in its fullest measures.

The study of values is fundamental to the understanding and managing of organizational behaviour. The value orientations of managers underlie managerial behaviour. Values are pervasive because they are involved in the selection of missions, goals and objectives. The job of planning, organizing and controlling the behaviour of individuals should also be compatible with manager's values. Values lay the foundation for the understanding of attitudes, motivation and perceptions

To quote Shri S.K. Bhatia, these values are:

Truth:	Treat others with uncompromising truth.
Trust:	Lavish trust on your associates.
Mentoring:	Mentor unselfishsly.
Openness:	Be receptive to new ideas.
Giving-credit:	Give credit where it is due.
Risk-taking:	Take personal risks for the good of the organization.
Honesty:	Be honest in all dealings, do not touch dishonest money.
Caring:	Put the interests of others before your own social conscience.

(6) Women leaders in education should promote Harmony and Peace

In the world today, we are living through an age of confusions and tensions, both within and without. The external challenges persecute us and render our lives unhappy and sorrow ridden. The intelligent philosophy of the Rishis advises man 'to live in harmony' with the situations in life and steadily work on to meet them with discretion and constant application. When we live thus for a period of time, a subjective poise develops, giving us inward peace and tranquillity, which, thereafter, remains unaffected by external threats and onslaughts.

Revered Shri Vethatheri, Maharishi says: 'Harmony is a precious treasure of human life'. Real success, satisfaction and happiness are the different facets of harmony. If one is to enjoy the benefits of life to the fullest, it is necessary to develop and maintain harmony; and for this understanding the philosophy of nature is required.

- Harmony should be maintained in all spheres of life, and these:
- Between body and life;
- Between wisdom and habits;
- Between self and society;
- Between the purpose of life and the method of living; and
- Between will and nature

The more one understands life, the more one will achieve harmony; and success will be proportionate to that. No doubt, harmonizing life is a difficult task, but is worth all the striving, for it is the only way to equip oneself to enjoy life to the fullest extent and to reach the goal of life, which is the perfection of consciousness. By the development of knowledge man comes to understand the cause and effect system, which is the law of nature.

(7) Training for Creativity

Creativity is defined as, "Energizing connected mental communication to bring out something original, new and different." In other words, it means "creativity is the imaginatively gifted recombination of known elements into some thing new." We are here more concerned about the problem-solving element. It therefore suffices to say, "Creativity is keeping blocked minds open."

Creativity plays a vital role in decision-making and problem-solving. It helps individuals and the groups to arrive at better decision-making. Creative decisions are good to the extent that they depart from the routine and cut new grounds, nor for its own sake, but for improving the quality of the outcomes.

Creativity is also a high risk activity. A great deal of time and efforts are required to generate new ideas. Excessive use of policies, procedures, rules and schedules impede creativity. Proper training in creativity for solving problems is very essential, so that the right type of technique is used.

Leadership of Women in Education should be an example for men as they possess better qualities especially integrity, sincerity and professionalism. Even, women leaders in local institutions, i.e. Panchayati Raj Institutions are proving their worth and have great enthusiasm.

Women in rural Punjab have secured more than their rightful 33 per cent share in the grass-root democratic institution of gram panchayats by heading more than 4,200 of the 22,446 panchayats in June 2003. Though those elected are a mixed group, both illiterate and educated, they mostly have a common minimum programme to work for upliftment of the weaker sections of society. Adult literacy, pension for the aged and poor, better educational and healthcare facilities and overall development of villages is all they want to achieve in their five-year term.

Many of them promise to do it on their own, with the support of fellow panches, while some others, inexperienced and introvert, will depend upon either their husbands or educated sons to help them discharge their responsibilities. In some cases, even experience of in-laws is promised to be utilised in running day-to-day affairs of the panchayat.

Prabhjot Singh while interviewing Balwinder Kaur, aged 30, Sarpanch of Mullanpur Garibdass village (Ropar) finds her views which indicate her potential for effective leadership. To quote her views: (*The Tribune* dated July 4, 2003).

"My endeavour would be to work for overall development of the village and see it come up as a model village." The first and foremost task will be laying proper sewerage and drainage, besides providing proper toilet facilities for women. Emphasis will also be on making the village lanes 'pucca' and providing adequate street lighting facilities. She will also strive to get the Notified Area Committee (NAC) status for the village. Balwinder attributes her success to her father-in-law, Mr. Naib Singh Dhaliwal, a former surpanch of this village, and goodwill of the family in the village. A widow, she has been staying with her in-laws. "Though I will continue to have the support of my family. I would try and take independent decisions and come up to the expectations of those who have reposed confidence in my abilities."

Other women also possess enthusiasm and they are keen to change the life of the people in villages. The need is to provide them training so that women can face the challenges both internal and external. Women in education must learn from these village women, the qualities of leadership to make their place in education system and other areas.

The "Sub-committee on Women's Role in Planned Economy", set-up by the National Planning Committee of the Congress Party, in 1939 observed as follows:

> "We do not wish to turn woman into a cheap imitation of man or to render her useless for the great tasks of motherhood and nation-building. But in demanding equal status and opportunity, we desire to achieve for women the possibility of development under favourable circumstances of education and opportunity. . . . We would like to displace the picture so deeply impressed upon the racial imagination of man striding forward to conquer new worlds, woman following wearily behind with a baby in her arms. The picture which we now envisage is that of man and woman, comrades of the road, going forward together. . ."

Subramanya Bharathi was perhaps one of the greatest exponents of the cause of the status of women. He believed:

- Women are equal to men in their mental faculties.
- Women shall rule the land.
- Women shall take up making laws.

Training is essential for building confidence, commitment and competence. Mahabir Singh Kasana, rightly observes, "Training is very important component of Human Resource Development. It is, perhaps the most cost effective method of improving competencies amongst the manpower of any organisation. Training has been defined as a planned process to impart knowledge, develop skills and motify attitude of the work force through learning processes to achieve the effective performance in any activity or range of activities. The right mix of knowledge, skills and attitudinal components in a training course or a training programme is essential for performance improvement. Performance calls for upgrading confidence, competence and commitment of the persons to enable them to handle the situation and show the results on the ground. Whereas, increase in knowledge, arguability imparts confidence, the skills contribute to enhancement of competence of individuals. The attitude primarily leads to commitment to job. Possessing of the right aptitude, combined with appropriate knowledge and skills is required to be assured through training efforts. It is, therefore, necessary that a systematic approach to training linking it with performance is necessary. Developing confidence, competence and commitments require enriching learning experience consisting of Tell, Show, Do, Check and Act through systematic approach to training.

Training to women in Education Leadership is a right step to women development and empowerment. The scheme run by UGC and NAAC is full of potentialities. There should be linkage between training and promotion of women in higher echelons of educational administration. Instead of arranging these programmes at selected places, why not these, may be got done through Academic Staff Colleges, on a regular basis.

It is hoped that UGC and NAAC would find success in their venture when more than 50 per cent of women would be occupying positions of leadership in higher education system.

Pure, We Must be,
Sincere, We Must Become.
Earnestness, We Must Befriend,
Dedicated Living, We Must Bequeath.
Joyous Living We Must Behold,
When We Live in And For the Beloved Alone.

Globalization has put a premium on skills and higher levels of education, which are often out of reach of women in the unorganized sector. A key issue in the Eleventh Plan is to enable these women to secure higher level and better paid jobs through vocational training and skills development. Women need technology support, credit facilities, and marketing support to take up entrepreneurial activities in new and emerging trades. At the same time, women's traditional skills such as knowledge of herbal plants, weaving, food processing, or providing 'care' will be recognized and marketed.[9]

Notes and References

1. Lok Sabha Secretariat, Committee on Empowerment of Women, (2001-02), Sixth Report, Thirteenth Lok Sabha, Education Programmes for Women, Ministry of HRD, Dec. 2001, p. 1.
2. GOI, Planning Commission, Xth Plan (Draft), 2002-07.
3. First Five Year Plan, Government of India, 1951, Chapter XXXIII.
4. Report of the Secondary Education Commission, Govt. of India, 1953, Chapter IV.
5. Report of the Committee on Differentiation of Curricula for boys and girls, Govt. of India, 1954, Chapter IV.
6. Report of the University Education Commission, 1949, GOI, Chapter 12.
7. National Policy of Education, GOI, 1965.
8. Committee on Empowerment of Women, 2001-02, Sixth Report, 13th Lok Sabha, *op. cit.*, pp. 107.
9. GOI, Planning Commission, XIth Five Year Plan, 2007-12, p. 192.

Violence against Women (VAW)

Road Block for Women Empowerment

"It is important to walk a mile in another person's shoes. As it is possible to grow up in the same family, neighbourhood, school, etc. and yet have totally different experiences depending on whether you are a man or a woman. The way to resolve differences therefore is not to suppress those who are different but to notice them and not try to see our reflection in them."

—Justice L'Heureux Dube, Supreme Court of Canada

INTRODUCTION

Gender-based violence has only recently emerged as a global issue extending across regional, social, cultural and economic boundaries. As a near universal phenomenon, gender based violence threatens the well-being, rights and dignity of women. [Fischback, 1997] Violence against women is being documented across cultures and nations. The United States, where the feminist movement had opportunity to flourish has not even ratified the CEDAW. According to state statistics, about 18% of women are being sexually abused in the U.S. The condition in other developed countries is not any better. The UN Rapporteur on violence against women regretted that even countries such as Denmark, Germany, Spain, Switzerland, the United Kingdom, among others, could not provide accurate documentation and statistics on domestic violence (United Nations, 1999). The Available data on wife abuse is even more appalling. In the U.S., The Department of Justice reported that, every year, 3-4 million women are battered by their husbands or partners (UN, 1999). Even in Sweden which ranks high in the gender-related index, 66 percent of the 18,650 reported cases of violence on women in 1996 were of domestic assault. Further 45

CHART 7.1

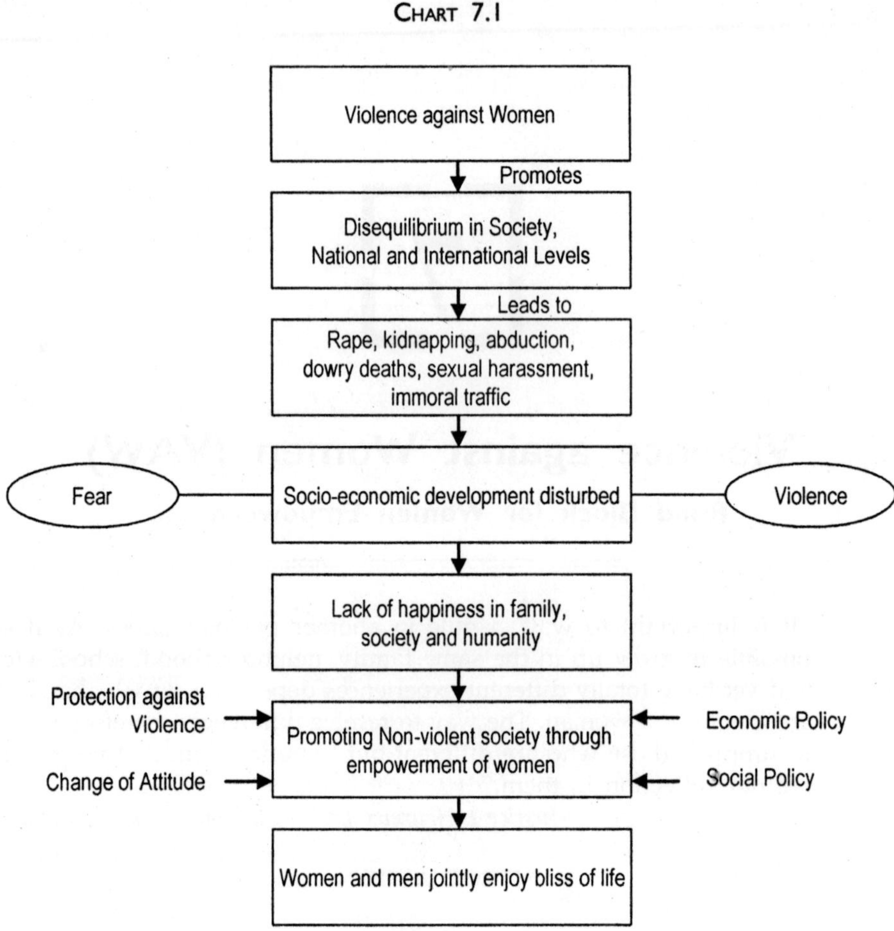

percent of 681 offences of homicide recorded in England and Wales in 1996 were cases of homicides in which women were killed by current or former spouses or lovers (UN, 1999).

Women victims needed to be treated with sensitivity. Victims of sexual violence suffered from a sense of shame, self-guilt, fear and feel humiliated, abandoned, traumatised and stigmatised. In case of domestic violence, offences were committed in the privacy of the home, by a person on whom the women was emotionally and economically dependent. Moreover even though she was a victim, she was compelled to live with the assaulter, as she had no other alternative. In such cases, the role of the police was not one of an interrogator but of a facilitator and emphathiser.[1]

In recent years, the issue of violence against women has been recognised as a basic human rights issue and the elimination of gender-based violence has been seen as central to equality, development and peace. Violence against women includes not only physical violence, but also sexual, psychological and emotional abuse. Many forms of violence are not even recognised as such and are ignored, condoned or justified, by involving religious, cultural or traditional beliefs. There is increasing evidence to show that women regardless of age, educational level, class, caste, community and family living arrangement, are vulnerable to violence. They face violence both inside and outside the family, at all stages of their lives. Official statistics show that there has been a dramatic increase in the number of reported crimes against women over the last decade. Between 1980 and 1990, there was an increase of nearly 74 percent in crimes against women, with rape, molestation and torture by husbands and in-laws showing the highest rate of growth. The National Crime Records Bureau reported in 1998 that the growth rate of crimes against women would be higher than the population growth rate by 2010 (Sen and Shivkumar, 2001).[2]

Inspite of plethora of agencies and large number of laws to make the life of women decent, yet we do not find any newspaper or T.V. or Radio not narrating the one form or the other of violence against women. The violence is more prevalent in rural areas, urban slums and backward areas. Before, we discuss the methods of containment of violence against women, let us discuss its meaning and the various forms in which it is exhibited.

MEANING AND SCOPE

According to the United Nations, violence against women consists of "any act of gender-based violence that results in, or is likely to result in, physical, sexual or psychological harm or suffering to women, including threats of such acts, coercion or arbitrary deprivation of liberty, whether occurring in public or private life. Violence against women shall be understood to encompass but not be limited to: physical, sexual and psychological violence occurring in the family and in the community, including battering, sexual abuse of female children, dowry-related violence, marital rape, female genital mutilation and other traditional practices harmful to women, non-spousal violence, violence related to exploitation, sexual harassment and intimidation at work, in educational institutions and elsewhere, trafficking in women, forced prostitution, and violence perpetrated or condoned by the State."

Violence against women is viewed as one of the most crucial societal mechanism by which women are forced into a subordinate position. It is a manifestation of unequal power relation, which has led to man's domination over and discrimination against woman.

Violence is defined as a physical act of aggression of one individual or group against another or others. Violence results in or is likely to result in physical, sexual, psychological harm or suffering. This also includes the threat of such act, coercion or arbitrary deprivation of liberty in public or private life and violation of human rights of women in situation of armed conflicts.

While the basic reason for violence against women is their inferior status in a male dominated society educationally, economically, politically and socially, there are other factors too. The increasing criminalisation of society, media images of violence, poor enforcement of legal provision, unabashed consumerism and erosion of traditional values have all added to it.

The issue of violence against women has been the most pervasive themes of the new women's liberation movement in India since its rise in 1974-75. First, it was the horrifying rising toll of fire in the growing number of dowry deaths, then from 1980 with the cases of Mathura, Maya Tayagi and Rameeza Bi, the problem of rape burst out of the shadows to stand as the symbol of women's oppression. Finally, the last few years have seen dramatic revivals of the ancient customs of Sati as well as female infanticide and female foeticide.[3]

Violence against women is an important force that helps to keep the structure of patriarchy intact. It makes gender discrimination a live and terrifying experience for women, and ensures their subjugation. We have used the term gender-based violence to describe acts that cause physical, sexual or psychological harm to women. Such acts are based in the unequals relations that exist between men and women in society. The most important thing to remember about gender-based violence is that, it is all pervasive—it can occur in all kinds of situations (within the family, at the workplace, in public places, in the community, and even when in the custody of the state) and at all stages of a womens life.[4]

'Violence against women' means any act of gender-based violence that results in, or is likely to result in, physical, sexual or psychological harm or suffering to women, including threats of such acts, coercion or arbitrary deprivation of liberty, whether occurring in public or private life. Violence against women, including threats or fear of violence is a permanent constraint on the mobility of women and limits their access to resources and basic activities. Such violence are impediments to the achievement of the objectives of equality, development and peace. It violates and impairs or nullifies the enjoyment by women of their human rights and fundamental freedoms.

The term "violence against women" following the declaration of UN Commission on the Status of Women (1993), is usually defined as "any act of gender-based violence that results in or is likely to result in, physical, sexual or psychological harm or suffering to women, including threats such as acts, coercion or arbitrary deprivations of liberty, whether occurring in public or private life."[5]

Broadly, violence against women can be divided in two categories:

(a) Physical, sexual and psychological violence occurring within the community, including rape, sexual abuse, sexual harassment and intimidation at work, in educational institutions and elsewhere, trafficking in women and forced prostitution;

(b) Physical, sexual and psychological violence occurring in the family, including bettering, sexual abuse of female children in the household, dowry-related violence and other traditional practices harmful to women, non-spousal violence and violence related to exploitation.

The nature and forms of violence is intertwined within physical, mental and psychological levels. Prevailing forms of violence are wife beating and cruelty at home, molestation, rape, sexual harassment at workplace, etc. It occurs regardless of age, marital status, caste, relation, culture and class or income level.

Violence includes physical, sexual, emotional, psychological, social and economic abuse by one member of a family/society to control or dominate women in the family/society.

Physical violence includes slapping, punching, beating, shoving with or without weapons.

Sexual violence includes rape, molestations harassment. Rape is forcing a woman to have sex against her will. It is a violation of an individual's rights over her body.

Emotional violence can include all intentional attempts to minimise the victim's concern and to make them feel bad. Humiliating the victim in public and private places.

Psychological violence is any threats that are made or carried out with the intent of financial or emotional injury, blackmail or humiliation.

Economic violence creates financial dependence.

Intimidation as a form of violence can include making women afraid by using looks, action and gestures: by destroying their property or by displaying weapons.

Isolation can be used to control and limit what woman does, whom they see and where they go.

Using privilege to control is also a form of violence. By treating a woman or child like a servant and having the last word about everything, the abuser is acting like a master. He is defining and rigidly abiding by the traditional roles of men and women.[6]

Extent

Violence against women is an impediment to the achievement of the objectives of equality, development and peace. Fear of violence is a permanent constraint on the mobility of women and limits their access to resources and basic needs. The subject "Violence Against Women" is broad-based and comprehensive and includes different types of violence against women, viz. domestic violence, violence at the work place, violence by the State and its functionaries, violence during war and social disturbances, sexual harassment and abuse, female foeticide, rape, trafficking, dowry-related issues, etc. The innumerable forms of violence against women are so inter-connected that there is need to understand the ways in which women become susceptible to those who prey on their socially constructed vulnerability. The Committee on Empowerment on Women have therefore taken up the subject "Violence Against Women" for detailed examination.

It is provided in Section 10 of the National Commission for Women Act, 1990 that the Commission shall "investigate and examine all matters relating to the safeguards provided for women under the Constitution and other laws [Sec. 19(1)(a)] and "look into complaints and take *suo motu* notice of matters relating to: (i) deprivation of women's rights; (ii) non-implementation of laws enacted to provide protection to women and also achieve the objective of equality and development; and (iii) non-compliance of policy decisions, guidelines or instructions aimed at mitigating hardships and ensuring welfare and providing relief to women, and take up the issues arising out of such matters with appropriate authorities." [Section 10(1)].

She is today not only dishonoured in Panchayats but also in the city transport buses, in the city streets and even in her own homes. It is high time that we get rid of this inequality and indignity to women in our country."

Manisha Joshi in her Article "A cry for justice" in Social Welfare 2002, rightly states:

The phenomenon of violence against women arises from patriarchal notions of ownership over women's bodies, sexuality, labour, reproductive rights, mobility and level of autonomy. Deep rooted ideas about male superiority enable men to freely exercise unlimited power over women's lives and effectively legitimize it too. Violence is thus a tool that men use constantly to control women as a result of highly internalized patriarchal conditioning coupled with legitimacy for coercion to enforce compliance and increasing aspirations, frustrations and 'might is right' becoming a legitimate view and increasing need for assertion of individual egos and control. Within this context, several developments serve as a backdrop to the discussion and analysis of increased violence against women. In the wake of liberalization new modes of living are being introduced. Consumerism, unreal aspirations incited by the barrage of the advertising industry and get rich quick schemes have been increasingly influencing the thinking and behaviour. So much so that even the remote hilly areas are being affected by the market forces and are increasingly adopting the system of dowry, which was virtually non-existent earlier (Krengel, 2000). An increasingly growing gap is being witnessed between the aspirations and their fulfilment. As per women speak this is reflected in an increased violence in human interactions and increasingly cases are being reported of small differences leading to inexplicably violent reactions. In such a situation women have become more vulnerable.[7]

Aditi Pandey in her Article, 'Violation of Human Rights' in *Social Welfare,* April 2002 states:

Violence against women should be viewed as one of the most crucial social mechanisms by which they are forced into a subordinate position. It is a manifestation of unequal power relations which has led to men's domination over and discrimination against women.

The term Violence Against Women can be defined as "any act of gender-based violence that results in, or is likely to result in physical, sexual or psychological harm or suffering to women including threats of such acts, coercion or arbitrary deprivations of liberty, whether occurring in public or private life and violation of human rights of women."

All women, whether they live in the rich North or the poor South, the backward East or the progressive West are subject to violence. This is a deprivation of their fundamental human rights. Any act of gender-based violence that results in physical or mental harm or suffering to a woman or the threat of such an act constitutes gender violence.[8]

Indira Gandhi, Former Prime Minister of India has stated that:

"In few countries do women hold higher positions in Politics and public life than in India. But this should not lead us to think that the old inequalities and disabilities from which the women of India suffered have all ended. Ours is a country in which oppositions and contradictions thrive, and nowhere is this more so than as regards women. If we have women who are among the most progressive in the world, we also have women who are among the most backward. In law, discrimination between men and women has been abolished. Yet, we all know the social and economic hardships which our women suffer in addition to the general hardships which every individual suffers in a society so poor and still so largely medieval as ours."

Violence against women during riots pose peculiar problems. These are:

(i) During riots women have suffered immensely as they have lost their husbands, parents and children; and many have lost the only earning member of the family.

(ii) The women who have faced violence are totally shattered and are yet to recover from the shock. They feel traumatized and will need trauma counselling for a long period.

(iii) There have been cases where police have not registered the crimes or have registered FIRs against the entire village equating the victims with the culprits. And wherever they have registered the cases, the progress of investigation is very slow. Special efforts are needed to help those women who want to register FIRs through free legal aid services and guidance.

(iv) As regards cases of sexual assault, it was mentioned that women, though sexually abused were hesitant to speak out of fear of reprisals.

(v) While praising the media for highlighting the instances of violence perpetrated on women and children, some NGOs were of the opinion that at times of both the print and electronic reports provoked both the communities to further violence.

(vi) There was a consistent demand that cases of atrocities on women should be investigated by an unbiased independent commission not only to do justice to the affected persons but also to verify the reports published in the media.

(vii) The compensation paid for damaged/destroyed houses is too inadequate and with that it is impossible for them to repair/reconstruct their houses.

(viii) Many families have lost their earning assets. A comprehensive survey is needed to assess the extent of loss and to take steps to adequately compensate them.

(ix) Camps are being closed down even though people have not been able to repair/reconstruct their houses and the monsoon season is on.

(x) Women are reluctant to go to their respective villages on account of security concerns and threats from their old neighbours.

(xi) Comprehensive rehabilitation schemes need to be formulated and implemented for all riots affected women and children.

(xii) Special efforts must be made by the Government to provide livelihood means by way of jobs to members of those families who have lost their earning members.

(xiii) Self-employed women need to be provided marketing linkages and credit facilities, in view of the economic boycott call of the Muslims by some organizations.

(xiv) Confidence building measures need to be launched in a serious and systematic way:

(a) Majority of the women have seen/experienced violence and are still to recover from the trauma experienced by them. They continue to feel insecure and need trauma counselling for longer periods. For this, Government ought to get assistance of trained counsellors and professionals from TISS, Mumbai and NIMHANS, Bangalore.

(b) There are complaints that police have not registered several FIRs in cases of crimes against women, and the progress of investigations where the cases have been registered, is too slow. Women are asked to identify the attackers or produce witnesses when they are in camps while on the other hand they are under threats/pressure to withdraw their complaints. Free legal aid and assistance to those women who have so far not been able to register their FIRs is an urgent need. For this the concerned police officials need to be instructed to visit relief camps which are still operating and also the riot affected areas. While women in general did not complain of sexual harassment at Lunawada and Dariakhan Ghummat camps, women in Shah Alam Camp complained of sexual harassment and attack during riots. A list of 58 women who have allegedly been sexually assaulted was given by the organisers of the Shah Alam Camp to the Committee, a copy of which was handed over to the State Police for investigation. The Committee desire that all cases of sexual harassment which have been reported and these 58 cases be properly investigated so as to do justice to the affected women, and to follow up report sent to the Committee.

(c) Though *ex-gratia* death relief amounting to Rs. 1.5 lakh is claimed to have been paid in respect of 767 cases, most of the women the Committee met in the Ahmedabad Camps did not know anything about it. Out of 983 death cases, the payment has not been made in the balance of 216 cases, (the Committee were told) for various technical reasons like lack of proof of death, failure to identify the bodies in morgues, etc. The Committee hope that efforts would be made to complete the process of payment for the remaining cases including the cases of unidentified dead bodies.

(d) It has been brought to the notice of the Committee by the affected women that no *ex-gratia* payment has been made in respect of missing persons. The Committee feel that a sympathetic attitude needs to be taken in respect of these cases and after necessary affidavits are obtained from the dependents/near relatives of the victims, the compensation to them must be paid at the earliest.

(e) Another fact which was brought to the notice of the Committee was the inadequate compensation that has been paid for damaged/destroyed houses by the State Government, the upper limit of which is Rs. 50,000. Further, earning assets of many families had been destroyed during the riots and very few of them have received the compensation and those who got it said it was absolutely inadequate. Moreover, the surveys were made in an *ad-hoc* manner when the affected families were in camps. They also complained of discrimination based on the community they belonged to. In many cases the landlords had claimed the compensation and were now refusing to let the tenants return. The Committee were informed that fresh surveys are being conducted to ascertain the exact extent of damage to the houses of the victims and their earning assets.

The Committee hope that the fresh surveys in this connection would be completed soon and fair compensation to the victims paid. If the victims need more financial help over and above the compensation they are paid as per the revised surveys, the help of agencies such as Banks, HUDCO, and other Financial Institutions should be taken to extend loans on easy terms to them.

(f) The houses of the majority of the affected persons have not yet been repaired/reconstructed so far. With the monsoon season on and the camps being closed they have no shelter and nowhere to go. The Committee hope that the camps which are still operating would be closed only after the monsoons so that the affected persons are able to get their houses repaired/reconstructed.

(g) Another matter of concern was that though they are eager to go back to their villages/areas, the security aspect still haunts them. Though the State Government claimed that it had taken steps to provide security to the affected persons when they move back to their localities, the Committee are of the view that the confidence building process in the affected areas has not been seriously initiated. Women complained of threats meted out to them when they returned, forcing them to take shelter in the camps again. It is necessary to ensure that victims who have left the camps and returned to their localities are provided proper security.

(h) Many NGOs pleaded for a separate rehabilitation colony for the affected families. If the Government gave the land they are prepared to build it. The Committee feel this should be considered where there is real danger to their lives.

(i) At Shah Alam Camp, the Committee noticed that there was lack of beddings especially for pregnant women and new born babies. There was also shortage of milk for children and lactating mothers. The Committee had pointed out this shortcoming during their discussion with the State Government officials, and hope that suitable steps would have been taken to remedy this situation.

(j) Having suffered immensely, the major problem confronting the affected people especially women, is to work out livelihood measures for the rest of their lives. The relief operations undertaken for the riot victims require provision for not only relief but also for rehabilitation, with the objective of enabling the affected women regain the courage to achieve sustainable long-term earning capacity. Programmes for meaningful resettlement of these women and their families have, therefore, to be worked out. The Committee note that Red Cross, SEWA and some NGOs have offered support to run such programmes in camps by giving sewing machines and ensuring wages for women to earn. Some NGOs have also offered help to women to upgrade their skills under NORAD with market tie ups so that they may earn their livelihood, despite the economic boycott call against them, by some religious groups.[9]

Violence against women must be seen in the socio-economic and political context of gender relations. In every country of the world where reliable, large scale studies have been conducted, including two in the South-East Asia Region, results indicate that between 16% and 52% of women have been assaulted by an intimate partner. The "silence" of violence is breaking. To listen to women's voices is the first step in making their lives safer.

Ending violence against women –in our families, communities and societies remains the greatest challenge facing humanity on the eve of the 21st century. Women are attacked on the street, in the workplace, in the home, in situations of armed conflict, and while in state custody. Violence against women devastates lives, fractures communities and is a barrier to development in every nation.

Because violence against women and girls underlies all human societies, we are all the poorer for it; world development is impeded by exactly the measure of the harm dealt out to women; the common future of all of us shrinks to exactly the degree that women are impeded from nourishing themselves and their families. In 1993 alone, the World Bank estimated that violence against women was as serious a cause of death and incapacity among women of reproductive age as cancer, and a greater cause of ill-health than traffic accidents and malaria combined. The World Health Organistion estimates that at least 20 percent of women in the world have been physically or sexually assaulted by a man at some point in their lives. In the United States alone, violence against women costs businesses $100 million in lost wages, sick leave, absenteeism, and non-productivity.[10]

In the ultimate analysis, there can be no two opinions about the need for stringent laws, sensitive judiciary, effective law and enforcement machinery and vigilant women's groups to deal with such atrocious crimes against women. But what is needed more than anything else is a total revolution in the thinking of our society that always blames the woman for the crime of which she is the victim, not the perpetrator.

The problem of violence against women has its roots in a socio-economic order that is heavily biased against women. A woman having an identity of her own is a concept alien to Indian culture.

When the entire milieu is steeped in the tradition of women's utter subjugation to men, there can be little hope for a dramatic improvement in the state of women.

The Supreme Court has recently expressed its serious concern at the leniency shown by the Allahabad High Court in discharging the accused in a dowry torture case. A division bench comprising M.B. Shah and S.N. Sariava observed: "It is a matter of shame that indiscriminate attacks and violence are directed against married women and the accused being let-off for various reasons . . . The result is that violence against women continues unabated as law loses its deterrent."

More than changing laws to fight crime against women, the courts must be seen as delivering justice. Society must also radically change the way it instinctively blames the women for such crimes.

Journey has just begun and that there is a long distance to be covered to reach the far pavilions of welfare, development and empowerment for women. But we may take some satisfaction in the fact that our road map is now clearer, our team energized, our organizational resources re-grouped and our gear refurbished so that the Commission's endeavours would be more fruitful.

Mahatma Gandhi strongly feels that, "If only the women of the world would come together they could display such heroic non-violence as to kick away the atom bomb like a mere ball. Women have been so gifted by God. If an ancestral treasure, lying buried in a corner of the house unknown to the members of the family were suddenly discovered, what a celebration if would occasion. Similarly, women's marvellous power is lying dormant. If the women of Asia wake up, they will dazzle the world. My experiment in non-violence would be instantly successful if I could secure women's help."

CONCLUSION

We are also on the threshold of the few millennium—a millennium which is unprecedented in terms of the hope and opportunities it holds out. It is exceptional in terms of resources, technological capacity, growth of civil society organistions, global connectivity and the sheer breadth of knowledge that is available for anyone to access. So much is within our grasp, so much more than even before, if only we have the courage to act differently. What is required to make this change? What can we really do together in South Asia to facilitate the realization of the Beijing vision. What can we really do together in South Asia to facilitate the realization of the Beijing vision. There are but some of the questions we will be trying to find answers to at this meeting? If we find even a few at the end of the meeting, we could have achieved a great deal. We owe it to ourselves and to the women of this region to find out what is that extra push that we need to make our dreams and visions a reality. Let us make this meeting an occasion for planning on doing just that: viz. how we can think and act differently so that we, through our collective efforts, can make a real difference to the lives of women in South Asia, especially those who are the most marginalized.

During the Eleventh Plan period, the justice delivery mechanism as well as the legislative environment under the PWDVA 2005 will be strengthened. VAW will be articulated as a Public Health issue and training will be provided to medical personnel at all levels from public health facilities (PHCs) to premier health facilities. It will be included in medical education because the medical and health establishments are often the first point of contact for women in a crisis situation. Training and sensitization of health personnel will include recognizing and dealing with injuries resulting from VAW and providing psychological support. Multiple forms of sexual VAW in conflict zones and in communal or sectarian violence, where they are specifically targeted as embodiment of community honour are cause for great concern. In the Eleventh Plan period, a National Task Force on VAW in Zones of Conflict will be set-up under the National Commission for Women (NCW) with adequate budgetary allocations to make it effective in monitoring VAW in conflict zones and facilitating relief and access to justice for affected women.[11]

Notes and References

1. NCW—Report of the Workshop on Gender and Law Enforcement held at Bangalore on 21-22, April, 2001, p. 5.
2. UNIFEM and Institute of Development Studies, Jaipur, Support Services to Counter Violence against Women in Rajasthan—A Resource Directory, Jaipur, 2002.
3. UNIFEM and Mary: Support Services to Counter Violence against Women in Haryana, A Resource Directory, New Delhi, 2003.
4. UNIFEM and Sanhito, Support Services to Counter Violence Against Women in West Bengal, Kolkata, 2002, p. 13.
5. UNIFEM and Sakhi, Support Services to Counter Violence Against in Kerala, A Resource Directory, 2002, p. 15.
6. *Ibid.*, pp. 15-16.
7. Manisha Joshi, Violence Against Women, A Cry For Justice in Social Welfare, April 2002.
8. Aditi Pandey, Vision of Human Rights, Social Welfare, April 2002.
9. Lok Sabha Secretariat, Committee on Empowerment of Women, 2002-03, Violence against Women During Riots, Ministry of HRD, Deptt. of Women and Child Development and Ministry of Home Affairs, Ninth Report, Thirteenth Lok Sabha, August 2002, pp. 5-7 and 74-75.
10. R.D. Sharma, Crime Against Women, *The Hindu*, Chennai, 15 May, 2001.
11. GOI, Planning Commission, Eleventh Plan, 2007-12, p. 194.

Annexure 7.1

State-wise Percentage Contribution to Total Crimes Committed against Women during 2000

S. No.	State/City	Total		
		I	R	P
1.	Andhra Pradesh	14299	18.9	10.1
2.	Arunachal Pradesh	143	11.9	0.1
3.	Assam	3732	14.2	2.6
4.	Bihar	6299	6.3	4.5
5.	Goa	100	6.2	0.1
6.	Gujarat	6140	12.7	4.3
7.	Haryana	3311	16.6	2.3
8.	Himachal Pradesh	842	12.5	0.6
9.	Jammu and Kashmir	1642	16.4	1.2
10.	Karataka	5852	11.2	4.1
11.	Kerala	4982	15.4	3.5
12.	Madhya Pradesh	17902	22.3	12.7
13.	Maharashtra	13177	14.4	9.3
14.	Manipur	74	2.9	0.1
15.	Meghalaya	69	2.8	0.0
16.	Mizoram	133	13.9	0.1
17.	Nagaland	22	1.3	0.0
18.	Orissa	4717	13.1	3.3
19.	Punjab	2156	9.1	1.5
20.	Rajasthan	12942	24.0	9.2
21.	Sikkim	21	3.7	0.0
22.	Tamil Nadu	13732	22.2	9.7
23.	Tripura	330	8.7	0.2
24.	Uttar Pradesh	19820	11.0	13.4
25.	West Bengal	7043	8.9	5.0
	TOTAL STATES	138572	14.1	98.0
26.	A and N islands	45	11.6	0.0
27.	Chandigarh	161	18.0	0.1
28.	D and N Haveli	17	8.9	0.0
29.	Daman and Diu	6	4.3	0.0
30.	Delhi	2439	17.3	1.7
31.	Lakshadweep	1	1.4	0.0
32.	Pondicherry	132	11.8	0.1
	TOTAL	2801	16.6	2.0
	TOTAL (All India)	141373	14.1	100.0
33.	Ahmedabad	510	11.9	3.0
34.	Bangalore	1255	11.0	7.5

35.	Bhopal	320	19.0	1.9
36.	Chennai	4037	59.8	24.0
37.	Coimbatore	283	21.8	1.7
38.	Delhi (City)	2122	17.6	12.6
39.	Hyderabad	1227	17.2	7.3
40.	Indore	372	25.6	2.2
41.	Jaipur	804	36.4	4.8
42.	Kanpur	659	38.6	5.7
43.	Kochi	125	6.8	0.7
44.	Kolkata	558	4.3	3.3
45.	Kucknow	683	25.3	4.1
46.	Ludhiana	289	16.7	1.7
47.	Madurai	380	29.6	2.3
48.	Mumbai	888	4.7	5.3
49.	Nagpur	443	21.2	2.6
50.	Patna	212	16.3	1.3
51.	Pune	352	9.8	2.1
52.	Surat	243	10.0	1.4
53.	Vadodara	240	14.5	1.4
54.	Varanasi	206	15.7	1.4
55.	Vishakhapatnam	282	15.8	1.7
	TOTAL (CITIES)	16787	15.8	100.00

Source: Official Documents.

8

Administration Machinery for Women Empowerment

Part A

"In every country, whether it is new or long established, whether it is underdeveloped or highly developed, any programme of economic or fiscal development, of improvement in education, health, labour and social conditions and of reform and reconstruction in any of the women services can only succeed if it is supported by machinery and methods established under sound principles of public administration and adapted to the circumstances of the country concerned."

MINISTRY OF WOMEN AND CHILD WELFARE

At the top is the Minister of Women and Child Welfare. The administrative organization consists of the secretary who is assisted by four Joint Secretaries who head the four Bureaux of the Department, namely, the child Development, Child Welfare, Women's Development and Women's Welfare.

The work of the Department is divided in nine Divisions or Units, each headed by an officer of the rank of Director or Deputy Secretary. The Department has three Director and six Deputy Secretary ranking officers, besides eighteen Under Secretaries, and thirteen Desk Officers/Section Officers. In addition one Joint Director, three Deputy Directors and six Assistant Directors hold various technical posts in the Department.

The WCD department is the nodal Ministry of the Government of India for the welfare and development of women and children of the country. The specific issues like health, education. Employment, etc. of women and children are looked after by the sectoral Ministries/

Departments, but the Department of women and child Development has the overall responsibility to coordinate the activities of all other Ministries and organizations on this subject.

The Ministry has four autonomous organizations working under its aegis viz. National Commission for Women (NCW), National Institute of Public Cooperation and Child Development (NIPCCD), Rashtriya Mahila Kosh (RMK) and the Central Social Welfare Board (CSWB). NIPCCD and RMK are registered under the Societies Registration Act, 1860, whereas CSWB is a charitable company registered under Section 25 of the Indian Companies Act, 1956. The National Commission for Women was constituted in 1992 by an act of Parliament as the national apex body for protecting and safeguarding the rights of women. These organizations are fully funded by the Government of India.

National Policy for Empowerment of Women

One of the landmark achievements of the year 2001 was the approval of the first ever National Policy for the Empowerment of Women. The main objective of this Policy is to bring about the advancement, development and empowerment of women and to eliminate all forms of discrimination against women and to ensure their active participation in all spheres of life and activities.

The policy prescribes affirmative action in areas such as Legal System, decision-making structure, Mainstreaming of Gender Perspective in Development Process, Economic Empowerment through increased access to resources like micro-credit, better resource allocation through Women's component Plan, Gender Budget exercises and development of Gender Development Indices and Social Empowerment of Women through, *inter-alia,* universalisation of education, adoption of holistic approach to women's health, etc. the policy commits to making compulsory the registration of marriages and to eliminate child marriage by 2010. This Policy takes into account the new developments initiated by the process of economic reforms and the impact of globalization and liberalization of women, particularly in the informal sector. The policy further prescribes that the provisions of various legislation including personal laws, which are discriminatory against women shall be reviewed and amended with the support and initiatives of concerned communities. Review of women-oriented legislations has been completed by 2003.

The Policy envisages setting up of a Council at the National level to oversee the implementation of the Policy. The National Council will be headed by the Prime Minister. Similar Councils will also be set-up at the State levels to be headed by the concerned Chief Ministers. All Central and State Ministries/Departments would be required to draw up Action Plans with measurable goals to be achieved in a time frame of the next 10 years.

National Resource Centre for Women (NRCW)

This Ministry has proposed to set-up National Resource Centre for

Women. The objectives of the centre will be to:

(i) Orient and sensitize elected representatives, policy planners, administrators, members of the judiciary, policy, bankers, etc. towards gender issues;
(ii) Facilitate leadership training for grass-root level workers, newly elected panchayat leaders, members of NGOs, etc.;
(iii) Create an information base and disseminate information in the fields of women's development and also facilitate generation of data on contemporary issues of women in development;
(iv) Facilitate and coordinate the monitoring and evaluation of existing government programmes relating to women development;
(v) Undertake and coordinate policy and programme-related research on women's development;
(vi) Provide networking facilities to institutions and individuals actively engaged in the field of women's development;
(vii) Strengthen institutional capacity of Department of Women and Child Development in relation to planning and implementation processes which are gender sensitive and participatory;
(viii) Assimilate gender perspective; in policies, planning, implementation and monitoring in selected sectors;
(ix) Undertake advocacy and provide policy support on women's issues; and
(x) Take up all or any other activity for the holistic development for women.

The proposal has been approved by the Standing Finance Committee of the Ministry, but in view of the restrictions imposed by the Government on the creation of new organization the possibility of anchoring the proposed Resource Centre with an existing institution is being explored.

National perspective plan of action for women, 1988-2000 AD Report of the core group set-up by the department of child and women development, Ministry of HRD, Govt. of India, recommends the following which should be followed by Ministry of Women and Child Welfare, Government of India. Certain important issues, however, impinge on all spheres of women's lives and work. With a view to enhancing women's status and capacities to participate in the process of nation-building, the following general recommendations are made:

1. The overall approach of this National perspective Plan is to perceive women in a holistic manner. While the programmes for women will continue to be implemented by different ministries as part of their department plans, it is essential to have a strong inter-ministerial coordination and monitoring body along with its own supportive facilities service by the Department of Women and Child Development.

2. All ministries must reflect the concern for the all round development of women. The concerned ministries must all have a women's cell which currently only exists in the Ministries of Labour, Small Scale Industry, Science and Technology and Rural Development. It is essential that the new policy thrust for women's development should be reflected in the Planning Commission as well as the State Planning Boards. The National Commission on Self-employed Women and Women in the Informal Sector, has also independently concluded that the Planning Commission and State Planning Boards need to focus their attention sharply on the realistic situation of (Labouring) women.
3. An essential pre-requisite for the implementation of these new policy directives would be a women's unit in the Planning Commission, to redefine categories of data collection for women, modify existing terminology and identify gaps in data collection relating to women and to give direction to plans and programmes for women's development. It is also essential to analyse the impact of the different macro-policies on women while planning new endeavours.
4. Financial and fiscal resources should be apportioned and preferential allocations for women's employment in mainstream programmes and projects should be made. This would imply the rationalization of resource allocation within mainstream programmes so as to benefit women, rather than only seeking separate allocations for women. Critical emphasis must be placed on rate of investment in women preferred industries and occupations.
5. At the state level, the Departments/Directorates of Women's Development should be initiated. Currently, there is no separate department for women in many States. Social welfare, handicapped, Scheduled Castes and Tribes are subjects that are bracketed together with the development of women at the State level. This new department could also be the State level implementation body for the programmes/policies of the Department of Women and Child Development of the Government of India.
6. In terms of programme implementation, the two major implementing bodies envisaged, are the Social Welfare Boards and the Women's Development Corporations. There can be a rationalization of service provision between these two bodies. The State Social Welfare Advisory Boards could eventually concentrate on implementing welfare/supportive programs for women (homes for women in distress, working women's hostels, counseling centres for legal aid and paralegal training, condensed courses, etc.); Women's Development Corporations

would be responsible for the implementation of economic programmes through non-governmental and governmental agencies/departments wherever necessary, concentrating on technical inputs like credit, marketing, design development, etc. and reaching out to women at the district and village level.

7. Women should be entitled to a package of services at the block level created by the convergence of schemes such as Development of Women and Children in Rural Areas (DWCRA), Integrated Child Development Schemes (ICDS), Adult Education, health Care, etc. at the grass-roots administrative level. Every district should have a coordinator to assist in the integration of these programmes aimed at the development of women. The coordinator will also be responsible for motivating local planning of programmes and assist in their implementation and provide feed-back for effective planning and evaluation. Since decentralization of planning, monitoring and implementation of development programmes for women is suggested as also devolution of finance at district level, appointment of District coordinators for women's programmes would facilitate this process and control over finance would empower them. The National Commission on Self-Employed Women and Women in the Informal Sector has also recommended the appointment of District Coordination Officers to be responsible for planning, monitoring, coordination and evaluation of the programmes affecting women. Rationalization of functionaries at the block and village level to ensure coordination of programmes affecting women at the grass-roots level also needs to be undertaken.
8. There are today sufficient number of programmes in the government of India as well as innovative programmes in many States and sectors. What is needed is not merely larger resource allocation but technical inputs for greater effectiveness of these programmes, to guarantee better resource utilization. Emphasis has to be placed on more effective planning, monitoring and evaluation of existing programmes through a result-oriented mechanism operating at different levels.
9. Recognizing that a critical input for women's development would be New thrust to training and wider dissemination of information backed by research data and documentation, it is proposed to set-up a National Resource Centre for Women. This resource centre would translate national developmental needs of women into a systematic grid of programmes and schemes for training at different levels in skills/knowledge/attitudes. The centre would identify and if necessary, strengthen existing governmental and non-governmental agencies including women's universities/women's centres and colleges through which the training, research/dissemination could be carried out.

The National Commission on Self-employed women and women in Informal sector has also recommended the need for a national Institution to cater to women's training as well as formulate guidelines and help the other constituent units at the state level, divisional level and district level to carry out training programmes.

10. Reorientation and sensitization of the administrative machinery at all levels in the government of India, the States, as well as specialized technical agencies (both government and Voluntary) to the issues of women in development is essential. Three levels of orientation are necessary, i.e. at the policy and planning level, at the district or intermediary level, and at the block and village level. The training of functionaries and their orientation to women's issues must also be in the right perspective, i.e. women should be perceived as producers and participants, not clients for welfare. The dynamic role of women's contribution to the national economy as partners and equal citizens must be reiterated and translated into programmes and projects. The National Resource Centre would be responsible for revamping the existing content/methodology and monitoring of training at all levels.
11. A special division should be created in the Department of Women and Child Development for the enforcement of law for women. The officer-in-charge may be designated Commissioner for Women's Rights and must liaise with the various Special Cells for women created by the police, the CBI as well as with the Departments of Public Grievances at Centre and State levels as also the women's Cell in the Home Ministry. This division will be concerned with the enforcement of law to ensure women's rights, to facilitate action-oriented research in fields such as discrimination against women, protection at work, etc.
12. This Plan recommends that the Census in future must take into account women's unpaid work in the household and outside as well as the value added in performing her many survival tasks for the family. A greater conceptual clarity has to emerge on 'work' and 'non-work' as well as a distinction between work that produces economic value and other activities that are consumption-oriented. Data relating to women, especially in the unorganized sector should be reflected in the data of the National Sample Survey and the Central Statistical Organization.
13. It has been observed through various studies, that education of citizens not only builds up knowledge and information but also helps the citizen understand the complexities of the political process. It is therefore, recommended that the programme of free universal education upto the age of 14 should be vigorously

implemented. Further, serious attention needs to be paid to the content of education. The courses of studies and the text books should inculcate values of gender equality, self-respect, courage, independence, etc., which would help develop the personalities of women.

14. The Planning Commissions and all ministries and government departments must have a Women's Cell. All government delegations to international meetings must include at least one or more women members. Wherever a Committee or Commission is set-up by Government for any purpose, 30 per cent of its representation must be of women. The Union and all State level Public Service Commissions must have women representatives. The Planning Commission and State Planning Boards must have adequate representation of women.
15. All women members of panchayats and other executive bodies must be trained and empowered to exercise their authority. Both men and women members must be sensitized to women's issues. A committee should be formed to look into the training needs of women panchayat members and to help in designing modules separate allocations may be made for this purpose. Particular attention must be paid to the development of interpersonal communication skills amongst the trainees/ community leaders.
16. Media should play a productive role in enhancing women's participation. It should give wider coverage to various activities and measures taken by women, and should highlight the problems of women. In order to project women's issues and achievements, perhaps mainstream media may not be adequate and, therefore, it is necessary to develop an alternate media system that could portray women's struggles and experiences, help generate values which encourage gender equality and justice, and build up a positive image of women participating in public life.

PART B

[NATIONAL COMMISSION FOR WOMEN (NCW)]

The National Commission for Women Bill was passed by the Lok Sabha and the Rajya Sabha on 9th and 23rd August 1990 respectively. The Bill received the assent of the President on the 30th August, 1990.

In pursuance of the National Commission for Women Act, 1990 the National Commission for Women was constituted on 30th January, 1992 as an autonomous statutory body. The State Governments were also requested to set-up similar State Commissions for Women in their respective States. The Department of Women and Child Development is the nodal Department for the National Commission for Women.

The State Commissions for Women have been set-up in the following States under their own executive or statutory orders:

1. Andhra Pradesh
2. Assam
3. Delhi
4. Goa
5. Haryana
6. Himachal Pradesh
7. Karnataka
8. Kerala
9. Madhya Pradesh
10. Mizoram
11. Maharashtra
12. Orissa
13. Punjab
14. Rajasthan
15. Tamil Nadu
16. Tripura
17. West Bengal
18. Jammu and Kashmir

Organisational Structure

The National Commission for Women consists of a full time Chairperson, five Members and a Member Secretary. They are all appointed by the Government of India (Department of Women and Child Development) for a period of three years from the date of assumption of office.

The Standing Committee on Empowerment of Women interacted with the former Chairpersons and Members of the National Commission for Women on 22nd February, 2001 and the following suggestions have emerged therefrom:

(i) There should not be any *ad-hocism* in the appointment of the Chairperson and Members.
(ii) There should not be any post of Members-Secretary. There should be only a Secretary for the administrative set-up for the Commission and Secretary should facilitate the functioning of the Commission in administrative matters only.
(iii) The Commission should have the powers to appoint experts.
(iv) The Commission must be consulted by the various Departments whenever they frame policies pertaining to women and the girl child.
(v) Commission ought to be totally accessible to the public.
(vi) National and State Commissions should identify the areas of work and there should not be any overlapping of their activities.

CHART 8.1

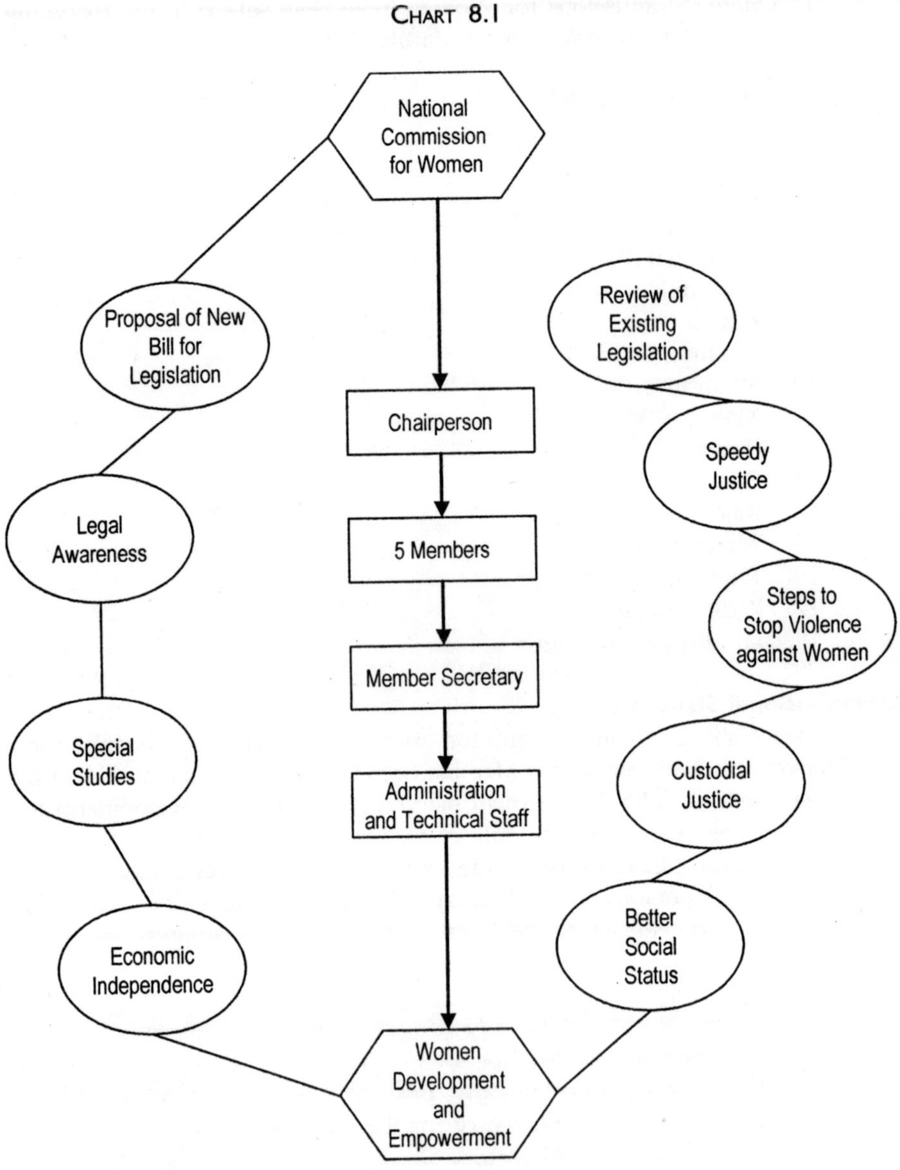

The various points/suggestions put forth by the NGOs in its meeting were as under:

(i) NCW should be strengthened to work as a high powered autonomous and statutory body to protect the constitutional rights of women.

(ii) National Commission for Women must be given autonomous status along the line of National Human Rights Commission and the status of the Chairperson and Members of the Commission should be suitably enhanced.

(iii) There ought to be strong network of State Commissions that should work in coordination with National Commission for Women.

(iv) There should be time limit within which the new appointments are made at all levels in the Commission.

(v) The Chairperson should have the powers to authenticate the decisions taken by the Commission.

(vi) More publicity needs to be given to the work and powers of National Commission for Women.

(vii) Autonomous functioning of the Commission, its role as a watchdog body as well as mandatory consultations by Government on policy matters has been under severe pressure by Government at various times.

(viii) The necessary staff and infrastructural facilities essential to ensure proper functioning of the Commission need to be provided.

(ix) Delay on the part of the Government in taking action on the specific recommendations made by the commission.

During interaction by the Committee with State Commissions, the following points emerged:

(i) Status of Chairperson and Members of the Commission to be defined to invoke better response.

(ii) Lack of adequate powers and statutory status to the Commissions need attention.

(iii) Need to fill up the vacancies for Members in some State Commissions.

(iv) Powers to appoint its own staff rather than getting staff of deputation basis from the Government.

(v) Shortage of adequate and competent staff support.

(vi) Allocation of insufficient funds to the commission.

(vii) Most of the commissions do not have their own building.

(viii) Non-availability of computers, fax and other facilities to some of the Commissions.

(ix) Non-availability of adequate infrastructure, conveyance and other facilities.

(x) Delay in acceptance of recommendations made by the State commissions by the Government.

(xi) In order to ensure continuity of its functions, amendment to the Act needed to ensure that 1/3rd of Members retire every year.

FUNCTIONS OF THE COMMISSION

(1) The Commission shall perform all or any of the following functions, namely:

(a) investigate and examine all matters relating to the legal safeguards provided for women under the Constitution and other laws;
(b) present to the Central Government, annually and at such other times as the Commission may deem fit, reports upon the working of those safeguards;
(c) make in such reports recommendations for the effective implementation of those safeguards for improving the conditions of women by the Union or any State;
(d) review, from time to time, the existing provisions of the Constitution and other laws affecting women and recommend amendments thereto so as to suggest remedial legislative measures to meet any lacunae, inadequacies or shortcomings in such legislations;
(e) take up the cases of violation of the provisions of the Constitution and of other laws relating to women with the appropriate authorities;
(f) look into complaints and take *suo moto* notice of matters relating to:
  (i) deprivation of women's rights;
  (ii) non-implementation of laws enacted to provide protection to women and also to achieve the objective of equality and development;
  (iii) non-compliance of policy decisions, guidelines or instructions aimed at mitigating hardships and ensuring welfare and providing relief to women, and take up the issues arising out of such matters with appropriate authorities;
(g) call for special studies or investigations into specific problems or situations arising out of discrimination and atrocities against women and identify the constraints so as to recommend strategies for their removal;
(h) undertake promotional and educational research so as to suggest ways of ensuring due representation of women in all spheres and identify factors responsible for impeding their advancement, such as, lack of access to housing and basic services, inadequate support services and technologies for reducing drudgery and occupational health hazards and for increasing their productivity;
(i) participate and advise on the planning process of socio-economic development of women;

(j) evaluate the progress of the development of women under the Union and any State;
(k) inspect or cause to be inspected a jail, remand home, women's institution or other place of custody where women are kept as prisoners or otherwise and take with the concerned authorities for remedial action, if found necessary;
(l) fund litigation involving issues affecting a large body of women;
(m) make periodical reports to the Government on any matter pertaining to women and in particular various difficulties under which women toil; and
(n) any other matter which may be referred to it by Central Government.

(2) The Central Government shall cause all the reports referred to in clause (b) of sub-section (1) to be laid before each House of Parliament along with a memorandum explaining the action taken or proposed to be taken on the recommendations relating to the Union and the reasons for the non-acceptance, if any, of any of such recommendations.

(3) Where any such report or any part thereof relates to any matter with which any State Government is concerned, the Commission shall forward a copy of such report or part to such State Government who shall cause it to be laid before the Legislature of the State along with a memorandum explaining the action taken or proposed to be taken on the recommendations relating to the State and the reasons for the non-acceptance, if any, of any of such recommendations.

(4) The Commission shall, while investigating any matter referred to in clause (a) or sub-clause (i) of clause (f) of sub-section (1), have all the powers of a civil court trying a suit and, in particular in respect of the following matters, namely:

(a) summoning and enforcing the attendance of any person from any part of India and examining him on oath;
(b) requiring the discovery and production of any document;
(c) receiving evidence on affidavits;
(d) requisitioning any public record or copy thereof from any court or office;
(e) issuing instructions for the examination of witnesses and documents; and
(f) any other matter which may be prescribed.

PART C

CENTRAL SOCIAL WELFARE BOARD (See Chart 8.2)

Central Social Welfare Board (CSWB) was conceived as an institution to be instrumental in bringing the neglected, weak, handicapped and

CHART 8.2

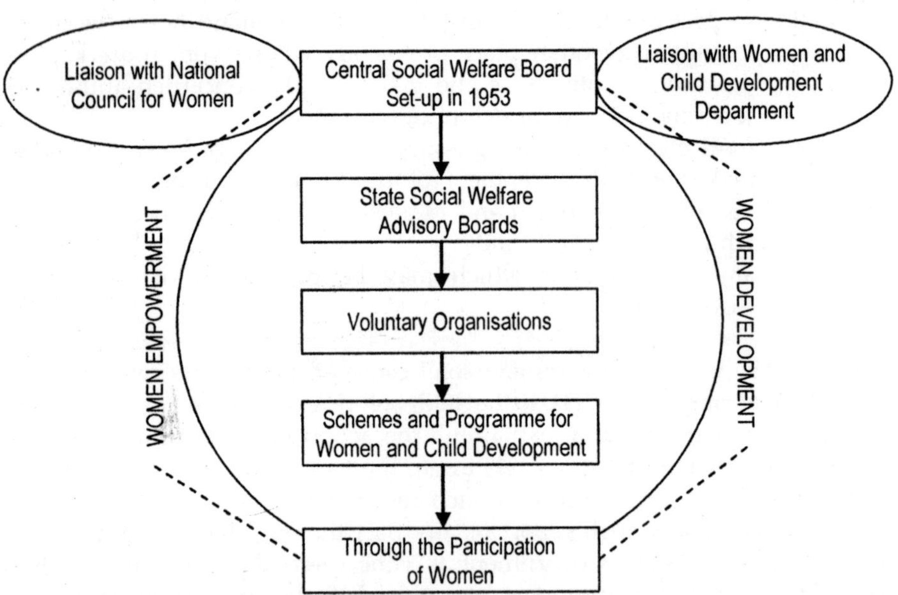

backward sections of society into the national mainstream. Established on 13th August 1953, the Board initiated several programmes for delivering welfare services to the most backward, marginalized and deserving sections of the society. As a follow up, the State Social Welfare Advisory Boards were set-up with the task of implementing and monitoring of different programmes of the CSWB. Over the years, the Board has not only widened the scope of its programmes but has also moved in policy approach from welfare to development to empowerment. Today it is the pioneering national level organization in the field of development and empowerment of women in the country. (See Chart 8.2)

It was declared by Jawaharlal Nehru, (the then Prime Minister of India) that "this attempt that we are making to encourage social welfare activities is in a sense rather unique. It is not some 'Central Authority' that is doing it and by itself, nor does the burden of this fall on the local social welfare organisations. It is certainly a combination of the two where the Central Social Welfare Board comes as a helper and adviser and at the same time the local welfare organisations which are best suited for it, undertake the work. In this case, we can utilise the energy, enthusiasm-and initiative of vast number of persons all over the country."[1]

The CSWB was also envisaged as an interface between the Government and the voluntary sector for social development in the country. It has made a signal contribution in encouraging, assisting and promoting the growth of nearly twenty-five thousand voluntary organizations for reaching the neglected women and children of the country.

Economic growth means not only creation of wealth but also creating people's capacity to create wealth and that resides in their health, education, knowledge, skills, etc. It is very difficult to separate the two. Social welfare has to be the society's organized expression of concern for the total well-being of its members. It is not some temporary relief measures but consists of long-term rehabilitation.

—Durgabhai Deshmukh

PART D

RASHTRIYA MAHILA KOSH

The objective of this institution set-up on 30 March, 1993 under Societies Registration Act, 1860 is to facilitate credit support to poor women for their socio-economic upliftment. The support is extended through NGOs, Women Development Corporation, suitable state government agencies like DRDAs, Dairy Federations, Municipal Councils, etc.

PART E

NATIONAL INSTITUTE OF PUBLIC COOPERATION AND CHILD DEVELOPMENT

The objectives of the Institutė are to develop and promote voluntary action in social development, take a comprehensive view of women and child development and develop and promote programmes in pursuance of the National Policy of children; develop measures for coordination of government and voluntary action in social development, and evolve framework and perspective for organizing children's programmes though governmental and voluntary efforts.

CONCLUSION

Platform for Action, set-up five years after, by the Ministry of Women and Child Development rightly observes that over a period of nearly five developmental decades, multi-sectoral interventions by significant components of civil society—the State, non-governmental organizations, and women's groups have brought about perceptible improvement in the status of women and increasing awareness on gender issues. However, certain grey areas do remain. Violence against women (including domestic violence), the unfavourable sex ratio (927 women to 1000 men), and the largely ignored contribution of women farm workers and home makers deserve greater attention. Developing and establishing systems for the collection and analysis of data desegregated by sex, age, and location is a priority concern. Enhanced resources for the National Women's Machinery will also be crucial for sustaining and augmenting attempts to realize the goal of gender equality.

In the Eleventh Plan institutional mechanism will carry forward the. process of gender mainstreaming and will be strengthened. National Commission for Women (NCW) and State Commissions for Women will be strengthened to enable them to effectively play their role as the nodal agencies for the protection of rights of women. Towards this end, effort will be made in the Eleventh Plan to suitably amend the NCW Act to give the Commission more powers. The States likewise, will be urged to review the powers of their Women's Commissions. In addition to this, more functional and financial autonomy and a statutory base will have to be ensured for these organizations to strengthen their legal status. This will not only ensure that these bodies remain non-partisan, it will also increase their credibility. A mechanism will be created to periodically report to the National Development Council the progress on Women's Plans with respect to the National Policy for Empowerment of Women. Action Plans for Women's Empowerment at national and State levels will be drawn up in consultation with all sectoral agencies and civil society including women's groups, lawyers, activists, women's study centres, etc. Corss-cutting issues such as unpaid work, land and asset entitlements, skill development health, wages, Violence against Women will be mainstreamed. Parivarik Mahila Lok Adalat will be organized, which will supplement the efforts of District Legal Service Authority. Resource Centres for women will be set-up at national and State Levels and linked with Women's Study Centres.

Gender Budgeting and Gender Outcome assessment will be encouraged in all ministries/departments at the Central and State levels. Gender Budgeting helps assess the gender differential impact of the budget and takes forward the translation of gender commitments to budgetary allocations. During the Eleventh Plan efforts will continue to create Gender Budgeting cells in all ministers and departments. Data from these cells will be collected on a regular basis and made available in the public domain.[2]

Lord, Why have you not given Women
The Right to Conquer her Destiny
Why does she have to wait head Bowed
By the Road side waiting with tired patience
Hoping for a miracle in the narrow.

—*Rabindernath Tagore*

Notes and References

1. Prime Minister's Letter No. 32-PMH/54, dated the April 23, 1954, addressed to Chief Ministers of all states.
2. GOI, Planning Commission, XIth Five Year Plan, Volume II, Social Sector, 2007-12, p. 188.

9

Legal Measures

LEGISLATIVE MEASURES

To make the *de-jure* equality into a *de-facto* one, the State has enacted both women-specific and women-related legislations to safeguard the rights and interests of women, besides protecting against social discrimination, violence and atrocities and also to prevent social evils like child marriages, dowry, rape, practice of *Sati*, etc. Efforts of the Government have been to review and amend these legislations from time to time to take care of the interests of women in the changing situations and societal demands/ obligations. The National Commission for Women was attending to this responsibility since its inception in 1992 as it was mandated to. Of the total 41 legislations having direct/indirect bearing on women, the Commission has reviewed and suggested certain amendments in 32 Acts and forwarded the same to the Government for necessary action. The recommendations of the Commission in respect of 14 Acts were further examined in detail in 2000 by a Task Force on Women and Children headed by Shri K.C. Pant, the then Deputy Chairman, Planning Commission. To start with, the nodal Department of Women and Child Development has initiated action to move amendments in respect of 4 women-specific legislations, viz. The Immoral Traffic (Prevention) Act, 1956; The Dowry Prohibition Act, 1961; The Indecent Representation of Women (Prohibition) Act, 1986 and The Commission of Sati (Prevention) Act, 1987, Domestic Violence Act, 2005.[1] (See Chart 9.1)

Let us discuss recently passed Domestic Violent Act, 2005

According to the United Nations, violence against women consists of "any act of gender-based violence that results in, or is likely to result in, physical, sexual or psychological harm or suffering to women, including threats of such acts, coercion or arbitrary deprivation of liberty, whether

CHART 9.1

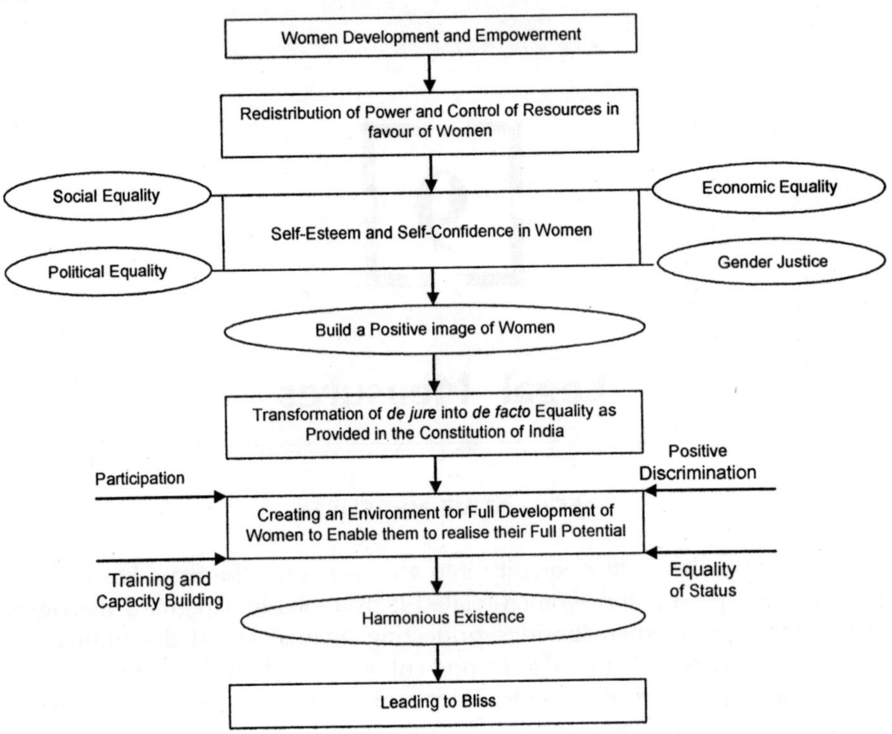

occurring in public or private life. Violence against women shall be understood to encompass but not be limited to: physical, sexual and psychological violence occurring in the family and in the community, including battering, sexual abuse of female children, dowry-related violence, marital rape, female genital mutilation and other traditional practices harmful to women, non-spousal violence, violence related to exploitation, sexual harassment and intimidation at work, in educational institutions and elsewhere, trafficking in women, forced prostitution, and violence perpetrated or condoned by the State."

Violence against women is viewed as one of the most crucial societal mechanism by which women are forced into a subordinate position. It is a manifestation of unequal power relation, which has led to man's domination over and discrimination against women leading to poor governance at home, in society and the country.

Violence is defined as a physical act of aggression of one individual or group against another or others. Violence results in or is likely to result in physical, sexual, psychological harm or suffering. This also includes the threat of such act, coercion or arbitrary deprivation of liberty in public or private life and violation of human rights of women in situation of armed conflicts.

While the basic reason for violence against women is their inferior status in a male dominated society educationally, economically, politically and socially, there are other factors too. The increasing criminalisation of society, media images of violence, poor enforcement of legal provision, unabashed consumerism and erosion of traditional values have all added to it.

The issue of violence against women has been the most pervasive theme of the new women's liberation movement in India since its rise in 1974-75. First, it was the horrifying rising toll of fire in the growing number of dowry deaths, then from 1980 with the cases of Mathura, Maya Tayagi and Rameeza Bi, the problem of rape burst out of the shadows to stand as the symbol of women's oppression. Finally, the last few years have seen dramatic revivals of the ancient customs of Sati as well as female infanticide and female foeticide.[2] Violence against women is an important force that helps to keep the structure of patriarchy intact. It makes gender discrimination a live and terrifying experience for women, and ensures their subjugation. We have used the term gender-based violence to describe acts that cause physical, sexual or psychological harm to women. Such acts are based in the unequals relations that exist between men and women in society. The most important thing to remember about gender-based violence is that, it is all pervasive—it can occur in all kinds of situations (within the family, at the workplace, in public places, in the community, and even when in the custody of the state) and at all stages of women's life.[3]

'Violence against women' means any act of gender-based violence that results in, or is likely to result in, physical, sexual or psychological harm or suffering to women, including threats of such acts, coercion or arbitrary deprivation of liberty, whether occurring in public or private life. Violence against women, including threats or fear of violence is a permanent constraint on the mobility of women and limits their access to resources and basic activities. Such violence's are impediments to the achievement of the objectives of equality, development and peace. It violates and impairs or nullifies the enjoyment by women of their human rights and fundamental freedoms.

The term "violence against women" following the declaration of UN Commission on the Status of Women (1993), is usually defined as "any act of gender-based violence that results in or is likely to result in, physical, sexual or psychological harm or suffering to women, including threats such as acts, coercion or arbitrary deprivations of liberty, whether occurring in public or private life."[4]

Broadly, violence against women can be divided in two categories:

(a) Physical, sexual and psychological violence occurring within the community, including rape, sexual abuse, sexual harassment and intimidation at work, in educational institutions and elsewhere, trafficking in women and forced prostitution; and

(b) Physical, sexual and psychological violence occurring in the family, including battering, sexual abuse of female children in the household, dowry-related violence and other traditional practices harmful to women, non-spousal violence and violence related to exploitation.

The nature and forms of violence is intertwined within physical, mental and psychological levels. Prevailing forms of violence are wife beating and cruelty at home, molestation, rape, sexual harassment at workplace, etc. It occurs regardless of age, marital status, caste, relation, culture and class or income level. Violence includes physical, sexual-emotional, psychological, social and economic abuse by one member of a family/society to control or dominate women in the family/society. Physical violence includes slapping, punching, beating, shoving with or without weapons.

Sexual violence includes rape, molestation, harassment. Rape is forcing a woman to have sex against her will. It is a violation of an individual's rights over her body. Emotional violence can include all intentional attempts to minimise the victim's concern and to make them feel bad. Humiliating the victim in public and private places is also violence.

Psychological violence is any threats that are made or carried out with the intent of financial or emotional injury, blackmail or humiliation. Economic violence creates financial dependence. Intimidation as a form of violence can include making women afraid by using looks, actions and gestures.

Isolation can be used to control and limit what woman does, whom they see and where they go. Using privilege to control is also a form of violence. By treating a woman or child like a servant and having the last word about everything, the abuser is acting like a master. He is defining and rigidly abiding by the traditional roles of men and women.[5]

Violence against women is an impediment to the achievement of the objectives of equality, development and peace. Fear of violence is a permanent constraint on the mobility of women and limits their access to resources and basic needs. The subject "Violence Against Women" is broad-based and comprehensive and includes different types of violence against women, viz. domestic violence, violence at the workplace, violence by the State and its functionaries, violence during war and social disturbances, sexual harassment and abuse, female foeticide, rape, trafficking, dowry-related issues, etc. The innumerable forms of violence against women are so inter-connected that there is need to understand the ways in which women become susceptible to those who prey on their socially constructed vulnerability. The Committee on Empowerment on Women have therefore taken up the subject "Violence against Women" for detailed examination.

It is provided in Section 10 of the National Commission for Women Act, 1990 that the Commission shall "investigate and examine all matters relating to the safeguards provided for women under the Constitution and other laws [Sec. 19(1)(a)] and look into complaints and take *suo motu* notice of matters relating to: (i) depreviation of women's rights; (ii) non-implementation of laws enacted to provide protection to women and also achieve the objective of equality and development, and (iii) non-compliance of policy decisions, guidelines or instructions aimed at mitigating hardships and ensuring welfare and providing relief to women, and take up the issues arising out of such matters with appropriate authorities." (Section 10(1)].

NCW in its report, "A Decade of Endeavour", Vol. II, 1990-2001, rightly states, "Domestic violence is a serious human rights threat to women in every society—rich and poor, developed and industrialized. Particularly in patriarchal societies, it is used as a weapon for subjugating women and suppressing their rights as equal partners in the family structure." Domestic Violence is widespread and cuts across caste, creed, class, and all educational levels. Around the world, on an average, one in every three women has experienced violence in an intimate relationship. It strikes in various forms—physical, sexual, emotional and psychological. It is not only damaging to women but causes deep psychological effect on their children, too, because of the constant fear and humiliation they live with. Largely viewed as a family matter, neighbours, friends and even the relations of the battered women rarely interfere in situations of domestic violence, because a wife is regarded as her husband's property and there is a social acceptance of his rights to chastise her, if she has displeased or disobeyed him in any way, howsoever minor.

The term domestic violence is wide and encompasses in its scope the types of violence resorted to within the home. The overwhelming majority of victims of domestic violence are women. Domestic violence not only includes conduct which amount to cruelty on a women by her husband or by any of his relative but also includes any act which is unbecoming of the dignity of the women. The women are brutally beaten or abused by their husbands or in-laws. Dowry is one of the most obvious causes of domestic crime prevalent in India.

(1) Domestic violence in a draft for Domestic Violence Bill was defined as any of the following acts committed on a woman by her husband or any of his or her relatives, namely:

(i) any wilful conduct which—

(A) is of such a nature as is likely to drive the woman out of the house or commit suicide or to injure herself; or

(B) causes injury or danger to the life, limb or health (whether mental or physical) of the woman; or

(C) (i) emotional, verbal and psychological abuse; or

(ii) harassment or intimidation which causes distress to a woman; or

(iii) any act which compels the woman to have sexual intercourse against her will either with the husband or any of his relatives or with any other persons; or

(iv) any act which is unbecoming of the dignity of the woman; or

(v) economic abuse; or

(vi) any other act of omission or commission which may either cause the threat or mental torture or mental agony to the woman or child in her custody.

(2) "Emotional, verbal and psychological abuse" amounted to degrading or humiliating conduct that adversely affects or is likely to adversely affect the psychological or mental state of the person aggrieved and includes, but is not limited to:

(i) insults, ridicule or name calling, including insults, specially with regard to not having a child or a male child, or for having got insufficient dowry;

(ii) compelling a woman to undergo a sex determination test and/or followed by selective abortion of a female foetus;

(iii) repeated and false allegations of adultery or infidelity;

(iv) repeated threats to cause emotional, psychological or physical pain to the person aggrieved or to any person to whom the person aggrieved is emotionally attached;

(v) threat of suicide; or

(vi) repeated exhibition of obsessive possessiveness or jealousy, which is such as to constitute a serious invasion of the privacy, liberty, integrity or security of the person aggrieved. "Economic abuse": any act, omission or conduct that has resulted in or has the effect of depriving, reducing or hindering access and control of the person aggrieved to economic resources.

(3) The provisions were in addition to, and not in derogation of the provisions of any other law, for the time being in force.

(4) Notwithstanding any other law in force, the court may, at any stage of the hearing of the petition, grant temporary custody of any child or children to the person aggrieved and specify, if necessary, arrangements for visitation by the respondent.

(5) Execution of a warrant: Upon a complaint by the person aggrieved or otherwise if the appropriate police officer of the concerned police station is satisfied that a condition exists for the execution of the warrant of arrest, he shall execute the warrant and arrest the respondent.

(6) A breach of an order directing payment of emergency momentary relief shall be an offence and shall be punishable

with imprisonment which may extend up to one year or with fine which may extend up to Rupees twenty thousand or with both.

(7) A person aggrieved shall not be disentitled or barred from claiming relief under any other law merely because she has sought protection under this Act and has initiated proceedings hereunder.

(8) The Court may at any stage of the hearing on the petition for an order direct the respondent or the person aggrieved either singly or jointly to undergo mandatory counselling with any accredited services provider.[6]

REASONS FOR INCREASING DOMESTIC VIOLENCE

1. Joint Families disintegrated into nuclear families. Joint family system has disintegrated resulting into lack of guidance, control, and affection to newly married. Joint family system was a shock absorber.
2. Husband dominates wife causing irritations. The husband dominates wife which is not acceptable to her. It becomes more serious when wife is also employed. There is no body to help them to sort out differences.
3. Husband and wife start doubting about extra-marital relations causing quarrels, fights and even suicides. It is very difficult to amicably settle such issues.
4 Interference of the parents of the girl in the husband's family-frequent visit of parents and other family members of girl's side cause tension and interference. This makes the husband and his family angry resulting into quarrels and disputes.
5. Husband if in business or service is starved of funds, he asks the wife to make arrangements from her parents causing domestic violence. This is not one time activity but a long-term problem. This results into all sorts of domestic violence.
6. Drinking habits of the husband make the life of the wife a hell. The drinking is becoming a common phenomenon. This results into wastage of money, poor health and bad habits like beating wife, children causing Domestic Violence.

The Protection of Women through Domestic Violence Act, 2005 (43 of 2005)

An Act to provide for more effective protection of the rights of women guaranteed under the Constitution who are victims of violence of any kind occurring within the family and for matters connected therewith or incidental thereto.

Definition of Domestic Violence

For the purpose of this Act, any act, omission or commission or conduct of the respondent shall constitute domestic violence in case it:

(a) harms or injures or endangers the health, safety, life, limb or well-being, whether mental or physical, of the aggrieved person or tends to do so and includes causing physical abuse, sexual abuse, verbal and emotional abuse and economic abuse; or

(b) harasses, harms, injures or endangers the aggrieved person with a view to coerce her or any other person related to her to meet any unlawful demand for any dowry or other property or valuable security; or

(c) has the effect of threatening the aggrieved person or any person related to her by a conduct mentioned in clause (a) or clause (b); or

(d) otherwise injures or causes harm, whether physical or mental, to the aggrieved person.

Appointment of Protection Officer for Dealing with Cases of Domestic Violence

(1) The State Government shall, by notification, appoint such number of Protection Officers in each district as it may consider necessary and shall also notify the area or areas within which a Protection Officer shall exercise the powers and perform the duties conferred on him by or under this Act.

(2) The Protection Officers shall as far as possible be women and shall possess such qualifications and experience as may be prescribed.

(3) The terms and conditions of service of the Protection Officer and the other officers subordinate to him shall be such as may be prescribed.

Duties and Functions of Protection Officer

(1) It shall be the duty of the Protection Officer—

   (a) to assist the Magistrate in the discharge of his functions under this Act;

   (b) to make a domestic incident report to the Magistrate, in such form and in such manner as may be prescribed, upon receipt of a complaint of domestic violence and forward copies thereof to the police officer in charge of the police station within the local limits of whose jurisdiction domestic violence is alleged to have been committed and to the service providers in that area;

(c) to make an application in such form and in such manner as may be prescribed to the magistrate, if the aggrieved person so desires, claiming relief for issuance of a protection order;

(d) to ensure that the aggrieved person is provided legal aid under the Legal Services Authorities Act, 1987 (39 of 1987) and make available free of cost the prescribed form in which a complaint is to be made;

(e) to maintain a list of all service providers providing legal aid or counselling, shelter homes and medical facilities in a local area within the jurisdiction of the Magistrate;

(f) to make available a safe shelter home, if the aggrieved person so requires and forward a copy of his report of having lodged the aggrieved person in a shelter home to the police station and the Magistrate having jurisdiction in the area where the shelter home is situated;

(g) to get the aggrieved person medically examined, if she has sustained bodily injuries and forward a copy of the medical report to the police station and the Magistrate having jurisdiction in the area where the domestic violence is alleged to have been taken place;

(h) to ensure that the order for monetary relief under section 20 is complied with and executed, in accordance with the procedure prescribed under the Code of Criminal Procedure, 1973 (2 of 1974); and

(i) to perform such other duties as may be prescribed.

(2) The Protection Officer shall be under the control and supervision of the Magistrate, and shall perform the duties imposed on him by the Magistrate and the Government by, or under, this Act.

Duties of Government

The Central Government and every State Government, shall take all measures to ensure that:

(a) the provisions of this Act are given wide publicity through public media including the television, radio and the print media at regular intervals;

(b) the Central Government and State Government officers including the police officers and the members of the judicial services are given periodic sensitization and awareness training on the issues and addressed by the Act.

(c) Effective co-ordination between the services provided by concerned Ministers and Departments dealing with law, home affairs including law and order, health and human resources to address issues of domestic violence is established and periodical review of the same is conducted; and

(d) protocols for the various Ministries concerned with the delivery of services to women under this Act including the courts are prepared and put in place.

Protection Order

The Magistrate may, after giving the aggrieved person and the respondent an opportunity of being heard and on being *prima facie* satisfied that domestic violence has taken place or is likely to take place, pass a protection order in favour of the aggrieved person and prohibit the respondent from—

(a) committing any act of domestic violence;
(b) aiding or abetting in the commission of acts of domestic violence;
(c) entering the place of employment of the aggrieved person or, if the person aggrieved is a child, its school or any other place frequented by the aggrieved person;
(d) attempting to communicate in any form, whatsoever, with the aggrieved person, including personal, oral or written or electronic or telephonic contact;
(e) alienating any assets, operating bank lockers or bank accounts used or held or enjoyed by both the parties, jointly by the aggrieved person and the respondent or singly by the respondent, including her *stridhan* or any other property held either jointly by the parties or separately by them without the leave of the Magistrate;
(f) causing violence to the dependants, other relatives or any person who give the aggrieved person assistance from domestic violence; and
(g) committing any other act as specified in the protection order.

Residence Orders

(1) While disposing of an application under sub-section (1) of section 12, the Magistrate may, on being satisfied that domestic violence has taken place, pass a residence order—
   (a) restraining the responded from dispossessing or in any other manner disturbing the possession of the aggrieved person from the shared household, whether or not the respondent has a legal or equitable interest in the shared household;
   (b) directing the respondent to remove himself from the shared household;
   (c) restraining the respondent or any of his relatives from entering any portion of the shared household in which the aggrieved person resides;

(d) restraining the respondent from alienating or disposing of the shared household or encumbering the same;

(e) restraining the respondent from renouncing his rights in the shared household except with the permissions of the Magistrate; and

(f) directing the respondent to secure same level of alternate accommodation for the aggrieved person as enjoyed by her in the shared household or to pay rent for the same, if the circumstances so require:

Provided that no order under clause (b) shall be passed against any person who is a woman.

(2) The Magistrate may impose any additional conditions or pass any other direction which he may deem reasonably necessary to protect or to provide for the safety of the aggrieved person or any child of such aggrieved person.

(3) The Magistrate may require from the respondent to execute a bond with or without sureties for preventing the commission of domestic violence.

(4) An order under sub-section (3) shall be deemed to be an order under Chapter VIII of the Code of Criminal Procedure, 1973 (2 of 1974) and shall be dealt with accordingly.

(5) While passing an order under sub-section (1), sub-section (2) or sub-section (3), the court may also pass an order directing the officer-in-charge of the nearest police station to give protection to the aggrieved person or to assist her or the person making an application on her behalf in the implementation of the order.

(6) While making an order under sub-section (1), the Magistrate may impose on the respondent obligations relating to the discharge of rent and other payments, having regard to the financial needs and resources of the parties.

(7) The Magistrate may direct the officer-in-charge of the police station in whose jurisdiction the Magistrate has been approached to assist in the implementation of the protection order.

(8) The Magistrate may direct the respondent to return to the possession of the aggrieved person her *stridhan* or any other property or valuable security to which she is entitled to.

Monetary Reliefs

(1) While disposing of an application under sub-section (1) of section 12, the Magistrate may direct the respondent to pay monetary relief to meet the expenses incurred and losses suffered by the aggrieved person and any child of the aggrieved person as a result of the domestic violence and such relief may include but is not limited to—

(a) the loss of earnings;
(b) the medical expenses;
(c) the loss caused due to the destruction, damage or removal of any property from the control of the aggrieved person;
(d) the maintenance for the aggrieved person as well as her children, if any, including an order under or in addition to an order of maintenance under section 125 of the Code of Criminal Procedure, 1973 (2 of 1974) or any other law for the time being in force.

(2) The monetary relief granted under this section shall be adequate, fair and reasonable and consistent with the standard of living to which the aggrieved person is accustomed.
(3) The Magistrate shall have the power to order an appropriate lump sum payment or monthly payments of maintenance, as the nature and circumstances of the case may require.
(4) The Magistrate shall send a copy of the order for monetary relief made under sub-section (1) to the parties to the application and to the in-charge of the police station within the local limits of whose jurisdiction the respondent resides.
(5) The respondent shall pay the monetary relief granted to the aggrieved person within the period specified in the order under sub-section (1).
(6) Upon the failure on the part of the respondent to make payment in terms of the order under sub-section (1), the Magistrate may direct the employer or a debtor of the respondent, to directly pay to the aggrieved person or to deposit with the court a portion of the wages or salaries or debt due to or accrued to the credit of the respondent, which amount may be adjusted towards the monetary relief payable by the respondent.

Implementation of Domestic Violence Act, 2005

In the 21st Century, domestic violence would increase more due to the changed life style, i.e. increasing use of alcohol, luxuries of life beyond capacity, lust for more money, etc. This is going to be a world phenomenon. Domestic violence is a slow poison which is swallowing the ingredients of family life. Such a situation is causing problems of health to the members of the family and is a source of constant tension.[6]

Most women, however, choose to suffer silently rather than report such incidents to the police and are unwilling to admit the causes of their injuries for fear of further victimization or bringing shame or dishonour to the family. The police, on the other hand, treat such incidents as marital disputes and often refuse to register them. Even if they are registered, they are rarely prosecuted with zeal. Similar gender bias is reflected in the judiciary, who treat cases of domestic violence as 'trivial matters', often giving lenient punishment to the perpetrators.

The menace of domestic violence is beyond description as it is like an iceberg and whatever we see outside in public, it is negligible. If we take up the definition of Domestic Violence in a broader sense then hardly any house is saved from its clutches. However, here we may take a narrow definition when domestic violence takes physical form and results in torture, beating, causing physical and mental tensions to women so that they get tired of their life. The women are denied food and good place to sleep, etc. it is not restricted to a particular area or types of people. Its tentacles are spreading in every area. However, the gravitation of violence against women in rural areas are more prevalent as compared to cities. The interesting feature of this is that it is found even among educated religious-minded people as well. Such a horrible situation causes havoc and make life of women miserable. What are the causes of it? Why is it on the increase? Why do we not make it a sweet home where peace prevails.

The Government especially the Department of Women and Child Welfare deserves appreciation and credit for enforcing a bold legislation in the area of Domestic Violence.

The daily *Tribune* dated Oct. 26, 2006 under the heading "Domestic Violence Act comes into effect" observes that the Protection of Women from Domestic Violence Act 2005 comes into effect from Oct. 26 aiming to provide protection to wife or female live in partner from the husband or male live-in partner and also his relatives. The Act, passed by Parliament in August, 2005 was approved by President A.P.J. Abdul Kalam on Sept. 12, 2005, following which the Minister of Women and Child Development issued a notification bringing Domestic Violence Act into force. Domestic violence under the Act included actual abuse or the threat of abuse whether physical, sexual, verbal, emotional or economical. Harassment by way of unlawful dowry demands to the women or her relatives would also be covered under the notification. The Ministry simultaneously issued another notification laying down rules framed for the implementation of the Act which will provide for, among other things, appointment of protection officers, service providers and counsellors.

Renuka Chowdhury, Minister for women and Child development. Said around 70 per cent of women in India were victims of domestic violence in some form or the other. The enactment of the law is a historic step towards ending gender discrimination. The law addresses sexual abuse of children, or forcing girls to marry against their whishes as well. The act also gives a married woman the right to remain in her husband's home, or under the same roof in a joint-family household, even if she does not have any rights to the property. The definition includes threats of abuse and dowry demands.

To quote the *Tribune* dated Oct. 26, 2006 under the heading "Domestic Violence Act comes into effect." According to Minister of Women and Child Development Renuka Chowdhary, the law will go a long way to provide relief to women from domestic violence and get their due. To ensure this, the ministry has also asked all state governments and union territories to ensure that necessary administrative arrangements are immediately put in place for the commencement of the Act. As per the statement, the law will cover all those women who are or have been in a relationship with the abuser where both parties have lived together in a shared household and are related by consanguinity, marriage or a relationship in the nature of marriage or adoption.

Besides, relationship with family members living together as a joint family is also included. Sisters, widows, mothers, single women or women living with the abuser are entitled to get legal protection under the proposed bill.

In Delhi alone there were 8,000 reports of Domestic Violence last year but there was very little the police could do because there was no teeth to the law. The act has empowered them. There is a sudden spurt of activity in all the states and more and more cases are being resolved. Honourable Renuka Chowdhary, Union Minister for Women and Child Welfare in her interview by Vibha Sharma, pertaining to the implementation of Domestic Violence Act, 2005 published in the *Tribune* dated Nov. 5, 2006 under the heading "New Act will check violence on women" observes that the new law for Protection of Women from Domestic Violence is a Diwali gift. In an exclusive interview she says, When we implement a law, we expect the civil society to use it in letter and spirit. We enact a law to set directions for society. There would have been no need for this Act if other laws had not been abused. Where is the law that says that a man can beat his woman? That a women must keep quite even if her husband comes home drunk and rapes his daughter? That in-laws can sit and watch a human being burnt alive? That a man must have an educated woman, whose salary must belong to him but she will have no freedom? Where are the laws for all this, but they are being practiced, aren't they? Why is society not standing up and questioning that?

The most terrifying task is to educate the so-called educated men who drive a Mercedes Benz but use the filthiest of abusive languages against their wives and children, daughters. Men who provide their wives designer handbags and sunglasses but accuse them of sleeping with their servants. I get at least one "please help me" call every single night. The other day a lady, a very well known person, wife of a very powerful man, daughter-in-law of a very powerful man, called me up crying. She told me how she was going through hell and mental torture every single day of her life. It is hard to believe that domestic violence can happen at those level also.

It is the upbringing, the social condition that these men have been given over the years that they are the lords and the masters, beholders of all that they see. That the wife is a disposable and removeable commodity. Look at their fate—women can be kicked out by their husbands, they have no right over their inheritance, they cannot return to their parents home. There was an incident when a husband kicked his wife out of their home in midnight after an argument. She had no money, no slippers. The husband did not even allow her to put on a dressing gown over the night dress.

It is absurd that men want educated wives, Barbie dolls with no brains so that they can kick and push them around and perform on order. But women are not some bandaariyas at India Gate who will dance at their order. What we need is a decent equitable equilibrium in society. Boys must grow up in the knowledge that they cannot take women in their lives for granted. For that the mindest at home has to change so that children do not grow up seeing their fathers abuse their mothers, using filthy language.

It will be an ongoing process. The information, the awareness will be disseminated right to the grassroots level. We plan to involve everyone, including the media, the police, the district level officers, panchayats, common people, volunteers in awareness building. It was not an easy task. Our first aim was to bring the law in its stark nascent form. But the law is not static. There are several things that can be worked upon.

Kiran Bedi feels that it is for women who genuinely need help. At no stage should this be used falsely by them. Magistrates, Protection Officers are for justice and not pro-women and anti-men.

The Acts empowers the court to pass protection orders to prevent an abusive husband from aiding or committing acts of domestic violence. The offender, for instance, can be restrained from communicating with the victim and from visiting her workplace or any other place she frequents.

The Protection of women from domestic violence Act, 2005 provides for the building of a cadre of protection officers who will operate in every district of the country, helping abused victims file cases before magistrates. The law has taken the unprecedented step of stipulating that the concerned magistrate hear the case within three days of its registration.

Under the Protection of Women from Domestic Violence Act, 2005, offenders can be jailed for a maximum of one year or fined up to Rs 20,000 or both. They can also be charged under other section of the Indian Penal Code (IPC), if applicable. The new law provides an all encompassing definition of domestic violence by the husband, such as beating or physical hurting his wife, or sexual violence like forced intercourse, but also verbal or emotional violence such as insulting the wife or preventing her from taking up a job, and even economic violence such as not allowing the wife to spend out of her income for personnel use.

However, some non-government agencies, dealing with crimes against women and child are not-so hopeful about successful implementation of the Act. Studies show that in India around 70 percent of women are victims of violence Acts in one or the other form, making it a massive task for enforcing agencies to successfully implement the Act. Advocates for Shaktivahini an NGO, actively involved in women and child welfare activities, Kamal Pandey says history of most of the social legislations, whether related to women or children or bonded labour, shows that implementation of these Acts is usually a long delayed process. "It is a step in the right direction. But I do not see any perceptible change in women's status overnight. Most of the social legislations are never implemented properly. . . It will take at least a decade before things change and that too provided the government puts proper machinery in place and the implementation agencies like the police and women are made adequately aware of the Act.

In addition to physical violence of beating, slapping, hitting, kicking and pushing, the act also covers sexual violence like forced intercourse, forcing his wife or mate to look at pornography or any other obscene picture or material and child sexual abuse. It also includes verbal and emotional violence such as name-calling and insults. Moreover, preventing one's wife from taking up a job or forcing her to leave job are also under the purview of the Act. An important features of the Act is the women's right to secure housing. The Bill provides for women right to reside in the matrimonial and shared household, whether or not she has any title in the household. This right is secured by a residence order, which is passed by a court.

The Act provides for breach of protection order or interim protection order or interim protection order by the respondent as a cognizable and non-bailable offence punishable with imprisonment for a term which may extend to one year or with fine which may extend to Rs. 20,000 or with both. The other relief envisaged is that the power of the court to pass protection orders that prevent the abuser from aiding or committing an act of domestic violence or any other specified act, entering a work-place or any other place frequented by the abused, attempting to communicate with the abused, isolating any assets used by both the parties.

Chetan Ji in his article, 'Will law go the Dowry Act way?" in the *HT*, Oct. 27, 2006 observed that the Protection of Women from Domestic Violence Act could well end up a paper tiger like the Dowry Prohibition Act. Even years after the Dowry Prohibition Act was enforced state government have provided only a few prohibition officers. A Women and child Development ministry official said this made the Act ineffective in checking the rising cases of dowry. The official said without prohibition officers, "most police officers are not even aware about the provisions of the dowry law."

Women's groups who pushed for the law have hailed it as a comprehensive legislation. This is a historic law. This is a Diwali and Ed gift for women. There can be no bigger happiness for us than seeing the law, which is our baby, come into being. National Commission for Women (NCM) chairperson Girija Vyas was quick to claim it a great achievement.

Centre for Social Research Director Ranjana Kumari agreed that the law was radical and tackled an ugly side of society that was often brushed under the carpet. This law recognizes new concepts like mental assault and torture, sexual violence within marriage and the legitimacy of live-in relationship. She pointed out that under the law, the victim could go directly to a court for protection.

In India, National Crime Record Bureau (NCRB) registers a case of cruelty by husbands and relatives every 9 minutes. National Commission for Women has in 2003-04 recorded 902 cases of dowry harassment and

310 cases of matrimonial disputes. Though welcoming the law, activists say these statistics do not account for growing crimes against women. They make the point that success of this legislation will depend on combating problems of illiteracy and ignorance amongst women as well as deep-rooted stigmas in reporting domestic violence

Doubts and Approaches

The protection of women from domestic violence Act could well end up a paper tiger like the Dowry Prohibition Act.

Even years after the Dowry Prohibition Act was enforced, state governments have provided only a few prohibition officers. A woman and Child Development ministry official said this made the Act in-effective in checking the rising cases of dowry. The official said without prohibition officers, "most police officers are not even aware about the provisions of the dowry law."

Domestic violence needs a coordinated and systemic response from the judicial system. While Sec 498A has been one of the most significant criminal law reforms protecting women's rights, this reform is not enough. Ultimately we need to remember that criminal law is indeed a blunt tool, as it is very difficult to change police culture; though the law may consider domestic violence against women an offence, the police may still not comply with the law and not implement it effectively. Therefore, in order to move towards an effective working of Sec. 498-A and other criminal law remedies, it is crucial that we put in place a new model of policing—the victim empowerment model as described above. A model that will put in place pro-arrest procedures and social service networks at the police station in order to give the victim alternative support services as needed. Most importantly, we need to work on standard and regular policing, which will ensure that domestic violence is taken seriously.

Hindustan Times Editorial heading "Home bitter home" dated Oct. 27, 2006, observes that IN THEORY, the Protection of Women from Domestic Violence Act, 2005 seems to be a conglomeration of loopholes tied together rather then a net to catch those guilty of committing violence against women. After all, how can one be sure that the law will not be misused by women? Or, for that matter, how will the law, never mind those who will wonder whether they are victims or not, define "verbal violence" that includes insults? These are valid questions. But in the Indian context, there have been too many occasions when a protective measure, either in the from of a law or a policy, has fallen by the wayside because of such head scratching.

What makes us come to the other end of the stick for a law to make any real sense, the victims must be made aware that they are victims. For a large majority of women, the suffering is silent simply because they are not aware of that, one, something is terribly wrong, and two, that there is a law to stop such suffering and punish the guilty. Crime against women is committed mostly by men. But women, too, have not been innocent of abusing women. Whether it be violence against the daughter-in-law, the mother-in-law or the domestic help, women have also played a role in this unsavory and continuing affair. With all its flaws and loopholes, the new law should identify and put a stop to domestic crime against women. A 21st century India does not only deserve to treat its women with dignity but also absolutely insists on it.

In addition to stepping up measures for better policing it is imperative to have a civil law which addresses domestic violence. The recently approved Domestic Violence Bill, 2005 contains remedies such as ex-parte injunctions without the need for filing for divorce or maintenance, protection orders, non-molestation orders and non-contact orders, which would help the woman while criminal action is being taken against the abuser to prevent him from making contact with her and inflicting more violence. Therefore, we need to look towards a co-ordinated legal approach to protect women facing domestic violence. Only such a coordinated and holistic approach would help persons facing domestic violence to get true relief from the legal system.

The legislation is expected to give women—wives, mothers, mothers in-law; sister, daughters and even adopted daughters—protection against physical, verbal and sexual abuse and the right to shelter and economic freedom.

CRITICAL APPRAISAL

There is no doubt that the implementation of Domestic Violence Act would promote good status for women suffering from centuries under the cruelty of family life. Many people in press are doubting about the success of implementation but we are sure that this landmark act would usher the freedom for women and would made them feel about the purpose and meaning of life. Let us analyse the views:

1. A Courageous and Bold Step

S.K. Nayyar from Panchkula in his views to *Hindustan Times* dated Nov. 6, 2006 observes that It is a welcome step by the Government of India to empower to women to raise their moral aptitude and voice against the violence they face at homes. Protection of women under Domestic Violence Act, 2005 will definitely change the relationship between the husband and wife. On the one hand the Act would protect the effected women, whereas on the other hand majority of people in the Indian society may exploit this Act similar to the Dowry Act.

In the words of Justice Krishna Iyer: "The poignancy of the Indian women's condition is that she is a slave, bonded labour, bought, sold, raped and murdered, eye-teased and dowry burnt, employment-wise exclude *de-facto* and even by rules profession-wise banished into the background and in industry and agriculture and science and technology silently barred from entry or promotion.

2. Promote Empowerment of Women and Better Status

Col. K.D. Pathak (Retd.) from Chandigarh in his views in *Hindustan Times* feels that in view of the above, protection of women under Domestic Violence Act, 2005 is a long awaited enactment to empower women legally to a better status in our society and raise their voice against the violence they are subjected to in our homes.

Empowerment of Women being one of primary objectives of the Ninth Plan, efforts were made to create an enabling environment where women can freely exercise their rights both within and outside home, as equal partners along with men. This was realized through early finalisation and equal partners along with men. This was realized through early finalisation and adoption of the 'National Policy for Empowerment of Women' which laid down definite goals, targets and policy prescriptions along with a well defined Gender Development Index to monitor the impact of its implementation in raising the status of women from time to time.

3. Well Researched and Framed Legislation

Praneet Bajwa reporting in *Hindustan Times* dated Nov. 6, 2006 rightly fees that this Act covers a wide range of domestic situations and has been well researched and framed, even consanguineous or adopted female relations are within its protection. The success of any law depends on its efficient enforcement. This Act shows direction to Indians to be have like responsible beings.

4. Sincere Efforts on the Part of Government

G.K. Chopra from Chandigarh reporting in Hindustan Times dated 6 Nov. 2006 really feels that the government has done a remarkable job buy implementing the Domestic Violence Act to protect Women. Now, all the men who are habitual drunkard and beat their wives for one excuse or the other will be brought to book. Women will have to take courage and come forward in case of atrocities by their husbands. No doubt this act will also be misused but the number of such cases will be negligible.

HT in its editorial "Home Better Home" on Oct. 27, 2006 observed that in theory, the protection of Women from Domestic Violence Act, 2005, seems to be a conglomeration of loopholes tied together rather than a net to catch those guilty of committing violence against women. After all, how will the law, never mind those who will wonder whether they are victims or not, define 'verbal violence' that includes insults? These are valid questions. But in the Indian context, there have been too many occasions when a protective measures, either in the form of a law or a policy, has fallen by the wayside because of such head-scratching. For a law to make any real sense, the victims must be made aware that they are victims. For a large majority of women, the suffering is silent simply because they are not aware that, one, something is terribly wrong, and, two, that there is a law to stop such suffering and punish the guilty. Crime against women is committed mostly by men. But women, too, have not been innocent of abusing women. Whether it be violence against the daughter-in-law, the mother-in-law or the domestic help, women have also played a role in this unsavoury and continuing affair. With all its flaws and loopholes, the new law should identify and put a stop to domestic crime against women. A 21st century India doesn't only deserve to treat its women with dignity but also absolutely insists on it.

5. Promote Safety and Welfare of Women

Vijay Bhardwaj from Chandigarh feels that after the domestic violence Act was passed recently, the genuinely suffering women must have had a sigh of relief and would be felling safe at home specially where the husband is a drunkard, a drug addict, wayward or uncaring. He will be cautious while taking any extreme step. In the scenario, where the so called educated liberated and modern women are concerned the act is bound to be misused liberally. It has been observed that majority of the working women emotionally and psychologically blackmail their husbands who have been already traumatized since the day they got married for the basic reasons that the wife neglects her basic duties.

6. Maintain Power Balance

Rita Raina from Jodhpur feels that The meaning of gender and sexuality and the balance of power between women and men at all levels of society must be reviewed. Combating violence against women requires challenging the way that gender roles and power relations are articulated in society. Increase sex equivalence counseling empower women to engage in extra earnings without hindering their basic wife and mother roles. Changing peoples attitude and mentality towards women will take a long time. Nevertheless, raising awareness of the issue of violence against women and educating boys and men to view women as valuable partner's life in the development of a society and in the attainment of peace are just as important as taking legal steps to protect women's human rights. It is also important in order to prevent violence that non-violent means be used to resolve conflict through family counselling and family courts of compromise and finding common means. The Act of quick hearing with police and courts for holding men culpable might spoil chances of common grounds of adjustments and further inflict men for greater infliction and all jails and remand house will fill to brim and women yet remain a bigger prey. I suggest NGO/area counseling members taking up the task at the premises of complaint of violence is better alternative than involving Law in the very beginning. Calling of male or female member to police, itself is a discomfort, whereas police also have no special attributes of consoling and compromise.

7. Cautious Approach

S.K. Khosla feels that It is not always that only women are subjected to domestic violence. Sometimes men and children become victims of

Chart 9.2

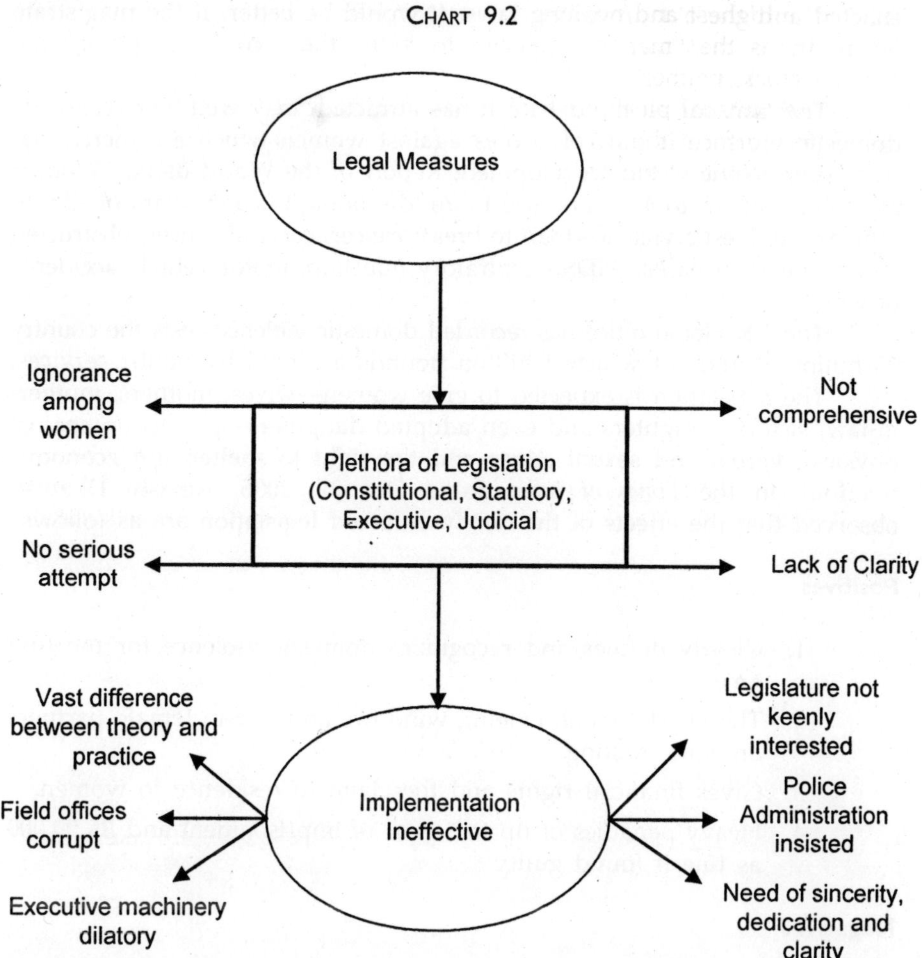

domestic violence. There should have been a provision in the Act that whosoever is the victim of domestic violence should be protected under this Act. In the absence of this provision, this act can be misused by women. There are a number of reasons of domestic violence such as dowry, sexual relations of husband or wife to an other person, joint family system, habitual behaviour like drinking, gambling, indulgence in latest fashion, etc. this Act shall have limited success, as only under extreme circumstances when all limits of decency crossed, the female dares to go out to get protection of this Act. Mental compatibility is the most sought thing in the family rather legislations. Secondly, the new law allowed the police to arrest an accused and also acts as a protection officer as had happened in the case of Josephy and Mary of Tamil Nadu the first ever case came to light under this Act. There should not be any role of the police to act as protection officer, if it is so, then there is no difference between the new enacted and the old prevailing laws. It would be better, if the magistrate where the application is supposed to lodge the complaint appoint the protection officer.

The law, for all the debate it has attracted, may well be overdue as domestic violence is part of crimes against women which are increasing. According to the world Development Report of the World Bank, "Women aged between 15 to 44 years lose more 'discounted health years of life' to rape and domestic violence than to breast cancer, cervical cancer, obstructed labour, heart diseases, AIDS, respiratory infection, motor vehicle accidents of war."

The UK Home office has recorded domestic violence costs the country 23 billion pounds of which 3 billion pounds are paid by public services.

The legislation is expected to give women—wives, mothers, mother-in-law, sisters, daughters and even adopted daughters—protection against physical, verbal and sexual abuse and the right to shelter and economic freedom. In the *Times of India* dated Oct. 27, 2006, Amashi Dhawan observed that the effects of the newly enforced legislation are as follows:

Positives

1. Clearly defines and recognizes domestic violence for the first time
2. The law treats all clueing windows and live-in female partners on equal footing.
3. Gives financial rights and the claim to residence to women.
4. Heavy penalties of up to 1 year of imprisonment and Rs 20,000 as fine if found guilty.

Negatives

1. Could be misused to settle scores out of vengeance. Anti-dowry legislation has also attracted similar criticism.
2. Social pressures may still lead to under-reporting and suppression of domestic violence.
3. No additional resources provided for setting up of shelters or homes and appointment of protection officers.
4. Slow bureaucratic and police process. It has taken a year for the act to be enforced.

SUGGESTIONS

Based upon the observations and comments from different people let me suggest to make the life of women and men happier rather than waste in police stations and courts.

1. Need of Constructive Actions

- A chapter on family life may be included in the school curriculum indicating the broad parameters of family life.
- Religious places may be encouraged to lecture on family life quoting ideal examples of Ramayana.
- Ethical values may be ingrained in the minds of children.
- Parents schools may be held on Sundays to have discussion on happy family and happiness.
- Nivedita R. Bhide in her article, "Values in family" rightly states.

In the Indian social system the unit of society is not an individual but a family. Traditionally, every person's life is divided into four stages.

In the second stage, called Grihasthashrama, a person takes to family life and is expected to serve society. Our forefathers, the rishis, had conscientiously set the family on firm foundations so as to ensure the stability of society. It is this admirable family system which led many historians to comment that the law and order, culture, and personal virtues did not suffer in India even under foreign rule or in times of war.

The principle which predominantly ruled in the family was dharma, a word which defies definition in English. 'family' does not mean a group of people related to each other by law or blood and living together. It is a social unit with a definite purpose—namely, man-making and nurturing of society.

Family is an institution. An institution can function effectively only if it follows the rule of continuity and change. The entry of a newly-wed bride into the house of her husband is an important landmark in any family. She is the child of the present and represents 'change' whereas the in-laws act as the link connecting the past to the present. They ensure continuity in a family. Both the bride and the in-laws have to understand and love each other to allow an uninterrupted progress in the family. The holding together or the breaking apart of a family generally gets decided at this point, namely, the entry of a daughter-in-law.

2. Holistic View

Hedi and Nik Boesten in their article, "three Points of View" rightly suggests.

If a man and woman marry for love, they are not in perfect harmony in thought and emotion right from the start. Instead, they want to accept one another just as they are, with different developments, and if possible complement one another. From then on, they should bear all responsibilities, perform duties and take decisions together and each can rely on the other. This helps enormously in coping with difficulties at work and in everyday life.

At the same time a process of mutual maturing begins: giving in, showing consideration, accepting the common fate, and giving up selfish desires. This takes place all the more quickly, the earlier the desire for children arises. Then selfless service is required. It culminates in the recognition of the fact that during the children's stay of about twenty years with the family, they are merely given into the care of their parents and that parents must learn to release them unconditionally when the time comes. In this way humility, contentment and kindness can grow and in old-age, wisdom, which we in our childhood so appreciated in the older generation.

Today the problem for parents in the West is that children are increasingly questioning the traditional family values. They no longer just want to take them over by way of obedience, but accept them only when they have understood their relevance and value after a period of time and a maturing process. Often the only help is if the parents have patiently and constantly set an example and are open to questions, even to have themselves called into question.

3. Promote Domestic Democracy

Radhika Chopra in her article, "Supportive Practices of Men: A Critical Assessment" rightly states that: In part that politics of entry seeks to change material conditions within households and encourage a form of domestic democracy to emerge. The efforts of this entry, via programmes of intervention, are geared toward persuading the "entitled" members—mainly the men—to play a more supportive role in the lives of their more deprived partners—mainly the women, but also children. Man-as-supportive-partners campaigns undertaken after the Cairo Conference, or the Men-in-Maternal Health Programmes of the Population Council (Directory: Research and Interventions; 2002) focus primarily on involving men in reproductive health care. However, both focus primarily on a single category of men in households—mainly, husbands. The campaigns also focus primarily on one category of women—wives in the reproductive phase of their lives. Within the focused terms of these campaigns husbands are being encouraged to play an active role in the lives of women in specific areas like women's reproductive health. The rationale for this encouragement is to animate the view that babies and their pre and post-natal care is not the work of women alone, but must include men. Such intervention in fact seeks to expand the role of men beyond the sexual and actively demystify the view that the only part men need to play is to make babies, not tend them. The attempt at involving men in the health care of their wives and children is to encourage men to think of reproductive health as 'their' work as well. Equally, encouraging men to participate in the reproductive health of women seeks to rework men's subject positions within the home by expanding and elaborating the role of men beyond the sexual, into the intimacies and the 'work of care.'

4. Addressing Domestic Violence Through Education

Prevention of domestic violence ultimately depends upon changing the norms of society regarding violence as a means of conflict resolution and traditional attitudes about gender. To achieve this, there must be introduction of gender and human rights in the curricula of schools, universities, professional colleges and other training colleges. Along with this, there must be recognition and commitment to the principle of the free compulsory primary and secondary education for girls. In Jawaharlal Nehru speech, "The habit of looking upon marriage as the sole economic refuge for women will have to go before women can have any freedom. Freedom, depends on economic conditions even more than political, and even if woman is not economically free and self-earning she will have to depend on the husband or someone else, and dependents are never free"

CONCLUSION

Darshan Singh has suggested the following to promote harmony in family:

- First of all, change is needed in the perception of society towards the dignity of women. She should be treated at par with her male counterpart because threat to male authority is the main cause of domestic violence against women.
- Violence against women is primarily a gender issue. So awareness against gender biases is necessary to minimize the problem. Legal education to fight against injustic must be imparted to girls at high school or secondary school level so that they stand up and fight for their rights.
- There is need to motivate poor families to utilize the various schemes started by the government for their welfare. The women in particular may be motivated to benefit from the on-going programmes for their economic empowerment.
- Strict legal action should be taken against those who are involved in violence-related activities against women. There is also a need to strictly implement the legal provisions of the various legislations which are meant for the protection of women. Moreover, there is a need for specific legislations which make wife beating and other similar problems a criminal offence and a ground of immediate divorce.
- There is need to strengthen and increase the non-governmental organizations which could take-up individual women's problems with their in-laws and police and court, etc.
- Women in general must be educated about their rights and also about the agency to be approached if they have any 'problem of violence' in their family.
- Family counselling centres must be set-up at lower level, so that at risk families may be identified and thorough counseling, supports and help may be given to such families before it takes the shape of conflict.

- Violence against women does not end by merely bestowing of judicial rights or by making women literate. Most urban women are literate today but they are also the victims of domestic violence. So to check the problem of domestic violence against women it is imperative that women must be morally strong empowered.

Inspite of the provision of family courts, women and men and children in a family would not co-operate with one another until and unless we make them our ancient values enshrined in our ancient literature.

We may conclude that Government should not plan Good governance merely on paper. It must be exhibited in practice as well. When our women would be safe, then one can think that Good Governance is beginning to emerge. As on today, one can safely conclude that women are discriminated in every sphere of life and no benefit of good governance is accruing them.

Amar Chandel in his article, "Protection Women at Home—Use the new law, but with care" dated Nov. 11, 2006 observes that the new Act is suitably harsh and all-encompassing to make sure that the perpetrators of atrocities do not manage to wriggle out. Ironically, that may also prove to be its undoing because now even a slight point of disagreement can be blown out of proportion and branded is "domestic violence." For instance, it is not only physical or sexual abuse which constitutes domestic violence but also "verbal and emotional abuse" that includes "insults, ridicule, humiliation, name calling and insults or ridicule, specially with regard to not having a child or a male child."

Indeed, such barbed comments have ruined the lives of many a woman, but at the same time there is need to be wary of the tendency of some to fly off the handle at the slightest provocation.

The intention of law-makers here apparently is to ensure that the guilty husband is not able to escape responsibility by merely denying that the complainant is his wife. It also aims to help women lured into a live-in relationship with a promise of marriage. The intent is laudable, but it is essential to be very particular as to what the nature and duration of a so-called live-in relationship is. When relationships sour, all too often, they have an unfortunate effect of bringing out the worst in both parties. The harshness of the Act too can become a handy tool in the hands of a crafty women hell-bent on blackmailing a male friend.

Domestic violence and abuse of women is a problem that should not be seen merely through a gender-oreinted prism. It is much more complex. Just as the endeavour of a good doctor zapping cancerous cells is also to ensure that the healthy ones are not damaged, the Domestic Violence Act should be geared to punish only the guilty. Swinging the pendulum to the other extreme will be a travesty.

Abhishek Singhvi in his article, "The Law lies in the detail" in the *HT* dated Dec. 6, 2006 observes that the juxtaposed with this, the definition of 'shared household' in Section 2(s) suggests that a person who has had a live-in relationship, but wants to break it to marry another partner, would have to reckon with the continued residence of his former live-in companion. Physical proximity through compulsory continuation of residence might mean, in a manner rather bizarre, that an ex-girlfriend can live with the spouse in the same 'shared household' through compulsion of law! This may or may not relieve the women's oppression but it would certainly create unheavals of an unthinkable kind.

We cannot ignore the structural realities of India. The use of wide, imprecise and subjective legislative language, coupled with a venal or malleable police force of enforcement machinery, can spell doom and destruction for any self-respecting and law-abiding male citizen of this country. Add to that, motivated or malafide invocation of the Act and we would end up with a remedy much worse than the disease.

This is not to suggest abrogation of this legislation. But a fair balance for different sections of society must be achieved. This alone is the best guarantee for the success of any legislation.

During the Tenth Plan period, some important legislations have been passed and amended. For example, besides the Hindu Succession (Amendment) Act, 2005 and PWDVA, 2005 mentioned earlier, the Dowry Prohibition Act was reviewed. A very active civil society has been relentlessly campaigning on these issues. Their experiences and recommendations will be taken on board to ascertain that the rights of every woman are enshrined in laws.

Under the Eleventh Plan budgetary allocations will be made for publicity and for creating the required infrastructure for effective implementation of these legislation. MoWCD will appoint Protection Officers and set-up district level cells to be responsible for monitoring and implementation of Protection of Women from Domestic Violence Act (PWDVA) and other Acts under its charge.[8]

Notes and References

1. GOI, Planning Commission, Xth Five Year Plan, 2002-07, pp. 228-29.
2. UNIFEM and Mary: Support Services to Counter Violence against Women in Haryana, A Resource Directory, New Delhi, 2003.
3. UNIFEM and Sanhito, Support Services to Counter Violence Against Women in West Bengal, Kolkata, 2002, p. 13.
4. *Ibid.*, p. 15
5. *Ibid.*, pp. 15-16.
6. NCW: Annual Report, 2000-2001, New Delhi, pp. 32-33.
7. UNIFEM and Support Services to Counter-Violence against Women in Haryana.
8. GOI, Planning Commission, XIth Plan, pp. 198-99.

10

Challenges of Women Development and Empowerment in 21st Century

We cannot continue doing
What we have always done
Tomorrow cannot be just more of yesterday
We need flexibility and Pragmatism
As much as innovation
But the stress must invariably be on action

It is also aimed at making women awakened, thinking persons, able to make balanced decisions and informed choices to be aware of their identity, to enhance their sense of self-esteem and acquire a belief in dignity– "preparing the women for tomorrow" is an integrated programme aspiring towards on all round development of the self NCW.

INTRODUCTION

There has been a slow movement towards the Development and Empowerment of Women during the last century in the developing countries including India. The reason behind all these is the lukewarm attitude and lack of sincerity in dealing with the women issues. It is paradoxical that all decision-makers whether politicians or administrators advocate in favour of women but in practice they are not inclined to this sincerely and earnestly, i.e. they provide only lip service. In addition, Women Organisations have failed to justify and pursue their issues persistently and consistently. All this has resulted in slow development of the Women's Welfare. However, in 21st Century, we have to wage a war to achieve all what has been agreed at the international forums and National Forums. It is high time that all those who are engaged in the development and Empowerment of Women should see that 21st Century must be the century of women wherein all the women enjoy not only equal status with men but go ahead to prove that women are second to none. This would require fresh approach and reforms which may be innovative, feasible, and cost-effective. The ultimate goal should aim at raising the status of women in practice and 21st century should see that no discrimination is made against women rather positive efforts should remove hurdles in their way.

United Nations Economic and social commission for Asia and the pacific in its report, "Asia and the pacific into the 21st century: prospect for social development" rightly sees the gains during the last century and indicates the problems in 21st century:

1. Wide Gap between Theory and Practice

As the twenty-first century approaches, it is clear that the Asian and Pacific region has witnessed impressive gains in standards of living, and many of these gains have accrued to women. In many countries, economic growth has been associated with increases in per capita consumption, life expectancy, literacy and educational attainment and declines in infant mortality, maternal mortality, and fertility. Other gains have included enhanced calorie intake and increased access to safe water, sanitation, electricity, public transportation, government-sponsored health care, and other services. For women, literacy and higher educational attainment have eased their entry into the paid labour force, which has provided many more women than in the past with social security and related benefits. Women's organizations and transnational feminist networks have been established virtually everywhere, and they have been active in raising consciousness about social injustice, economic hardships and gender inequalities. Women's groups throughout the Asian and pacific region have been pushing for policy and legal reforms to raise women's status, remove barriers to their social participation, ensure their rights, and expand their capabilities. Autonomy, equality and empowerment allow women to contribute more fully to the well-being of their families and societies.

Despite these significant improvements, at the end of the millennium, after three decades of development and four world conferences on women, problems remain with respect to the legal status and social positions of women. Throughout the world, gender ideologies assign differential roles, rights, and values to women and men, whether as workers, parents or citizens. Gender relations, therefore, are often unequal, even in the most developed countries, and this inequality manifests itself in the household, the economy and the polity. In some Asian countries, legal and customary barriers, including family laws, preclude women's full participation in economic development and in public life. The unemployment rates of women are often far higher than those of men; and in countries where women's employment has made significant contributions to national industries development and international competitiveness, the gender gap in wages remains very wide. Labour laws and social policies are often gender-blind, and they neglect working women's unique need to balance productive activities and reproductive responsibilities.

Poverty is a scourge that often affects females worse than males, for it exacerbates in household inequalities in favour of males and leads to the neglect of girl children and inadequate health care for expectant mothers. Violence against women, whether in the home, on the streets, or in war, continues unabated although it is now recognized as a major violation of women's human rights Economic crisis and restructuring have created difficulties for working people and for the urban poor, and especially for working women and poor women. In almost all sub-regions, women have been adversely affected by economic reforms, structural adjustments and market transitions which have occurred within the context of globalization.

Many Asian and Pacific countries have been deeply involved in the process of globalization, and this has presented both risks and opportunities for them. The risks associated with globalization became dramatically evident in late 1997 with the crisis of financial markets in Indonesia, Malaysia, Republic of Korea and Thailand. It is unlikely, however, that globalization will be reversed; indeed, more countries are seeking deeper integration into the global economy. This raises questions about the likely impact of globalization on women. What are the implications, both negative and positive, of a globalized economy for women workers? How are various countries preparing women, for example, in terns of education and skills, for a highly competitive global economy?

Globalization is not only an economic phenomenon; it has also political and cultural dimensions. If economic globalization refers to the worldwide liberalization of prices and trade and the increasing integration of world markets, political and cultural globalization refers in part to the internationalization of movements for democratization and discourses on human rights, women's rights and environmental protection. In its more negative connotation, globalization refers to the imposition of western liberal capitalism and "coca colonization." However, this outcome is not predetermined. Women and women's organizations can take advantage of global opportunities and new technologies to spread messages, form coalitions, and push for the implementation within their own countries of the objectives agreed upon at the Fourth World Conference on Women, held in Beijing in September 1995. In so doing, they will be influencing the direction of social change. Nor does the global eclipse the local. Indeed, the globalization of discourses of human rights, women's rights and environmental protection. In its more negative connotation, globalization refers to the imposition of western liberal capitalism and "coca colonization." However, this outcome is not predetermined. Women and women's organizations can take advantage of global opportunities and new technologies to spread messages, form coalitions, and push for the implementation within their own countries of the objectives agreed upon at the Fourth World Conference on Women, held in Beijing in September 1995. In so doing, they will be influencing the direction of social change. Nor does the global eclipse the local. Indeed, the globalization of discourses of human rights, women's rights and environmental protection gives added legitimacy to activists struggling at the local level.[1]

National Council for Women suggested the following to bridge the gap between theory and practice:

- Empowerment should be viewed as a two-fold process. Constructive activities to reorganize women's role system have to be accompanied by effective interventions leading to the community internalizing the idea of women's empowerment for its better future.
- Providing economic and political strength to women through collective activities, should be given the necessary focus. Clubbing of women's issues should be avoided.
- The need for women to have social space like "Sakhi Sabha", "Mahila Mandal", etc. within the community set-up through Panchayat Samitis should be given due recognition. Formalization of women NGOs net work to play a catalytic role in the social transformation should be given due attention. Development of leadership among women for advancement of the community is also necessary.
- Communication within the women's organizations and the community at large has to be fostered.[2]

2. Policymakers and Planners are merely Engaged in their Efforts for Women Development without Monitoring: Need of Reviewing Implementation

The Social scientists planners, policy-makers and administrators responsible for the improvement of the status of women has not to be satisfied only with effective planning and policy-making, but should think of the vehicle or administrative structure through which plans and policies are to be implemented. Myron Weinder has rightly pointed out:

> "India's forte is one of the crisis management. Instincts of leadership are to cope, rather than innovate, and to work within an existing framework not only of institutions but of ideas as well."

Thus, with the help of well-designed administrative machinery using modern management methods we should try to put the policy into action.

In this implementation process, women themselves will have to be most forceful agents for change and active participants in the development effort, wherever they have the opportunity to play a dynamic role. The contemporary social situations of women in India should not be frustrating and disheartening but should be rather challenging and it is the men and women of India, particularly, the women who have to face the challenge. It has been demonstrated by the women in the field that they are as capable and efficient as men in carrying out various kinds of work and have even much more endurance for hardships than is commonly believed. All of us who are associated with the development of the country in any capacity, must renew our dedication to the cause of women which would lead to national development and modernization.

The committee under the Chairmanship of justice V.R. Krishna Iyer submitted its report. The report states that womanhood and childhood even in criminal wrappings and behavioral aberrations deserve to be nursed in dignity and restored to working normally using all the material, moral and spiritual resources at the societies command. Despite constitutional mandates and recommendations of the committee, there is a serious shortfall in the delivery of services to women who are in custody in jails.

In 21st century, more emphasis is to be paid on implementation as words, written or spoken are of no use unless put to action. Mere provision in law would not remove the problems of women but action required to make the legal provisions a reality. This is to be assured through monitoring.

3. Lack of Vision for Women Development and Empowerment: Need of Defining Goals

We always talk about women development and empowerment but without definite goals resulting into the benefits for selected few. We have to see that all women achieve the goal especially those living in villages, Scheduled Castes and Scheduled Tribes women. Swami Chinmayananda has beautifully put it:[3]

Discovering a goal or vision in life, a great ideal to inspire, surrounding oneself to that ideal, and working in the world outside seems to be the secret of discovering new dynamism in our activities. We thereby raise the very standard of activity in us and thus bring about a greater happiness in the world outside. That goal each one will have to discover.

In order to live and to bring out the maximum happiness from ourselves, to work out the best for ourselves, everyone of us must have a goal in life, a mission, an inspiring ideal; looking up to that ideal and hitching our eyes to it, we must work on in the world outside. Thereby, the work becomes chastened; the work itself becomes its own reward for the individual and a great joy wells up in his mind, not in terms of what he gets on the first of the month, but what he gives to the society as best as he can, from the place where he is.

Thus, all the women have to do something for raising the status of women which is long overdue. The sporadic efforts will not bear the fruits but require persistent and consistent efforts from all of us to ensure parity of status of women with men and even more at the earliest as it is already too late.

Despite their infinite value in sustenance of family, shaping of society and destinies and in the development of economy as a whole, women generally are not treated at par in any of the aspects of life. While patriarchal system is undoubtedly the root cause of this subjugation of women, poverty, unemployment and societal attitudes have played no less a role in worsening the plight of the women's lot.

The measure of success of any developmental effort in a country is the qualitative difference it has been able to make in the life of the last person in the society. While there is no dearth of categories who may vie for this position in India's context due to the unfortunate socio-economic classification of the society, still the committee can come to the conclusion with some amount of certainty that of all such categories the rural women are the most underprivileged and neglected lot.

Although the Constitution of India has guaranteed certain rights and privileges to the women the fact however remains that no much headway has been made towards ameliorating the pathetic conditions of rural women. Successive legislative provisions have not made much difference in the social status, economic freedom or empowerment of rural women. The gender bias against them continues unabated.

The Committee note that the Government, as reflected in its planning process, has become increasingly conscious about development and empowerment of women. The progressive orientation of pogrammes and policies towards women and the women specific planning are some of the efforts made towards ensuring development and empowerment of women. What, however, has caused concern to the committee is the failure on the part of the Government to translate all these endeavours into qualitative improvement in the status of rural women.

The Committee, therefore, are of the firm opinion that the situation requires a radical reorientation of the planning process so as to make it truly women sensitive. Unless and until the andocentric bias is eliminated the formulation of women specific policies, plans, programmes, etc. and their successful implementation is very difficult to materialize.[4]

4. Department of Women and Child Development, National Commission for Women, Central Social Welfare Board, etc. are not concerned in building Women Organisation in Totality: Need of Holistic Approach

A population living in a geographical area would not by itself constitute a nation. It is just a mere number, a multitude of human beings. But, when the members live together with an integrated programme and strive with diligence and devotion for the achievement of a common goal, one sees the formation and glorious achievements of a nation. We cannot leave the women out of the focus of National Development. They are a part and parcel of the Nation.

As long as human beings live disintegrated; each one self-centered and seeking his private ends, regardless of others, with no allegiance whatsoever to a common cause, they can never make a nation. The scientific, economic and political philosophies have, time and again, given out revolutionary schemes, which present an artificial look of integration during the initial enthusiasm, but, by themselves, none of these schemes can ever succeed in creating or building up a true nation.

A united country, wherein each citizen is inspired to give out his very best in a spirit of selfless dedication, demanding nothing for himself except the privilege of serving the country, develops into a mighty nation asserting itself with power, prestige and strength.[5]

The dynamics of togetherness is, therefore, to be discovered immediately—more so in the context of the present world. The answer to this great challenge of the times assures us of a continued future as a happy, united and progressive nation serving as a beacon for the restless world to follow and gain a more rewarding peace and a more meaningful progress.

The platform of Action is an agenda for women's empowerment. It emphasis that women share common concerns that can be addressed only by working together and in partnership with men towards the common goal of gender equality around the world. IT respects and values the full diversity of women's situations and conditions and recognizes that some women face particular barriers to their empowerment.

The Platform of Action requires immediate and concerted action by all to creat a peaceful, just and humane world based on human rights and fundamental freedoms, including the principles of equality for all people of all ages and from all walks of life, especially for women and to this end, recognizes that broad-based and sustained economic growth in the context of sustainable development is necessary to sustain social development and social justice.

The success of the Platform for action will require a strong commitment on the part of governments, international organizations and institutions at all levels to provide positive discrimination to women.[6]

5. All those Engaged in Women Development and Empowerment are not doing from the core of their Heart: Need of Hope and Sincerity among them to Achieve Results in 21st Century

Love transports us beyond ourselves; it is like an inspiration that is constantly being renewed, a power that is always present, sustaining us.

—*Louis Lavelle: The Meaning of Holiness*

It is hardly necessary to stress the fact that the ability to love as an act of giving depends on the character development of the person. It presupposes the attainment of a predominantly productive orientation; in this orientation the person has overcome dependency, narcissistic omnipotence, the wish to exploit others, or to hoard, and has acquired faith in his own human powers, courage to rely on his powers in the attainment of his goals. To the degree that these qualities are lacking, he is afraid of giving himself—hence of loving.

Responsibility could easily deteriorate into domination and possessiveness, were it not for a third component of love, respect. Respect is not fear and awe; it denotes, in accordance with the root of the word (respicere—to look at), the ability to see a person as he is, to be aware of his unique individually. Respect means the concern that the other person should grow and unfold as he is. Such type of respect need to developed for women.

To make life worthwhile and fruitful, for women they must generate enthusiasm within themselves. Generation of enthusiasm will take place when they discover for themselves a goal and attach to the Altar with a spirit of dedication, reverence and love. The love for the ideal will overcome and vanquish all the hurdles from the ideal, and if it comes to that, life itself will be cast-off with a smile in dedication at that Altar. That was how Bhagat Singh could walk to the gallows with a smile on his face. What is important is that one should choose the right ideal . . . an ideal worthwhile even if it comes to sacrificing one's own life in the endeavour. The ideal should be inspiring, it should arouse the spring of activity in us. Thus, the discovering of the Ideal is the secret of generating in themselves Dynamism and vitality in its fullness.

Right actions strengthen and enrich women's vitality. The inspiration derived from the ideal has to be conserved, enriched and strengthened by cultivating and living right values of life. Living the right values of life is like building a dam on a river. Just as the dam raises the water-level, the right values raise the stock and wealth of their inner vitality.

The path of Action called Karma Yoga—is a highly scientific way-of-life which all of us can easily adopt, when once we have understood its entire implications. The world of objects and beings remaining the same, everyone of us, in whatever condition we may be at present, can learn to slowly grow to unbelievable heights-gathering to ourselves a new stature, undreamt by anyone around us at any time.

Life is ever active and positive. Life is never passive and negative. Dynamic expressions in action are "life." When all actions have ended, the organism is "dead", while living, no organism can ever remain, even for a moment, without activity; work expresses the life within in every living organism. All work outside and activities of thoughts within one, are stopped only when the organism is dead. To escape work is to escape "life" and run into "death", it is suicidal. All the women must work for their rights with great enthusiasm.

Face life and its upheavals around you. Be active and tirelessly dynamic. Each exertion undertaken is a shooting spark of "life" from the well of Existence in you. Fearlessly work. With a clear vision plan and selflessly execute it. Fear not sweat ! Hesitate not to face disappointments. Live life, so long as you are alive. Grow through work. Evolve in work. Expand while striving. Make your own life thus rich and sweet. You can. You must.

The highest and noblest type of an individual working in the world is known as the "man or women of achievement" (Yogi). Such men or women work, neither for the sake of wages, nor for success; they are not after mere sensual pleasures, nor do they aspire to reform the world; they delicately perform their obligatory duties finding peace and fulfilment in their very activity. Their fulfilment consists in doing their duties to the best of their ability without claiming any rights and they are totally unmindful to whether the society commends or condemns their actions.[7]

The Path of Action called karma-Yoga is a highly scientific way of life which all of us can easily adopt, when once we have understood its total implications. The world of objectives and beings remaining the same, everyone of us, in whatever condition we may at present, can learn and slowly grow to unbelievable heights, gathering to ourselves a new stature, undreamt of us by any one around at anytime.

Action is the answer, not inaction. Running away from problems is cowardice and the result of cowardice is sorrow, shame and defeat. Facing the situation is courage and the blessings of courage are sublimity, splendor and success. All the women should learn this and success is bound to touch their feet.[8]

6. Deterioration of Character among Persons Engaged in Women Development: Need of Engaging only Men of Character Swami Vivekanand says:

Character is that ensemble of actualized qualities of the head and heart of an individual through the help of which he masters facts and forces of life in a creative manner and gradually reaches self-fulfilment in a way helpful to others as well.

The man or women of character develops upwards, the man without character slips downwards. The man or women of character makes history, the man without it is marred by history. The man or women of character is the hope, solace, well-being, pace and inspiration of mankind; the man or women without character causes trouble, strife, worry, and misery in society. Therefore, we must select individuals with character to promote women development.

Character is so important for life that to have to live without it will be worse than not living at all. We may have filled the whole world with so much food that people refuse to have more. We may have succeeded in family planning to the extent that only adults are found sauntering around in the world. Gold bars stacked on the roadsides for people to take home at will may not be lifted. We may have industrialized the whole world to the extent of choking everybody with smog. And our established world Government may have been functioning without one jarring note. Even then, for want of one thing nobody is going to know how to cope with life's new and different problems of ennui. That one thing is character.

Character holds the key to any riddle of life. It can break each and every vicious circle. There is no mystery character cannot unravel. There is no wound it cannot heal, no want it cannot fill, and no loss it cannot make good. Hence, the most important thing among all creative endeavors of life is to know how to build one's own character and help build the character of others with whom one associates.

In the 21st century we have to locate persons of character who can change the fate of women since character has a multiplier effect. Most of the persons both men women engaged in women development and women empowerment try to get the maximum benefit for them and not to the women as a group. We have to be careful about them.

7. Lack of Adequate Educational Opportunities to Women Entreprenurship: Need of Education and Training to make Women Economically Independent and Self-confident

Freedom depends on economic conditions even more than political. If a woman is not economically free and self-reliant, she will have to depend on her husband or someone else, and dependents are never free. These were the ideas of Pandit Jawaharlal Nehru, first Prime Minister of India, which vividly highlighted the importance of economic independence of women.

"The emancipation of women and their equality with men are impossible and must remain so as long as women are excluded from socially productive work and restricted to house work, which is private."

"Today the sole occupation of a woman amongst us is supposed to be to bear children, to look after her husband and otherwise to drudge for the household . . . not only is the woman condemned to domestic slavery, but when she goes out as a labourer to earn wages, though she works harder than man she is paid less."[9]

"Discrimination against women is incompatible with human dignity and the welfare of the family and of society, prevents their participation on equal terms with men in the political, social, economic and cultural life of their countries and is an obstacle to the full development of the potentialities of women in the service of their countries and humanity."[10]

"To maintain the proper quantitative balance between various economic activities was one of the principal functions of the economic system, which, it was felt, should operate to give equal freedom of choice to men and women. The orientation of a society as a whole regarding the desirability that women should play an equal part in the country's development was taken as very important precondition for the advancement not only of the women but of the country as well."[11]

"This concept of women as a sort of balancing force in the family or national economy has a whole series of practical implications which have the net effect of making it difficult for women to become integrated as a permanent part of the work force and of rendering them particularly susceptible to unscrupulous or discriminatory treatment in the employment market."[12]

"In countries which are marked by labour surpluses, the need for providing employment for women when many men are available for work raises questions which cannot admit of categorical answers. It is in these developing countries that incomes by and large are low and the family requires the assistance of an additional earner. Where social conventions do not weigh oppressively against bringing women into paid employment, the family income can best be supplemented by a draft on the female population in the working age group."[13]

Nancy Reagan, wife of former US President, has rightly quoted, "A women is like a teabag—you can't tell how strong she is until you put her in hot water." And it is perhaps in the world of entrepreneurship that the recognition and value of women's contribution is the most vital to the making of a better tomorrow." An ILO Report in 1980 states that "Women are 50 percent of the worlds population, do the two-third of worlds work hours, receive 10 percent of worlds income and own less than one percent of world property. All because of an accident of birth." In the current age of rapid expansion of knowledge and frontiers of advanced information technology the need of training and re-training of work force including entrepreneurs cannot be overemphasized. Moreover, learning is a lifelong process. From the cradle and carryout days to the grave, if any things co-exists with life is learning. The broad objective of continuing education is to improve efficiency, quality and productivity in industries through better performance which ultimately lead to better living standards and economic conditions of people.

Potential women entrepreneurs must acquire formidable educational qualification (at least graduation) before venturing into entrepreneurial arena as education acts as a powerful tool in breaking down the barriers to successful entrepreneurship. This is more true in the case of women who are already burdened with too many social pressures and obligations.

Potential women entrepreneurs should prefer acquiring a few years of experience in Manufacturing or Trading or Servicing or more preferably in the line of activity they intend venturing into. This would give them as insight into the functioning of a business enterprise and will therefore, prepare them to better face the challenges ahead in the start up and management of their respective enterprises.

Running a business enterprise requires knowledge, skill and technique and therefore, the utility of undergoing, a properly designed training programme can never be wished away. The potential women entrepreneurs must therefore, undergo skill-oriented, managerial and/or business-related training like Entrepreneurship Development Programme before starting their units. Women who intend venturing into manufacturing sector must prepare themselves before hand and understand the intricacies of an industrial enterprise by having practical hands-on experience of a minimum six months to one year in a similar enterprise. It is also recommended that the financial institutions should involve a mechanism to link the credit delivery with acquisition of relevant training of a certain minimum duration by the women entrepreneurs.[14]

At the dawn of International Year of Women, the then Prime Minister of India Mrs. Indira Gandhi spoke firmly, "Since time immemorial, woman has been discussed, and written about mainly as a decorative object. But when she has stepped out of this niche, by and large, response has been one of cynicism and derision. Women's liberation is not a luxury for India, but an urgent necessity to enable the nation to move ahead to a life which is more than satisfying materially, intellectually and spiritually.

Training for Social Welfare

Broadly considered the training for women would aim at: (i) Increased confidence in one's own ability, (ii) Deeper appreciation of human and social problems as well as identification of problem areas, (iii) Enhancement of ability to look at older problem in newer ways, (iv) Wider tolerance of difference of opinion, (v) Enlargement and improvement of participant knowledge in the techniques, methods and tools of social welfare administration so as to deal with, the improvement of beneficiaries based on human approach theory, (vi) Creation of awareness and awakening towards improving administrative capacity and capability of the personnel, (vii) Extension of help in Reaction (i.e., satisfaction in turn favourable interaction to environment), Behaviour (i.e., change in outlook) and Attitudes, learning (i.e., development of skills and work-kits) and results (i.e., effectiveness and efficiency), (viii) Personnel growth (i.e., improvement, consolidation and expansion of skills to do a particular social welfare job in scientific manner based on system approach and staff development), (ix) Understanding of environmental or ecological intricacies and linkages to avoid duplication efforts, (x) Development of: (a) rational thinking, (b) objective thinking, (c) social understanding, and (d) aesthetic responsiveness and practical abilities, and (xi) Role performance and last but not the least to update the knowledge through motivation, life situations and self-development.[15]

To accomplish the institutional goals and objectives of the training, the existing as well as new training institutions provide or expected to provide the framework of: (a) assessment of the man-power needs and requirements in the field of social welfare and development. Physiological needs, safety and security needs, social needs, esteem or ego needs and self-actualisation needs are given weightage not in isolation but as a composite whole, (b) Drawing up of a perspective plan of training needs for the various categories of personnel required for social welfare from time to time, (c) extension of counselling, guidance and consultancy services to social welfare administrators at constant intervals, (d) producing of timely material aids and teaching aids for onwards adoption by fellow personnel, (e) organisation of surveys, seminars, workshops, symposia, refresher courses, panel discussions, etc. to elicit the public support and co-operation for further enlargement of programmes to uncovered, remote, backward and hilly areas, (f) bridging of communication and co-ordination gaps, (g) apprising the social welfare administrators, supervisors and the grassroot level workers with the latest developments in the field of social welfare at regular intervals, (h) undertaking of research projects so as to develop, formulate and implement Dew schemes required for down-trodden sections of the society in particular and last but not the least provision of policy framework, staff development and job enrichment.[16] Strategic Objectives, B1-B6 Platform for Action suggests for 21st Century: Ensure equal access to education. Eradicate illiteracy among women. Improve women's access to vocational training, science and technology, and continuing education. Develop non-discriminatory education and training. Allocate sufficient resources for and monitor the implementation of educational reforms.

As stated by UNDP, training may constitute the following areas:

- Advocacy in gender awareness in politics;
- Capacity-building through networking;
- Negotiation skills;
- Management;
- Constituency-building;
- Budget analysis;
- Gender mainstreaming skills;
- Use of mass media;
- Political and voter education;
- Mass mobilization; and
- Long-term strategies for engaging younger generations.

8. No Attention paid to General and Functional Literacy in Villages and Backward: Need of Priority in 21st Century

Education is the most potent factor for changing women's position in society. We must correct the imbalances by encouraging the education of girls. We can use the adult education or non-formal education system. What can be the future of a country where general illiteracy, especially among women, is very high? Besides, the women have also to handle the new generation, i.e. the child who is the future hope.

The importance of women's education cannot be overemphasized. Women centered society will also be a mother centred society. Mothers playing a crucial and primary role in the preparation of children for life and educating women yield spin-off benefits in several respects—child care, nutrition, delayed marriages, low fertility rates, enhancement of family income-levels through their own employment as well, participation of children in education, etc. But male-female disparities have all along been sharp over the years, whether it be in terms of literacy, or enrolment for education at various levels or access to employment-relevant vocational and technical education.

While there are several factors inhibiting women's education such as household chores like collection of water, fuel, fodder, etc. apart from sibling care, lack of schools near home, lack of female teachers, apprehension of molestation outside home, etc. the underlying reason, however, is still the strongly, prevailing societal attitude of gender discrimination. The situation cannot be altered by anything lesser than a social transformation.

All this would remain a dream unless women are themselves enlightened. Education is the key factor in elevating the status of women. It equips them to contribute in different fields more meaningfully. Late Dr. (Mrs.) P.K. Devi, Professor of Gynaecology, in Post-Graduate Institute of Medical Education and Research, Chandigarh, has rightly stated on the basis of her critical examination amongst the various States of the Indian Union, that "Literacy, especially of women seems to be a significant factor in differences in the morality and morbility rates between various Indian states and infant mortality rates coincide with a very low female literacy rate."

In India, social scientists, development planners, statesmen, educationists and administrators have come to realise that the pace of development cannot accelerate unless women are also properly qualified. So to improve the education of women quantitatively and qualitatively the following steps are submitted for consideration of implementation in 21st century:

(a) Expansion of the facilities of women education including adult and vocational education tremendously so that the literacy in respect of this group may be increased.

(b) Removal of disparity between rural and urban literacy by (i) provision of good institutions in villages to avoid the attraction for cities; (ii) to bring awareness towards hygiene among women through community development programmes; (iii) preference in employment to rural people; (iv) setting up of professional and other training institutions in the villages; (v) setting up of rural-based industries in villages, (vi) training of women in modern methods of agriculture, (vii) encouraging the formation of *mahila mandals* to provide the information on various problems facing the nation; and (viii) setting up of model villages.

(c) The contents of women education may be somewhat different from men as women have to devote a lot of their time in homes as well. Jobs in the country are limited and hence the women education (general) can create more frustration rather than prove an asset. Hence, along with general education, some courses like Home Science, Agriculture, Music, etc. may also be imparted.

(d) Involvement of women at the policy-making, planning and implementation of all the programmes aimed at national reconstruction, e.g., Social Welfare, Family Planning, Rural Development, etc. This would give the impetus to women education.

(e) The share of the women in the Government jobs is very limited at present as the men presume, without any justification that women cannot be effective in good administration. The State must employ more and more women if eligible and even, it is suggested that preference may be given till they are properly represented. Strangely, when one sees the University results, the girls are surpassing the boys but the same is not true in Government jobs. More and more women may also be assigned gazetted jobs of responsibility. Women may be encouraged even to take up part-time jobs.

(f) Women may be imparted education in the fields like management, marketing, etc. so that they can actively participate in co-operative organisations. They can make the co-operative movement a success.

(g) Incentive like mid-day meals, scholarships, free school uniforms, free books and study material, stipends, awards, etc. should be extended to all girls in the rural areas and urban slums.

(h) Scheme to activise dropouts may be planned.

It may be concluded that women education can help in nation building. Napoleon once said:

"Give me good mothers, I will give you a good nation."

Illiteracy is a great obstruction in the path of development and education is the backbone of democracy. The Director-General of UNESCO has described illiteracy as "the most" monstrous of all the many instances of wasted human potential which still at the present time keeps more than one-third of the human race in a state of hopelessness below the level of modern civilisation. Therefore, in order to translate the essence of the Preamble and the Directive Principles of the State Policy enshrined in the Constitution of India to practical life, it is imperative for us to increase the literacy in general and of women in particular.

"The general purpose and objective of women's education cannot, of course be different from the purpose and objective of men's education . . . At the Secondary and even at the university stage women's education should have a vocational or occupational bias."[17]

"In a democratic society where all citizens have to discharge their civic and social obligations, differences which may lead to variation in the standard of intellectual development achieved by boys and girls cannot be envisaged."[18]

"In the progress society of tomorrow, life should be a joint venture for men and women. Men should share the responsibility of parenthood and home-making with women and women in their turn should share the social and economic responsibilities of men."[19]

"Women's and men's education should have many elements in common, but should not in general be identical in all respects, as is usually the case today. A woman should learn something of problems that are certain to come up in all marriages, and in the relations of parents and children, and how they may be met. Her education should make her familiar with problems of home management and skilled in meeting them, so that she may take her place in a home with the same interest and the same sense of competence that a well trained man has in working at his calling."[20]

The educational trends promise a better position for women in the labour force particularly in an era of urbanistion and globalisation. Increasing women's Educational attainments and upgrading skills will serve to make women more socially, physically aware, and it creates a stronger workforce.

The empowerment of women is a function of social development but it is best captured by indicators that measure women political participation, their role in economic decision-making, and their share of earned income. Empowerment is also reflected in the legal framework pertaining to women's rights as workers, citizens and human beings and in the capacity of women to organize and mobilize on their own behalf.

9. Lack of Credit

Need of self-employment for Rural Women—as well as credit plus approach—M. Lalitha in an Article, "Self-Employment for Rural Women—Need for Credit Plus" Approach rightly sums:

> Majority of the third world women are involved in the informal sector of economic activities in which they are disproportionately represented among the poorest of the poor.[21] With limited education, skills and few formal employment opportunities, poor rural women in developing countries often turn to self-employment as the means of supporting themselves and their families. Rural women's self-employment in the informal sector[22] is based on various types of activities like: (a) farm-based activities and allied activities, (b) home-based production using non-traditional and acquired skills, (c) retail trading and services like flower and vegetable selling, garment-making, catering, petty shop, retail business in paddy, etc.

Yet most of these informal activities do not yield sufficient income to extricate women out of poverty. They lack capital, technical and managerial know-how, access to credit, market and materials as well as services necessary to expand or even to make marginal improvements in productivity and income. Though self-employment is seen as the panacea for rural poverty, initiating self-employment activity is not easy, either for men or for women in the informal sector. It is made doubly so for women by high rate of illiteracy, lack of access to resources along with socio-cultural taboos. The lack of funds and lack of staying power, limit self-employment and the scale of operation of self-employed women. As the majority of rural women do not own capital or tools and equipments of their trade, they remain vulnerable in the clutches of the private money-lenders. Indebtedness puts them in a weak bargaining position with the middlemen and traders of their own business on whom they are dependent for their livelihood, thus perpetuating state of high interest payment, low income, insecurity of work opportunities and completing the vicious circle of indebtedness. Out of the variety of ameliorative strategies proposed, to improve the income earning activities of women, provision of finance at reasonable rates on regular basis for women in the informal sector is the crucial one.

Promotion of poor rural women through bank credit facilities is a challenging task. The strategy should facilitate access of these women to skill training, and other support services like raw-material supplies, proper marketing linkages, and regular monitoring.

Given the 'credit plus approach' with necessary forward and backward linkage facilities under an organizational set-up, the credit promoted activities of women borrowers will result in emergence of potential women borrowers, productive utilization of bank loan, high income generation and better repayment thereby bringing women into the mainstream of economic development, paving the way for sustainable development.[23]

10. Wide Differences between Law and Practice: Need of Narrowing down the Gap to provide Justice to Women in Distress

After the critical examination of the legal provisions revealed that most of the protective laws for women suffer from various loopholes. The provisions of the law are not clear and precise. Certain laws remain confined to statute books, because the enforcement machinery is inadequate or the penalties are not awarded according to the stipulations. Many of these protective laws like Act prohibiting Sati were passed hurriedly without thinking about the various aspects of the enactment. The law on Sati is heartless, it treats Sati as a case of suicide. The definition of glorification of Sati is vague and ambiguous. Indecent Representation of Women Act was passed in great hurry, but the rules implementing that law were; not made for years, shows the unenthusiastic reaction of the enforcement authorities.

The Dowry (Prohibition) Act does not take into account the social realities of a woman's life. The procedural law should be changed to make it compulsory to record the statement of a victim of bride- burning immediately. The dying' declaration should be recorded by S.P., in case magistrate does not reach in time. The minimum sentence for 10 years for dowry death should be increased to life imprisonment. The provision of legal aid and advice should be available to the women victim and her family and her case should be decided at the earliest. Cruelty to wife by husband or the in-laws has been declared a crime under Section 498A of Indian Penal Code, but the definition *of* cruelty is vague. Discussion with the victims bring out, that in most of the cases, the reasons for the cruel treatment of the wife was not dowry, it is suspicion of illicit sexual relations, mutual incompatibility or girl friend, yet the enforcement authorities show reluctance to register crimes on these grounds. The procedural requirement of Section 498A, that only the woman victim, her parents or relation by blood can file a complaint, make it very difficult for the victim to get a complaint lodged in critical cases. Legal aid cells should be established. They should provide lawyer to fight their case and give legal aid to those who seek assistance either directly or through Public Interest Litigation.

The Amendment Act on Prostitution remains the same. The Act neglects the root cause of this evil. In fact, the new Act has only pushed the trade underground but it is flourishing nevertheless. The law starts with the presumption that it is an inevitable evil and cannot be curbed. It treats prostitutes, the victims of social injustice, as criminals and is silent on the punishment of those who hire them. There is no provision of providing legal assistance to these women.

In Indian condition, it is very rare for a woman or girl to make false allegation of rape, yet a women's credibility is always open to suspicion. Section 114A of the Evidence Act implicitly assumes that the moral character of a woman is not a relevant character, yet the legislature has not rescued clause 155{4) of the Evidence Act. This objectionable clause should be deleted without any delay. The undue emphasis on consent should be done away with. Marital rape within marriage should be given legal recognition so that the husband cannot ill-treat wives with impunity. Legal and medical assistance should be available at State's cost.

The ability of the legislature to pass an effective law banning various sex determination tests and resultant death of girls before birth have added to the woes of women. There seems to be a total lack of empathetic law favouring battered women of a broken marriage or a sufferer of an unhealthy marriage. Battered women struggle in the courts for years before they can get justice.

The concept and reality of legal aid in India can be achieved only if the measures discussed above are seriously taken by the Government and Public. The opinion of the public in favour of legal aid to women is lacking in the present scheme which must be achieved for a successful implementation of the Legal Aid Scheme. Crimes against women should be treated as an epidemic. A long drawn battle has to be thought with courage, determination and the consequences will definitely be rewarding.[24]

> "That country and that nation which do not respect women have never become great, nor will ever be in future "
>
> —*Swami Vivekananda*

In addition, there has been a great misuse of Lok Adalts by Vested interests.

To quote Madhava Menon:[25]

> "Lok Adalat has the potential for social reconstruction and legal mobilization for social change. It can influence the style of administration of justice and the role of lawyers and judges in it. It can take law closer to the life of the people and reduce disparity between law in books and law in action. Of course, in wrong hand it has also the potential to undermine stability and respect for the system of justice and to act as yet another forum of exploitation of ignorant and poor masses. It may be used by self-seeking politicians, lawyers and judges to advance their own interests and malign their enemies in the profession. It may become another bureaucracy if attempted, to be stereo-typed and made an appendage of the formal court system. The dangers are infinite and the potentialities are limitless."

In addition Legal Aid cells are limited due to paucity of funds. In this venture university law departments can help to a substantial extent.

M.A. Qureshi in his forward to Women Law and Free Legal Aid in India by Roma Mukherjee has rightly said,

> The various laws made by legislature and the law enforced are not successful because their whole concentration is only on legal measures. Their efforts were superficial. Section 376A, 376B, 376C and 376D were added to the Indian Penal Code to stop sexual abuse of women. It was expected that due to these amendments the incidence to rape will show a downward trend and it will be easy to get the culprit punished but the record shows that the incidence of rape has not only increased but became more brutal. Despite, the passing of the Dowry Prohibition Act and subsequent amendments women are still harassed, tortured and murdered. The incidence of cruelty and wife beating have increased over the past few decades. Inspite of relevant sections of Indian Penal Code, cases of harassment specially at work places are at sharp increase.

United Nations Economic and Social Commission for Asia and the Pacific in its report, "Asia and the Pacific into the Twenty-first Century: Prospects for Social Development" 1998 rightly concludes the Challenges of 21st Century for Women Development and Empowerment:

This paper has highlighted, as areas of priority, the impact on the social development prospects of women of: (See Chart 10.1)

(a) Gender Ideologies

At the heart of most of the situations adversely affecting the social development prospects of women are strongly prevailing ideologies which differentiate between women and men to the disadvantage of women. A

CHART 10.1

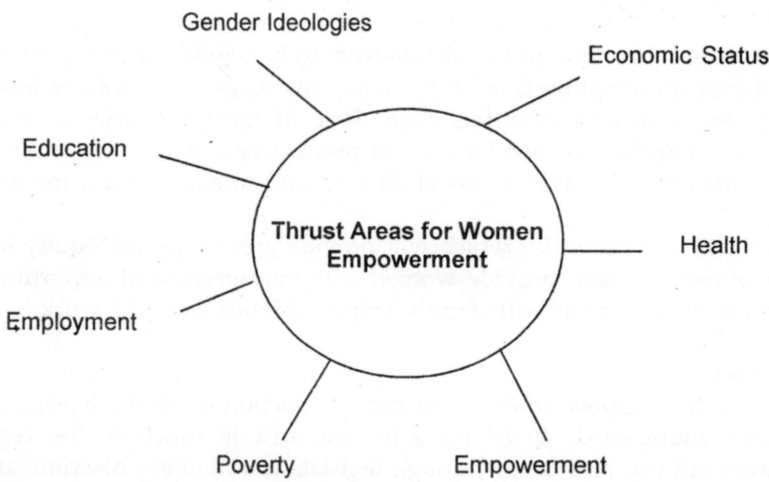

perception of women and men as different means that different roles, rights and values are attributed to women and men; while a perception of women as inferior means that anything perceived as women's roles or work is regarded as inferior. So there can be found in most countries a gender gap in employment, wages, rights regimes, access to services and so on.

If the social development prospects of women are to be enhanced, these gender ideologies must be countered through education and awareness-raising, and the gender gap addressed through legislation, policies and programmes aimed at achieving greater equality.

(b) Poverty

The situation of women in relation to poverty is one of extreme urgency. With the region-wide eradication of poverty making little progress in terms of an overall reduction in numbers, increasingly it is women who are bearing the brunt of that poverty. Older women, women in female-headed households, unemployed women and women prevented from inheriting from their families make up the majority of these women. The need to alleviate if not eradicate poverty is very important for the future of women in the region.

(c) Education

As a result largely of gender ideologies and poverty, girls have far less access than boys to education, literacy training and skills development. The gender gap is highly significant still in many countries, and improving only very slowly. There is a major need for affirmative action programmes to ensure that females receive at least an equal share of available education facilities at all levels. If this does not occur the situation of women in employment and income terms cannot be expected to improve greatly.

(d) Employment

Many factors are increasing women's employability in some parts of the region, but the situation is far from uniform. In most countries, women are more likely than men to be unemployed, to be employed in the informal sector if they are employed, to be receiving low wages and to have less job security. In particular, little has been done in most countries to enable women to do justice to a combination of productive and reproductive roles. This requires more provision for child care and adequate paid maternity leave.

Policies are called for which will provide greater gender equity in all aspects of employment, provide women with entrepreneurial opportunities and ensure that women with family responsibilities can still work.

(d) Empowerment

Women's empowerment is, in part, a function of capability-building, and much more needs to be done in that area in much of the region. Empowerment can also occur through legislation outlawing discrimination, and nations need to ensure that relevant international conventions are reflected in their national legislation.

Finally, empowerment can be achieved by women themselves through women's movements and networks. Much has already been achieved through such developments, and it is one of the more hopeful trends in the social development of women in the region.

At all three levels, however, it is only through women's empowerment that the profile of women will be raised and policies and programmes introduced to enhance their social development prospects.

Major Issues for the Social Development of Women into the Twenty-first Century

The major issues concerning women which will remain a priority into the twenty-first century are:

(a) to improve women's health;
(b) to increase access to all levels of education;
(c) to raise women's employability levels;
(d) to provide adequate policies for working mothers;
(e) to provide for older women living alone;
(f) to provide support for female-headed households;
(g) To introduce laws and measures to end violence against women in all situations, and including through prostitution and trafficking in women and girls;
(h) To increase women's role in decision-making; and
(i) To address the special needs of women in the economies in transition and the least developed countries of the region.[26]

Women in 21st century have to be more bold, courageous. Swami Chinmayananda rightly says:

Today belongs to us. Yesterday was; tomorrow will be; but today is with us. Everyday is bursting with opportunities for us to do and to serve, to act and to express, to love and to live.
We must make use of these lush chances and diligently make our life rich, fruitful and useful for others at all times. When we have such a team of even a few courageous and honest servants of God, the nation is made, the world is saved.
Shall we waste a life in the futility of indolence, in the arrogance of hypocrisy—or, shall we peep into our glorious being through the purity of our sincerity and the earnestness of our dedications.

Pure, We must Be,
Sincere, We Must Become.
Earnestness, We Must Befriend,
Dedicated Living, We Must Bequeath.
Joyous Living, We Must Behold,
When we Live in And for the Beloved Alone.

"Woman is the companion of man gifted with equal mental capacities. She has the right to participate in the minutest details of the activities of man, and she has the same right of freedom and liberty as he. . . By sheer force of a vicious custom, even the most ignorant and worthless men have been enjoying a superiority over women which they do not deserve and ought not to have."[27]
"Since resistance in satyagraha is offered through self-suffering. It is a weapon pre-eminently open to women . . . She can become the leader in satyagraha which does not require the learning that books give but does require the stout heart that comes from suffering and faith."[28]

The overall development process envisages a share in the development generated by the Plans-equally for women and men. Since the Constitution stresses the need for promoting with special care the educational and economic interests of the weaker sections of the people, the welfare and development of women received particular attention from the beginning.

"We talk about a welfare State and direct our energies towards its realization. That welfare must be the common property of everyone in India and not the monopoly of the privileged groups as it is today. If I may be allowed to lay greater stress on some, they would be the welfare of children, the status of women and the welfare of the tribal and hilly people in our country. Women in India have a background of history and tradition behind them, which is inspiring. It is true, however, that they have suffered much from various kinds of succession and all these have to go so that they can play their full part in the life of the nation."[29]

11. Lack of Good Governance and Ethical Values: Need of Injecting Moral Values in Government Machine

Until gender parity is reached in governance, women cannot reach full equality with men in any sphere. The absence of women's voices in shaping the most fundamental political instruments—the most critical of which is the national budget—has ensured the preservation of gender inequality even with regard to women's health and security in their own homes.

UNDP Management Development and Governance Division convened a meeting on Women's Political Participation: 21st Century Challenges. Held in New Delhi, India from 24-26 March, 1999, it brought together women parliamentarians, planners and civil society representatives, including those of grassroots organizations, to take stock of women's presence in government structures and to make recommendations for overcoming the fundamental obstacle that women face in politics: the division of the "public" and "private" spheres that relegates women to the latter.

A few months later UNDPs International Conference on Governance for Sustainable Growth and Equity, held in New York in July 1999, drew attention, *inter alia,* to the low number of women parliamentarians and the high number of women in poverty. Subsequently, the conference of Good Governance and Gender sponsored by the Netherland's Ministry of Foreign Affairs and held in Harare, Zimbave from 18-20 May 1998, was largely devoted to inequities in the enabling environment for women—among these education, training ownership of the means of production or even decision-making power in the home that might be translated into the public sphere.

The UNDP Human Development Report 1995 showed that in no society do women enjoy the same opportunities as men. It also demonstrated that successful initiatives for removing gender inequalities do not depend on wealth of nations. And even though some countries have set targets for women's representation in national government structures, these often do not have significant impact elsewhere in governance. Nor have these targets, even when achieved, endured.

Considerable progress has taken place in women's political participation, particularly towards the end of this century. Despite this progress, however, the 21st Century begins with enormous unfinished business in this realm.

Twenty-five years after the First World Conference of Women in Mexcio City, more than 20 after CEDAW, and five after the Fourth World Conference in Beijing, gender equality has finally been inscribed on the political agenda of most of the world. For example, the Beijing Platform for Action set the goal of 30 percent for women in national decisions-making positions, as a milestone towards the ultimate objective of 50 percent. Five years after Beijing, the level of women in parliaments in the world has increased from 10 percent to 12 percent. However, regional variations are significant. They range from 37.6 percent in the Nordic countries to 15.5

percent in the Americas, 13.4 percent in Asia, 12.5 percent in Europe excluding the Nordic countries.

There is growing recognition that economic participation and political participation cannot be separated. Institutional transformations are needed to create the enabling environment for the economic and political empowerment of women. A more profound understanding of the barriers in labour markets and remuneration processes is also necessary as a precondition for their transformation. This is particularly important since women's economic independence is critical for their exercise of influence on decisions that affect their lives and their families.

There are strong linkages between processes that lead to poverty and those that result in gender disparities. Efforts at poverty reduction therefore need to be informed by a gender analysis. Transforming and increasing the accountability of institutions to women's interests, and especially the interests of poor women, is necessary for poverty reduction and good governance.

Mr. O.P. Dwivedi has beautifully explained the need of common good. To quote him:

> That essence and basis of the moral State, as per ancient Indian thinking depends on the triangle of those actions for governance which are undertaken for universal welfare (Sarv Loka Kalyankari Karma), maintaining and protecting each and everyone in the Creation (Sarva Loksangrahamevapi), and securing universal care for all and everyone (Sarva Hitey Ratah). But that triangle has a center point, the common-most good which is denoted by the term "happiness for all" (Sarve Bhavantu Sukhinah). However, these prerequisites as enunciated in ancient times in India are sadly missing among the stewards and practitioners of governance. There is need to operationalise this ancient wisdom through the re-arrangement of socio-economic and political institutions; however, first, a country like India would have to formulate a set of realistic indicators for achieving such a common good. It is to the credit of India's constitutional framers and freedom fighters that they left a solid foundation for good governance and liberal democratic tradition which although wakened, can be made resurgent. In this task, both the secular and spiritual institutions must work together rather than fencing out, in the name of secularism, the spiritual domain from contributing to good governance. There is a need to bring both together for sustaining the common good. Although they have different perspectives and objectives (one dealing with the welfare and care of life here and now, while the other striving for the life hereafter); nevertheless, both are needed to serve the common good of the Loka and the fight for good governance.

Vasundhara Raje, Minister of State, Personnel and Pensions, in a message to Platinum Jubilee Souvenir (1926-2001) of Union Public Service Commission has observed:

> "As we stand at the beginning of the 21st century, the greatest challenge before us is to steer the overall growth in the country along the lines of fairness, equality and sustainability, particularly when the role of the Government itself is being redefined. Good governance is of paramount importance in these times of far reaching changes. In this backdrop of major changes, we need to re-orient ourselves to devise ways and means to secure efficient civil servants for the country at the national and state levels, so as to guard the core values.
>
> Mr. Kidwai, former Chairman of the Union Public Service Commission, has rightly observed, "An efficient civil service is one of the essential ingredients of our democratic system and one of the best guarantees for sound and effective administration." Referring to the importance of both government and administration, an American scholar writes: "No government, of course, can hope to survive without a strong and effective administrative system; nor can an administrative system exist without the support of those it was established to serve."

However, the present crisis in public administration has not been able to carry out Good Governance. It emanates from our wrong approaches. We have to follow the knowledge available in our ancient literature to ensure Good Governance.

In the present day world, we find as increasing relevance of the statement made by Dr. Radhakrishnan, when he observed that the mind that invented the atom bomb was more powerful than the bomb itself. Every letter can be made into a mantra. Every root has a medicinal value. Every person has some competence and making him realize his potential is the Human Resource manager's challenges. Unfortunately, the yojakas, the visionaries, the leaders, the organizers or managers who can make these things happens, are rare. Can we come up with techniques/methods by which such managers can be multiplied so that their positive impact can help to create the right human capital to meet the challenge of the emerging future.

D.M. Nanjundappa in his article, "Management by Values" rightly stresses that work in life becomes worship, if it is in the service of the nation, poor, hungry and the helpless and not for self. The Vedantic human orientation finds an inspiring expression that inevitably raises the quality of life. To quote Swami Vivekanand's observations, "This life is short, the vanities of the world are transient; but they alone live who live for others. The rest are more dead than alive."

We are now on the threshold of the twenty-first century. In the new Millennium, above all, the government would need to reinvent itself to become 'women-centric and women-friendly'. It would need to limit its role to core functions of infrastructure and macro economic management. Greater delegation and decentralization of authority and responsibilities would need to be introduced at all levels. A combination of Citizens' Charters and the Right to Information would ensure greater accountability in the administrative system. The process of consultation with the participation of women in decision-making would gradually become more pronounced in order to ensure accountability. At the same time, good citizenry would also need to be emphasized for all round development of the society. Besides enjoying their rights, the citizens would need to behave responsibly and perform their duties towards the state. Clearly defined ethical standards would also need to be adopted by the civil servants as well as politicians. In order to achieve all this, innovative use of information technology would be critical. The mechanical steps which are incorporated in a sporadic manner to improve our system would lead us to more problems and decay. The need is to follow the eternal principles of Human Excellence as contained in Bhagavad Gita, Vedas, Upanisads and other literature aiming at building character, and spirituality which would impel individuals to lead a detached, moral, contended life and service to people and animals, non-possessive, simple life. There is no magic or formula which can transform our present governments into Ethical Government until and unless all those who are in Government as well as the people outside the Government follow ethical, moral, spiritual values and service to humanity as the cardinal principles of life. The present day reforms are an eyewash to quiten the people temporarily as well as superficial. The permanent solutions are possible if we take the help of the basic principles enshrined in ancient Sanskrit literature (Ram Rajya in Ramayan). Protecting the Fundamental Rights are key to Good Governance. Supreme Court in a case, (Maneka Gandhi *vs.* Union of India—1978 (I) SCC 248) has said that:

> "These fundamental rights represent the basic values cherished by the people of this country since the Vedic times and they are calculated to protect the dignity of the individual and create conditions in which every human being can develop his personality in the fullest extent."

No doubt, there have appeared, sky-rocketing towers and building, snake waved multi-storied bridges and roads, the underground metros and undersea water ways, which shows that technology of this century have covered miraculous potentialities. Even the international skies these days, are born with planes which are without thunder and without any microwaves, to be detectable by the refinely tuned new generation radars. But still the people are burning, as it is only the level of one's consciousness, which can give you calmness and peace of mind, as never the man can get bliss absolute by the power and pelf, titles or titans, money or materials. It is only the balance of mind, pure and pious thought, rhythmic civic behaviour, selfless service aptitudes, which can make the character and esteem of a nation strong and subtle. It is the dire need of the next century so that future of mankind including women may remain safe.

It is a great privilege
For all of us
to have been allowed
to do any thing for the world
In helping the world
We really help ourselves.

12. Absence of Decent Living to Girl Child and Adolescent—The Girl Child

Mounting evidence of the special needs of girl children is increasingly focusing world attention on this very vulnerable group of the young. Exploring the problems of the girl child in the Region has raised several important issues.

It is a common foot that girl children are less desired, largely for economic reasons and the roles they will play in adult life. Tradition does not consider them as future bread winners. In fact, they become an economic liability at the time of marriage, with large dowries expected from their families.

Such discrimination begins in intrauterine life. Selective abortions of female foetuses have been reported in some countries. A study in an urban area of one country in the Region showed that, out of 8000 abortions performed after parents learned the sex of the foetus, only one was a male. Female infanticide has also been reported in some countries.

There are also gender differences in childhood mortality, with under-five mortality rates higher in girl children in a few countries of the Region. Since female mortality is typically lower than male mortality during childhood, this suggests some gender-related differences in child-rearing practices, and possibly in feeding patterns and use of health care services.

Under nutrition is also more prevalent in girls. Inadequate feeding in childhood has serious health consequences. It can lead to impaired intellectual capacity, delayed puberty, possible impaired fertility and stunted growth, resulting in higher risks of complications during childbirth.

Child prostitution and sexual abuse of young girl including rape and incest are also issues of serious concern in some countries of the Region.

Education is less accessible to girls in some countries of the Region. Even in countries where primary and secondary school enrolment is relatively equal, dropout rates in girls are higher and enrolment at higher educational and vocational training courses is lower. Young girls, particularly in rural areas, contribute substantially to domestic chores and caring for smaller children in the family, and hence are often unable to attend school.

We have to take care of girl child in 21st century through positive discrimination.

A. Regional Health Report, 1998

Protection of the girl child is to be ensured through the following:

- Relief for those girls who are economically and socially deprived and belong to special groups;
- Intervention to sensitize various agencies on the need to protect thegirl child and adolescent girls from exploitation, assault and physical abuse;
- Education and sensitization of male members of the family to the special needs of the girl child;
- Equal treatment, dignity and respect for girl children in the family and community as well as providing support and helping their day to day work so that they get time to avail of the opportunities for self-development;
- Rehabilitation services to reduce the growing instances of exploitation of girl-children and adolescent girls; and
- Protection of girl-children and adolescent girls from prevalent social evils such as dowry, child marriage, prostitution, rape, incest, molestation, etc. through appropriate legislation and proper enforcement.

B. Absence of Decent Health Living for Adult Women

With the onset of puberty and with learning new ways of behaving that may lead to experimentation with sex, drugs and alcohol, adolescents find themselves exposed to a host of factors which can adversely affect their health. The female adolescent is especially vulnerable.

Maternal mortality is estimated to be three to four times higher in adolescent women than in adults, and pregnancy-related complications are the leading cause of mortality among adolescent girls in many countries. In addition, infants born to adolescents are more likely to have low birth weight, to be premature, to be injured at birth, or to be stillborn.

Adolescent girls are both biologically and socially more vulnerable to sexually transmitted diseases (STDs) including HIV infection.

Unwanted pregnancies in single adolescents are of increasing concern and could lead adolescent girls to seek abortions. Often such abortions are sought from illegal and unsafe sources, and may lead to serious complications and even death.[30]

The Committee on Empowerment of Women (2001-02) 13th Lok Sabha, Fourth Report has suggested the following to take care of health of women at all ages.

There is a growing reorganization that since women also suffer from other disabilities and morbidities, some of which are again very gender specific there is need to examine the adequacy of our strategies in ensuring that they are appropriately covered. The scanty data available has shown that women in reproductive age groups of 18-45 years, constituting a bulk of the working population, suffer from TB, Malaria, UTI, STDs, Cancer, Leprosy, etc. Women working in cities are also subject to stressful conditions and are seen to suffer from mental health problem as well as heart ailments, blood pressure and other stress induced diseases. Likewise the National Commission for Women had also brought out the special needs of women working in agriculture and informal sectors where they are exposed to chemicals and pesticides. Besides the longevity of life has resulted in a higher burden of diseases among the older aged women. The women in this age group suffer medical disorders such as Alzheimer's and arthritis, etc.

The various Disease Control Programmes are being implemented without any specific allocation for women. However, it is felt that the sensitization to women's health is the need of the hour. Certain areas on women's health may require specific interventions especially those disabilities and morbidities which are very gender specific such as cervical and breast cancer. Main constraints are inadequate funding and inadequate development of gender perspective in programme formulation.

Since the vast majority of women live in rural areas, where there are hardly any medical facilities available, women become victims of various diseases due to mal-nutrition, lack of clean and safe drinking water, unhygienic conditions, etc. the government ought to integrate various programmes and take a holistic approach to immunization, nutrition, health care, drinking water, cleanliness, health infrastructure, trained personnel, etc. so as to improve the health of the rural women. As 33 per cent women are now in panchayats and other local bodies they can be utilized for improving the condition of women all over the country. The Committee desire that the Government should coordinate with various concerned Departments in this regard to draw up appropriate programmes and schemes along these lines.

Committee have noted that important issues related to women's empowerment include awareness about women's rights, proper education, legal literacy, adequacy of health facilities and services for them. Studies have shown that women and adolescent girls have a very limited knowledge of their own body and biological processes and needs. The Department should, therefore, make concerted efforts to involve both women and adolescent girls in various programmes and enhance their understanding and awareness towards various issues. The Committee should be apprised about the various initiatives taken/to be taken by the Department to address the problems of adolescent girls. The Department should also consider the feasibility of making Sex Education part of school curriculum as well as of the Adult Education programmes.[31]

13. Environment and Work-related Health Problems

Health problems that are work related or those that arise out of adverse environmental conditions cover a broad range of illnesses and disabilities. Such problems arise out of injuries, infections, exposure to dust, chemicals and gases, from psychological stresses, and from the harmful effects of a degrading environment.

Women often work long hours, increasing their exposure to illness and injuries. A large proportion of women are engaged in agricultural work. This can expose them to worm infestations which aggravate anemia, to injuries, snake bites and insecticide poisoning as well as to disorders resulting from extreme climatic conditions. Exposure to pesticides and chemical fertilizers can also result in abortion and stillbirth. The health department must provide facilities against such risks.

Intensified advocacy over the past several years has led to widespread endorsement of a life-cycle approach to women's health and recognition of women's vital participation in national sustainable development.

Greater attention to women, health and development (WHD) issues has also been promoted through widespread dissemination of information material. A video was produced portraying gender-based inequalities in health and outlining the actions needed to improve women's health and enhance their role in development.

14. Absence of partnership in Governance

UNDP States Women's equal participation in political life plays a pivotal role in the general process of the advancement of women. Women's equal participation in decision-making is not only a demand for simple justice or democracy but can also be seen as a necessary condition for women's interests to be taken into account. Without the active participation of women and the incorporation of women's perspectives at all levels of decision-making, the goals of equality, development and peace can not be achieved.

In this broad context, the Conference highlighted a close relationship between the low number of women parliamentarians and the high number of women in poverty. It also underscored that the budget of any nation is the most important economic instrument for improving the well-being of its citizens. The reconfirmed what gender specialists have always maintained: that unless macro-economic policies are engendered and adequate budgetary allocations for health, education and social support systems are earmarked, an increasing number of women and their families will continue their drift into poverty. The Conference also called upon countries that have attained a 30 per cent representation of women in their parliaments to share their experience and strategies with others.[32]

Platform for Action—After five year after the departments of Women and Child Development enunciated the 12 point agenda of Beijing Platform for Action, which should guide us in new millennium.

"Gender" is used to describe those characteristics of men and women which are socially constructed and therefore can change, in contrast to those that are biologically determined and therefore cannot change. Gender is thus a dynamic concept which looks at the social divisions and the interrelations between men and women. (See Chart 10.2)

CHART 10.2

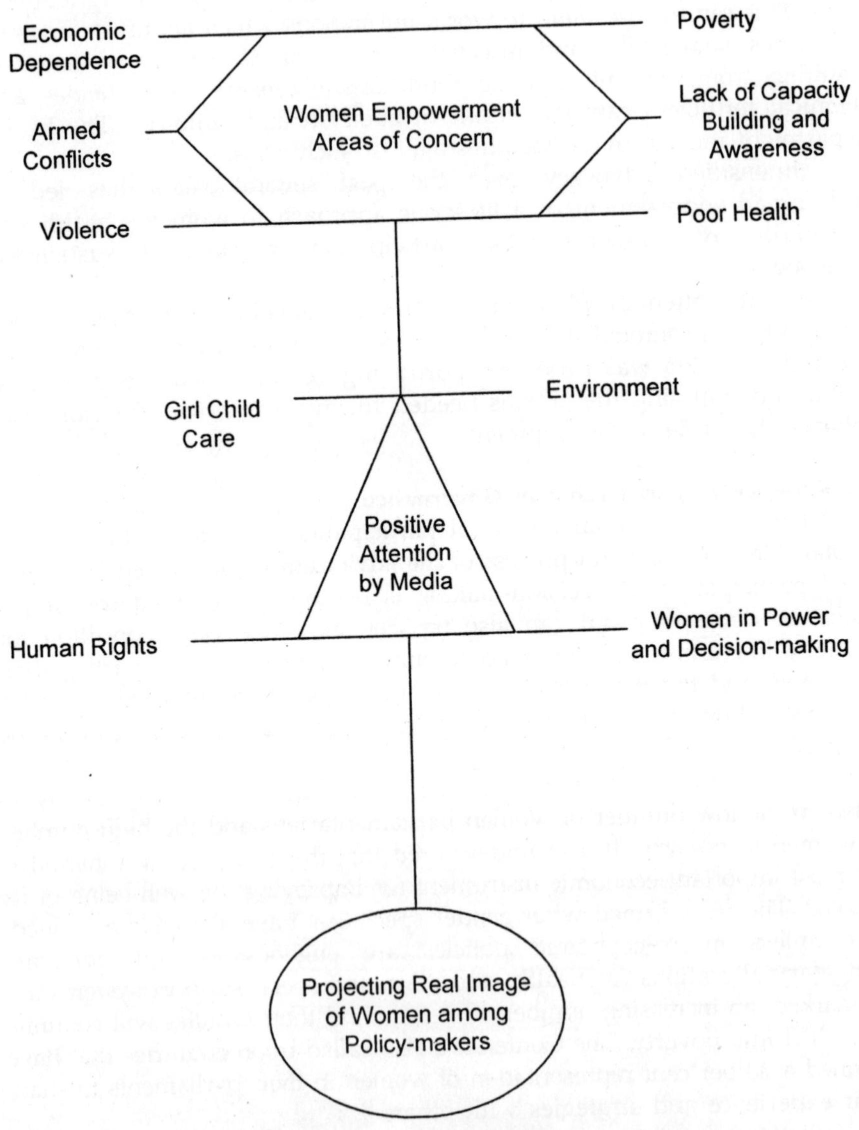

A "gender approach to health" is based on an analysis of how differences and disparities between women and men determine their differential exposure to risk, their access to technology and health care, their rights and responsibilities, and their control over their own lives.

A. Women and Poverty

Strategic Objective

A.1. Review, adopt and maintain macroeconomic policies and development strategies that address the needs and efforts of women in poverty.

A.2. Revise laws and administrative practices to ensure women's equal rights and access to economic resources.

A.3. Provide women with access to savings and credit mechanisms and institutions.

B. Education and Training of Women

B.1. Ensure equal access to education.

B.2. Eradicate illiteracy among women.

B.3. Improve women's access to vocational training, science and technology, and continuing education.

B.4. Develop non-discriminatory education and training.

B.5. Allocate sufficient resources for and monitor the implementation of educational reforms.

B.6. Promote lifelong education and training for girls and women.

C. Women and Health

C.1 Increase women's access throughout the life cycle to appropriate, affordable and quality health care, information and related services.

C.2. Strengthen preventive programmes that promote women's health.

C.3. Undertake gender-sensitive initiatives that address sexually transmitted diseases, HIV/AIDS, and sexual and reproductive health issues.

C.4. Promote research and dissemination information on women's health.

C.5. Increase resources and monitor follow-up for women's health.

D. Violence against Women

D.1. Take integrated measures to prevent and eliminate violence against women.

D.2. Study the causes and consequences of violence against women and the effectiveness of preventive measures.

D.3. Eliminate trafficking in women and assist victims due to prostitution and trafficking.

E. Women and Armed Conflict

E.1. Increase the participation of women in conflict resolution at decision-making levels and protect women living in situations of armed and other conflicts or under foreign occupation.

E.2. Reduce excessive military expenditures and control the availability of armaments.

E.3. Promote nonviolent forms of conflict resolution and reduce the incidence of human rights abuse in conflict situations.

E.4. Promote women's contribution to fostering a culture of peace.

E.5. Provide protection, assistance and training to refugee women, other displaced women in need of international protection and internally displaced women.

E.6. Provide assistance to the women of the colonies and non-self-governing territories.

F. Women and Economy

F.1. Promote women's economic rights and independence, including access to employment, appropriate working conditions and control over economic resources.

F.2. Facilitate women's equal access to resources, employment, markets and trade.

F.3. Provide business services, training and access to markets, information and technology, particularly to low-income women.

F.4. Strengthen women's economic capacity and commercial networks.

F.5. Eliminate occupational segregation and all forms of employment discrimination.

F.6. Promote harmonization of work and family responsibilities for women.

G. Women in Power and Decision-making

G.1. Take measures to ensure women's equal access to and full participation in power structures and decision-making.

G.2. Increase women's capacity to participate in decision-making and leadership.

H. Institutional Mechanisms for the Advancement of Women

H.1. Create or strengthen national machineries and other governmental bodies.

H.2. Integrate gender perspectives in legislation, public policies, programmes and projects.

H.3. Generate and disseminate gender-disaggregated data and information for planning and evaluation.

I. Human Rights of Women

I..1. Promote and protect the human rights of women, through the full implementation of all human rights instruments, especially the Convention on the Elimination of All Forms of Discrimination against Women.

I.2. Ensure equality and non-discrimination under the law and in practice.

I.3. Achieve legal literacy.

J. Women and the Media

J.1. Increase the participation and access of women to expression and decision-making in and through the media and new technologies of communication.

J.2. Promote a balanced and non-stereotyped portrayal of women in the media.

K. Women and the Environment

K.1. Involve women actively in environmental decision-making at all levels.

K.2. Integrate gender concerns and perspectives in policies and programmes for sustainable development.

K.3. Strengthen or establish mechanisms at the national, regional and international levels to assess the impact of development and environmental policies on women.

L. The Girl-child

L.1. Eliminate all forms of discrimination against the girl-child

L.2. Eliminate negative cultural attitudes and practices against girls.

L.3. Promote and protect the rights of the girl-child and increase awareness of her needs and potential.

L.4. Eliminate discrimination against girls in education, skills development and training.

L.5. Eliminate discrimination against girls in health and nutrition.

L.6. Eliminate the economic exploitation of child labour and protect young girls at work.

L.7. Eliminate violence against the girl-child.

L.8. Promote the girl-child's awareness of and participation in social, economic an political life.

L.9. Strengthen the role of the family in improving the status of the girl-child.

Notes and References

1. UN: ESCAP: Asia and the Pacific into the Twenty-first Century; Prospects for Social Development, 1998, pp. 179-80.
2. NCW: 1990-2000, New Delhi. p. 135.
3. Swami Chinmayananda, Kindle Life, CCMT, Mumbai, 2002, pp. 206-07 and 192.
4. Development Schemes for Rural Women, Ministry of Rural Areas and Employment, First Report, Committee on Empowerment of Women, 1988-89, Twelfth Lok Sabha, Lok Sabha Secretariat, New Delhi, pp. 1-3.
5. Swami Chinmayananda, Kindle Life, CCMT, Mumbai. 2002, pp. 48-50.
6. GOI, Department of Women and Child Development, Ministry of HRD, Mission Statement, Platform For Action, Five Years After—An Assessment, June 2000, p. 6.
7. Chinmayananda, The Source of Inspiration, CCMT, 2002, pp. 5, 24-15.
8. *Ibid.*
9. Karl Marx and Freidrick Engles, Selected Works, Vol. II, p. 310.
10. Declaration on the Elimination of Discrimination against Women—United Nations, 1967.
11. Report of the Inter-Regional Meeting of Experts on the Integration of Women in Development, UN Document SN/SOA, p. 5
12. ILO, Women Workers in a Changing World, 48th Session, p. 19
13. Report of the National Commission on Labour, Govt. of India, 1969, p. 379.
14. S.K. Dhameja, Women Entrepreneurs, New Delhi, Deep & Deep, 2002, pp. 143, 174-75.
15. James L. Marshall, Development Teaching, New York, 1949, pp. 190-306 and UN: Standards and Techniques of Public Administration, New York, 1951, pp. 20-54 and Mathur, Some aspects of Administering Teaching Aid Programme, *The IIPA Journal*, Vol. XVII, No. 20, April-June 1972, pp. 243-53.
16. Platform for Action, *op. cit.*, p. 16.
17. R.C. Majumdar, British Paramountcy and Indian Remanence, p. 289.
18. Report of the Secondary Education Commission, GOI, 1953, Chapter IV.
19. Report of the Committee on the Differentiation of Curricula for Boys and Girls, GOI, 1954, Chapter III.
20. Report of the University Education Commission, 1949, GOI, Chapter 12.
21. Ilsa Schumacher, Jennefer Sebstad and Mayra Buvinic, (1980): Limits to Productivity: Improving Access to Technology and Credit, International Centre for Research on Women, Washington, D.C.: US Aid.
22. The informal sector is the sector which encourages income generating activity that does not involve a formal wage contract; it is not capital-intensive , large-scale, publicly or corporately owned, regulated or unionized. It encompasses a variety of activities like petty trading, production and service activities that usually involve self-employment, and, sometimes, labour contract too.
23. N. Lalitha, Self-Employment for Rural Women—Need for Credit Plan Approaches in Anita Banerjee, Raj Kumar Sen (editors), Women and Economic Development, pp. 188, 195-96.
24. Roma Mukherjee, Women Law and Free Legal Aid in India, New Delhi, Deep & Deep, 2000, pp. 312-14.
25. This remarks was made by Bredam O'Brien, a former treasurer of the law society. It is quoted in 1968 Annual Report, Ontario Legal Aid Plan at p. 17, This first report contains a fairly comprehensive outline of the history).
26. UN ESCAP: Asia and the Pacific into the Twenty-First Century: Prospects for Social Development, 1988, pp. 209-10.

27. Mahatma Gandhi, *Young India*, 26.2, 1918.
28. *Ibid.*, 14.1.1932 and 24.2.1940.
29. Jawaharlal Nehru, Forewod to Social Welfare in India, The Planning Commission, 1935.
30. WHO: SEARO Regioal Health Report 1998, Focus on Women, New Delhi.
31. Committee on Empowerment of Women, 2001-02, 13th Lok Sabha, Fourth Report, Lok Sabha, Secretariat, New Delhi.
32. Line Hamdesh Banerjee and Paul Qurist, Over-view Women's Political Participation and Good Governance, 21st Century Challenges in UNDP, Sales No. E0011, B.7, pp. 2-4.

11

Women Empowerment in Eleventh Five Year Plan—A Case Study of Haryana

STATUS OF WOMEN IN HARYANA

Haryana State was carved on 1st November, 1966. Out of a total population 21,082,989, as per 2001 census there were 9,755,337 females, i.e. 48.27% of total population. Sex ratio per 1000 males is only 861 which is very low as compared to all India average of 933. Kerala is the highest in India with 1058 while Daman and Diu, is lowest in India, i.e. 709. Literacy rate for female as per 2001 census is 56.31% as compared to male 68.59% making a total of 69.25% expectation of life for female is 69.3 years against. All India Average of 65.43 years while expectation of life for male is 64.64 against on All India Average of 64.11 Infant Mortality Rate (IMR) is 72 (73 female and 70 male). The total percentage of female main workers, marginal workers and non-workers in 2001 is 13.37, 13.94 and 72.69 against the males 43.63, 6.86 and 49.51 respectively. Work Participation Rate according to Sex for Haryana during 2001 is 43.24% and 12.62% females in rural and urban areas respectively. Female Government employees in 2001 constituted only 25.72% of the total employees while at the decision-making level it is marginal, i.e. 3.4% The per capita income of Haryana is 21551, 2nd state in India while in Punjab it is 23040, i.e first state in India. (See Chart 11.1 and Map 11.1)

The elected women members in 2001 in Haryana in PRIS is as follows:

	Female	*Total*
1. Garm Pachayat	16704	54346
2. Intermediate Panchayat	858	2430
3. District Panchayat	182	226

CHART 11.1

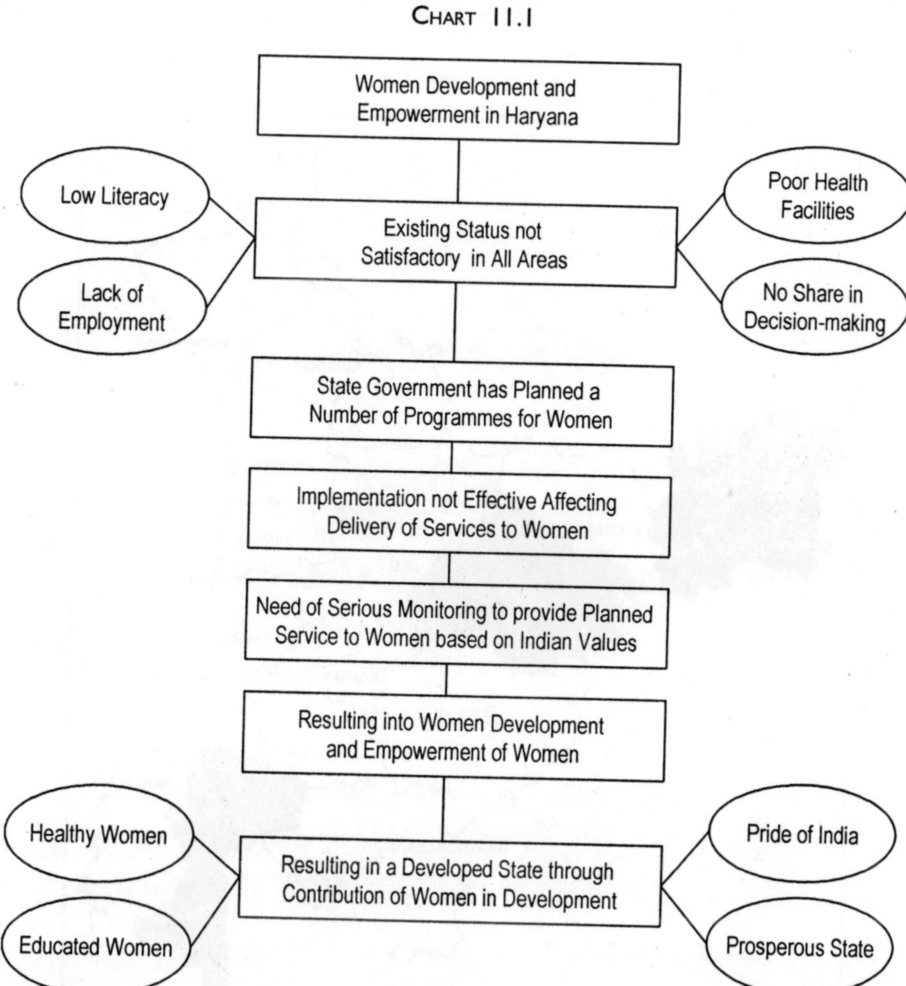

Women's Participation in polls in Haryana in 2001 is 58.27 percent as compared to men 63.68 percent. In 2001, there were 1695149 girls in schools, 2081038 boys and a total of 23776188 while in colleges and universities there were 84740 girls and 1880797 boys making a total of 1965537. Thus total girls undergoing education in Haryana in 2001 were 1779889 out of a total of 3972725 giving a percentage of 44 percent. Dropout rates for females in 2001 in percentage in Primary Classes (I-V) is 20.92 as compared to 25.82 for boys while in elementary Classes VI-VIII is 28.92 for girls and 19.17 for boys.

Nutritional Status

Gender Diaggregation for the state of Haryana in percentage of 2001. (See next page)

Map 11.1

Selected Districts of Haryana for Time Use Survey

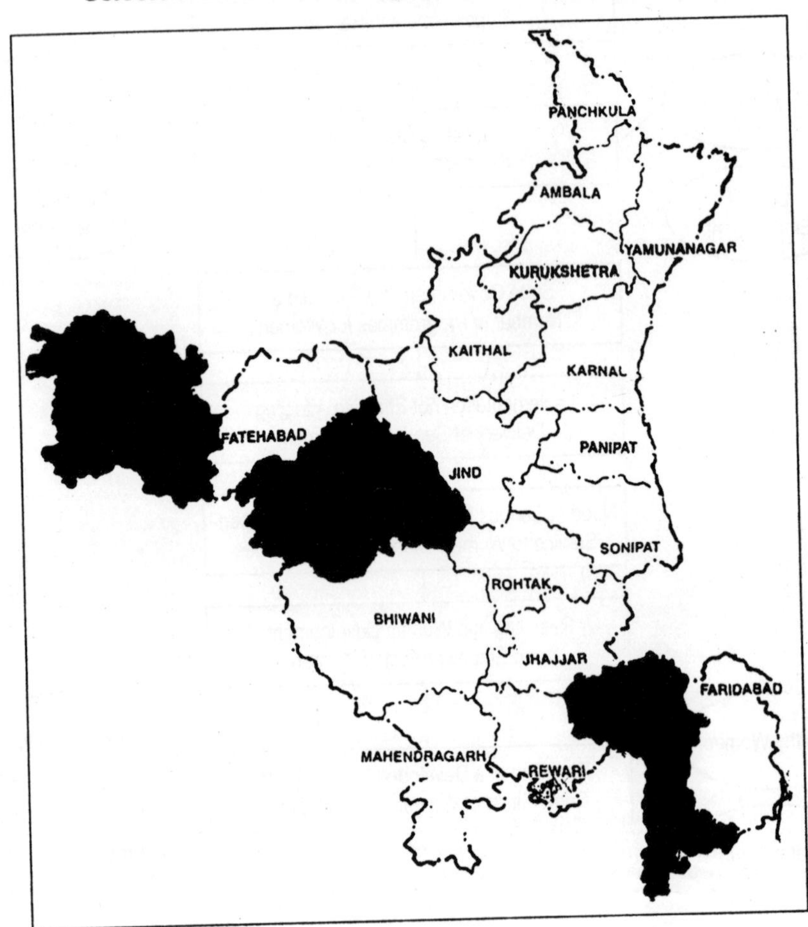

Nutritional Status	Male	Female	Total
A. Undernourished			
(i) Underweight (weight-for-age)	11.0	9.0	20.0
(ii) Stunted (height-for-age)	24.4	24.2	38.6
(iii) Wasted (weight-for-age)	1.0	0.5	1.5
B. Severely Undernourished			
(i) Underweight (weight-for-age)	31.8	38.1	69.9
(ii) Stunted (height-for-age)	47.5	53.1	100.6
(iii) Wasted (weight-for-age)	5.9	4.6	10.5

Source: National Family Health Survey, 1998-99, India.

Let us mention a special type of survey called Time Use Survey done in Haryana from July 1998 to June 1999 by Economic and Statistical Organisation, Planning Department, Haryana, Chandigarh. The main findings of the Survey are mentioned below:

In Haryana, Time Use Survey was conducted in 1344 households spread over six selected districts namely, Yamuna Nagar, Kurukshetra, Gurgaon, Rewari, Hissar and Sirsa. The main objective of this survey was to collect data for properly quantifying the economic contribution of the women in the national economy and to study the gender discrimination in the household activities. The field work of the survey was completed by the staff of Economic and Statistical Organisation, Planning Department, Haryana during July 1998 to June 1999.

The sampling design adopted in the survey was two stage stratified design. The census villages/urban blocks and households were first and second stages respectively for this survey. To ensure representation of all types of households in the survey, sub-stratification was also adopted in the villages/urban blocks level.

The main findings of the survey have been highlighted as follows:

1. The average household size varied from 4.17 in Yamuna Nagar district to 5.08 in Kurukshetra district. The average household size of the State comes out to be 4.52.
2. The trend of the surveyed households shows predominantly Hindus constituting 81.7% of the total households in the six districts combined. The Muslim and Sikh's households were 9.2% and 8.7% respectively.
3. Predominancy of Muslim households was found in Gurgaon district (37.9%) whereas percentage of Sikh's households was found highest (31.1%) in Sirsa district.
4. About 59% households were found to be living in *pucca* houses. This percentage was 52 for rural areas and 87 for urban areas.
5. The proportion of landless households was significantly more in urban areas (88%) as compared to rural areas (59%). The proportion of households possessing land 6 acres and above in rural areas was found to be highest (22.6%) in Sirsa district and lowest (5.8%) in Gurgaon district.
6. As expected, 87% of the scheduled caste households were found landless as compared to 53% of other castes. The percentage of female headed households was marginally higher (6.25%) in urban areas as compared to rural (6.11%) areas. The proportion of single member female headed household was significantly higher (30.4%) in urban areas as compared to (11.1%) rural areas.
7. About 25% households in rural areas were found to be having monthly per capita expenditure of more than Rs. 560 and about 21% households in urban areas were found to be having monthly per capita expenditure of more than Rs. 1055.

8. The percentage of surveyed population in the age group 0-14 was 37.8. Only 5.7% persons were of age 60 years and above. This percentage was highest (8.9%) in Yamuna Nagar district and lowest (37%) in Sirsa district
9. The males and females proportions in the age group 0-14 were 39.6% and 35.7% respectively whereas this proportion in the age group of 60 years and above found to be almost same.
10. 48.96% persons were found to be never married and 47.38% as currently married. The proportion of widowed population was about 3.5%. The percentage of currently married population was found to be marginally higher (48.8%) in urban areas as compared to 47.1% rural areas.
11. In all the six districts taken together 62.34% of the persons were found to be literate; the percentage being 74.55% for males and 47.84% for females. The literacy rate has increased from 1991-population census of 55.85% in the State. The literacy rate was found to be highest (70.33%) in Rewari district followed by 65.75% in Yamuna Nagar district.
12. The results of the survey show that about 35% of the respondents were employed whereas 64% were out of labour force. There was not much variation in the percentage of persons employed among districts. The percentage of employment was marginally higher (35.6%) in urban areas as compared to 35% in rural areas.
13. The prevalence of child labour was found to be marginally lower (2.45%) in this survey as compared to NSSO (1993-94) figure of 2.47% to the general perception, about 87% of the women aged 18 years and above reported that they participated in the household decision-making. Some difference was observed in the rural and urban sector as far as female participation in household decision-making was concerned. The participation in the household decision-making was found highest (88%) in the women having education level upto primary.
14. About 1.61% of surveyed population was found to be having some form of disability. Out of total disabled persons, 67% were males and remaining 33% females. The incidence of disability was highest (2.26%) in Kurukshetra district followed by Yamuna Nagar district (2.06%) and Gurgaon district (1.79%).
15. Out of 7 days, normal, weekly variant and abnormal days were reported to be 6.50, 0.42 and 0.08 respectively. Therefore, normal days, constituted about 93% of all the days covered in the survey. The normal days were higher (6.55) in rural areas as compared to urban areas (6.30). (Normal days for females (6.64) were marginally higher as compared to males (6.40).
16. On the average, 73% of the time spent on non-SNA activities,

18% on SNA and 9% on extended-SNA. On an average male spends about 38 hours in SNA activities as compared to about 21 hours by females in a week. However, situation completely changes when we consider extended-SNA activities. In these activities, male spends only about 2 hours as compared to 31 hours by females in a week. In non-SNA activities, male spends about 12 hours more as compared to females. However, going by districts, time spent by male on SNA activities was highest (43 hours) in Gurgaon district and lowest (29 hours) in Rewari district.

17. The percentage of time spent on SNA activities by male was 23% in rural areas as compared to 22% in urban areas. However, the percentage of time spent on SNA activities by females was only 7% urban areas as compared to 14% in rural areas.
18. The time spent on extended-SNA activities by rural female was higher than urban female in Yamuna Nagar, Kurukshetra and Gurgaon districts whereas it was found to be lower in Rewari, Hissar and Sirsa districts. If we take SNA and extended-SNA activities together, the average time spent by rural male (24 hours) was found to be much lower as compared to rural female (32 hours). However, in urban areas not much variation was observed in time spent by male (23 hours) and female (26 hours). Hence women are found to be working for longer hours than males. Therefore, if extended-SNA activities are included in the economic activities, the contribution of women will be higher as compared to men.
19. A number of economic activities are performed either by family labour or through exchange labour. No payment is made for such activities. The results of Time Use Survey reveal that payment was not made for about 52% of the time spent in SNA activities. The proportion of time spent on unpaid activities was highest in Rewari district (59%) followed by Hissar district (58%) and Gurgaon district (53%). The amount of unpaid activities was more (86%) for female as compared to only 35% for male. The predominance of female unpaid activities was visible in all the six selected districts. The proportion of time spent by females in unpaid activities was highest (92.2%) in Kurukshetra district followed by Rewari district (91.6%) and Gurgaon district (88.2%).

Whatever characteristics of respondents we take, it is generally found that females spent about more than double time as compared to males in activities relating to taking care of children, sick and elderly people for own household. No significant impact of educational level was found in such activities. Some difference was observed over the districts. The average time spent by female in taking care of children, sick and elderly people was found to be highest (16.82 hours) in Hissar district followed by Sirsa district (15.37 hours) and Kurukshetra district (14.44 hours). Currently married and widowed females spent more time than those for never married and divorced in such activities. The results of the survey also reveal that females aged 60 years and above spend more time in such activities as compared to females of other age categories.

The data on some peculiar activities which generally fall in the domain of women's life was also collected through Time Use Survey. About 1.6 hours per day was found to be spent by woman on cooking food and 1.3 hours on cleaning utensils. About 0.72 hours per day was spent by women for taking care of own children and teaching and supervising own children. The male spent only 0.06 hours per day on such activities.

Personal care and self-maintenance is necessary for the healthy life and individual's well-being. In this survey, data on such activities was also collected. Not much significant difference was observed in the time spent on personal care and self-maintenance by males and females. The time spent on personal care and self-maintenance was highest in the individual aged 60 years and above (.127 hours) followed by age group of 6-14 years (99 hours) and 15-59 years (.96 hours) in a week and women should get equal time for reading, personal hygiene, leisure such as reading, newspaper, watching T.V. and listening to music, sleep, etc. for proper individual development. The results of this survey reveal that women slept 2 hours less than men in a week. However, women spend more time in talking and gossiping as compared to men. Men in all the six selected districts spent much more time than women in reading newspaper, smoking and drinking intoxicants and physical exercise. There was marginal difference on time spent for watching T.V. by men and women. Time spent on travel relating to various activities was also collected through this survey. However, it will not be possible through this survey to find out the time spent by one individual travel in one day or one week. Rural male spends highest travel time (1.87 hours) in crop farming, kitchen, gardening, etc. followed by personal care and self-maintenance (1.22 hours) and services (0.70 hours). As expected travel time was highest (1.03 hours) per week in services in urban areas. Women spent highest travel time in collection of fruits (1.09 hours) followed by personal care and self-maintenance (0.84 hours) and learning (0.73 hours). Travel time for social and cultural activities was found to be higher in rural areas as compared to urban areas.

FACILITIES AND PROGRAMMES FOR DEVELOPMENT AND EMPOWERMENT OF WOMEN IN HARYANA

A Directorate of Women and Child Development is functioning in the State for overall development of women and children. Integrated Child Development Services scheme is being implemented in 116 blocks including five urban blocks through which supplementary nutrition is being provided to 9.80 lakh children between 6 months to 6 years of age and 2.29 lakh pregnant and nursing mothers (upto to December, 2001). During the year 2001-02, a sum of Rs. 2781.50 lakh is being spent on supplementary nutrition. In addition to this, 2.87 lakh, 2.76 lakh, 2.76 lakh and 2.59 lakh children have been immunized against BCG, DPT, Polio and Measles respectively and 2.65 lakh pregnant women have been immunized against Tetnus Toxite (TT) upto December 2001 through network of ICDS scheme. Under "Pardhan Mantri Gramodaya Yojana (PMGY)", the department is providing supplementary nutrition to malnourished children below three years of age.

Year 2001 was celebrated as "Women's Empowerment Year". During this year, a number of programmes focusing on issues concerning women's empowerment such as human rights and women, women and dowry, nutrition and health, women and education, entrepreneurship in women, women and police, etc. were conducted. For empowerment of women, the Haryana Government decided to prepare a five year perspective plan for women which is being prepared by the Haryana State Commission for Women through the task force constituted by the State Government. Women's Awareness and Management Academy, Rai (Sonipat) imparting training to grass-root level women workers, has been upgraded to the Regional Level Gender Training Institute to provide training on gender sensitisation. As per guidelines of Government of India, the State Government has constituted District Level Committees on 1.5.2001 to monitor and take steps for investigation, prosecution and trial relating to violence against women.

The 2nd phase of United Nations Fund for Population Activities (UNFPA) assisted "Integrated Women's Empowerment and Development Project" started from 1.1.1999 for three years was being implemented in Mehendergarh and Rewari districts at a total approved cost of Rs. 1561.10 lakh and UNFPA has agreed in principle to extend the period of project for further one year. The main aim of the project is to change the present scenario by generating awareness and mobilizing women into groups and making direct interventions in the areas of health and education. A sum of Rs. 1261.48 lakh has been spent on various activities upto December 2001. Similarly, "Rural Women's Development and Empowerment Project" known as Swashakti Pariyojana is being implemented through Haryana Women Development Corporation in three districts namely, Sonipat, Jind and Bhiwani with assistance of World Bank/International Fund for Agricultural Development (IFAD). The emphasis of the project is to promote Self Help Groups for Women Empowerment. So far, a sum of Rs. 216.44 lakh has been received under this project and forming 1200 women groups against which 1119 groups have been formed upto December 2001.

The State Government has set-up "State Commission for Women". The main functions of this Commission are to act as a consultative body to advise the Government on legislative and departmental policies concerning the women, to take necessary steps at the level of the government and public to protect the constitutional and legal rights of the women in order to improve their status. The Commission will monitor the implementation of laws and welfare measures, investigate complaints, demand prosecution in offences committed against women, inspect police station lock ups, sub-jails and rescue homes, etc., conduct public interest litigation and conduct studies and researches, etc.

Women and Child Development Department is also implementing many other programmes/schemes launched by State/Central Government like 'Apni Beti Apna Dhan', 'Balika Samridhi Yojana', "Kishori Shakti Yojana", "National Maternity Benefit Scheme" and "Mahila Mandal Scheme, etc. for the upliftment of the status of the girl child and women.

Under "Kanya Dan Scheme" girls belonging to the Scheduled Castes families living below poverty line are given Rs. 5100 on their wedding. During the year 2001-02 (upto December 2001) 3647 beneficiaries have received under this scheme as against 3312 beneficiaries covered during the previous years.

"Old Age Pension Scheme" now renamed as "Tau Devi Lal Old Age Pension Scheme" prevalent in the State has been based on economic criteria and the eligibility age is 60 years or more so as to give the benefit to the really poor and needy persons. Under this scheme, pension @ Rs. 200 per month is given to the eligible senior citizens of Haryana domicile. The norms of the existing scheme have also been relaxed to widen its scope. 9.25 lakh senior citizens have been covered under the scheme upto December 2001.

"A Widow Pension Scheme" is also being implemented to provide security and financial assistance to widows and destitute women. Under this scheme, widows and destitute women aged 18 years and above, who have no other financial support, are provided pension @ Rs. 200 per month. A total of 3.09 lakh such women had been benefited upto December 2001. In addition, the State is running 3 women homes one each at Karnal, Rohtak and Faridabad for young widows and destitute women and their dependent children to rehabilitate and provide the facilities of boarding, lodging, education and vocational training in various trades. A cash dole @ Rs. 200 per month and the clothing allowance @ Rs. 50 per month is provided to each inmate of these homes. At present (as on 31st December, 2001) there are 350 members of 112 families residing in Mahila Ashrams at Karnal, Rohtak and Faridabad.

The State has also taken a number of steps for rehabilitation of blind, deaf, handicapped and mentally retarded persons. As many as 66,113 physically handicapped persons are being provided pension @ Rs. 200 per month upto December 2001. Scholarships ranging from Rs. 100 to Rs. 500 per month are being given to handicapped students. Un-employment allowance to the educated handicapped persons ranging from Rs. 150 to Rs. 250 per month is being given. Retainership allowance @ Rs. 1500 per month is also being given to the blind.

The Five Year Perspective Plan for Women in Haryana State is the outcome of the decision taken by Hon'ble Chief Minister, Haryana in the meeting held on 13/09/2000. It shows that the Haryana Government has a determined commitment for empowerment and development of women to bring them in the mainstream of the economy by providing them opportunities and facilities and benefits under various schemes.

The Perspective Plan is a product of the Haryana State Commission for Women through a Task Force constituted by the State Government. The processes for its formulation included successive consultations and discussions among members of the Task Force, representatives of different Departments, agencies including NGOs across different sectors.

The Haryana government has launched innovative steps and schemes to improve the status of women like Kanyadaan Yojana, Devi Rupak Yojana, Swayamsiddha, Balika Samriddhi Yojana, Kishori Shakti Yojana and Women's Empowerment Project, Tau Devi Lal Vriddha Awastha Pension Yojana and Widow Pension, setting up of all-woman police stations at Divisional level and increase in number of women in the police-service in the State apart from setting up of State Commission for Women.

The members of the Task Force from different fields have contributed inputs from their area of specialization using reports/data/information from various sources which concentrate on the following concerns and strategies.

PROVISIONS IN ELEVENTH FIVE YEAR PLAN OF HARYANA FOR WOMEN EMPOWERMENT, 2007-12

1. Women Training-*cum*-Production Centres and Stipend Day School

In order to assist destitute, widows, handicapped, socially maladjusted and economically backward women to become self-reliant, the department has been running schemes of setting up voluntary Organization for imparting training and providing them employment avenue. These units will provide special vocational guidance-*cum*-residential opportunity for training and self-employment to destitute women and widows. An outlay of Rs. 500.00 lakh has been approved for 11th Five Year Plan and Rs. 75.00 lakh for Annual Plan, 2007-08 under this scheme.

2. Gender Sensitisation Programme

It is approved to gender sensitize Panches and Sarpanches, Medical Officers, and Police Personnel at the first instance. These gender sensitization training will be organized at district level consisting of panches, sarpanches, doctors and police personnel. Each batch will consist of 30 participants. A 3 days training manual will be used for orienting these functionaries. These trainings will be imparted through Expert Agencies/Gender Consultants/ NGOs @ 6 training programmes per block per year @ Rs. 10,000. An outlay of Rs. 600.00 lakh has been approved for 11th Five Year Plan and Rs. 85.00 lakh for Annual Plan, 2007-08 under this scheme.

3. Promotion of Self Help Group Strategy among Mahila Mandals

At presnt there are 6713 registered Mahila Mandals in Haryana State but the internal reviews by the grass-root level functionaries the department often revealed that these Mahila Mandals are not actively functioning as they could have. It is approved that each Mahila Mandals may be organized into Self Help Groups for which funds of the tune of Rs. 12,000 per SHG will be required for mobilizing them into group formation, their training capacity building during a period of 5 years.

4. Financial Assistance to Women's Awareness and Management Academy (WAMA)

WAMA at Rai was set-up in January 1995 which is registered under the Societies Act, 1860. This Institute has no resources of its own and depends upon States Government Grants that too are not regular. In order to achieve the desired goals, the institutional mechanism needs to be strengthened for regular and quality trainings. It is approved that grant-in-aid to WAMA may be granted on regular basis. An outlay of Rs. 50.00 lakh has been approved for 11th Five Year Plan and Rs. 10.00 lakh for Annual Plan 2007-08 under this scheme.

5. Award for Rural Adolescent Girls

In order to encourage rural girls for pursuing higher education, an award is approved for top 3 girls from each block, who will be given an award of Rs. 2000, Rs. 1500 and Rs. 1000 for 1st, 2nd and 3rd Positions respectively and who have passed their matriculation examination conducted by Haryana State Education Board from schools in rural areas. An oulay of Rs. 29.00 lakh has been approved for 11th Five Year Plan and Rs. 5.35 lakh for Plan 2007-08 under this scheme.

6. Swavlamban (NORAD)

Under this scheme grant in aid will be given to those women NGOs who are working for the welfare of women. This grant is for the training of women for capacity building and for innovative skills. As per norms fixed by GOI, Rs. 8,000 per capita will be spent on training of women. Earlier the scheme was implementing with the entire assistance from GOI under 100% Centrally Sponsored Scheme. Now GOI has informed that State Government should implement this scheme with their budget so the scheme has been included in the 11th Five Year Plan. An outlay of Rs. 200.00 lakh for 11th Plan and Rs. 25.00 lakh for Annual Plan 2007-08 has been approved under this scheme.

7. Subsidy and Share Capital to Haryana Women Development Corporation

Under this scheme Grant-in-Aid and Share Capital is provided to Haryana Women Development Corporation. The main objective of the Corporation is to promote activities for the welfare and development of women. An outlay of Rs. 5700.00 lakh has been approved for 11th Five Year Plan and Rs. 628.00 lakh for Annual Plan 2007-08 under this scheme.

8. Planning-cum-Monitoring Cell (Communication and Publicity)

The role of publicity in the context of child and women development is vital for furthering advocacy, social mobilization and community empowerment which will be area specific, need-based and target-oriented with a focus on child survival, protection and development, area of behaviour concern and empowerment of women. An outlay of Rs. 1500.00 lakh has been approved for 11th Five Year Plan and Rs. 150.00 lakh for Annual Plan, 2007-08 under this scheme.

9. Financial Assitance to Destitude Women and Widow (Widow Pension)

A woman in the age group of 18 years and above is eligible for grant of pension @ Rs. 300 p.m. if she is a widow or unmarried woman or a married woman who has been deprived of the financial support from her husband because of his physical/mental capacity or desertion by husband or any other reasons and her close relatives such as parents, sons, grandsons are not supporting her and her own income from all sources is upto Rs. 10,000 per annuam and she is a domicile of Haryana and has been residing in the Haryana State for the last one year. An outlay of Rs. 101100.00 lakh has been approved for 11th Plan and Rs. 12741.00 lakh for Annual Plan 2007-08.

CONCLUSION

In nutshell, the status of women is still not raised and they suffer on many counts. The state government should not only be satisfied with quantity but also help women in building confidence that will be the real development and empowerment of women. Being a woman, it was easy for me to do participatory observation and not mere statistical counting. The State Government must accelerate the steps for development and empowerment of women.

To make life worthwhile and fruitful, women must generate enthusiasm within themselves. Generation of enthusiasm will take place when they discover for themselves a Goal and attach themselves to the Altar with a spirit of dedication, reverence and love. The goal is the development and empowerment of women. Once they have accepted this, the ideal itself will provide us with the inspiration and strength. Then nothing can hinder the progress of their march towards that Goal and the ideal. The love for the ideal will overcome and vanquish all the hurdles from the ideal, and if it comes to that life itself will be cast off with a smile in dedication at that Altar. That was how Bhagat Singh could walk to the gallows with a smile on his face. What is important is that one should choose the right ideal. . . an Ideal worthwhile even if it comes to sacrificing one's own life in the endeavor. The Ideal should be inspiring, it should arouse the spring of activity in them. Thus, the discovering of the Ideal is the secret of generating in them Dynamism and Vitality in its fullness.

Total Outlay on Women Welfare in XIth Plan

S. No.	Major Head of Development	10th Plan Approved Outlay	Annual Plan 2006-07		Tenth Plan Actual Exp. outlay which Outpay capital capital content	11th Five Year Plan Approved which		Annual plan Approved of	
			Revised outlay	Actual outlay					
1	2	3	4	5	6	7	8	9	10
	Women welfare								
1.	Home-*cum*-training centres for Destitute Women and Widows	125.00	28.50	18.32	93.02	50.00	50.00	10.00	
2.	Financial Assistance to Destitute Women and Widows	30000.00	13848.00	13385.90	45074.58	101100.00		12741.00	
3.	Setting up of Vocational Training Centres for Women	15.00	2.00	0.80	6.78	—	—	—	—
4.	Financial Assistance for the marriage of daughter of widows and destitute women of economically weaker section of the society	10.00			0.00				
	Total IV Women Welfare	30150.00	13514.50	13405.03	45174.38	101150.00	50.00	12751.00	—

Source: Eleventh Five Year Plan, Government of Haryana, 2007-12.

12

Conclusion

Empowerment has been defined as a change in the context of a woman's life, which enables her increased capacity for leading a fulfilling human life. It gets reflected in external qualities such as health, mobility, education and awareness, status in the family, participation in decision-making, and also at the level of material security. It also includes internal qualities such as self-awareness and self-confidence.

—*From "Human Development in South Asia 2000"*

Women have shown the potential of challenging the iniquitous power relations in the public domain. Six million women's representatives in PRIs, directly and indirectly, have given an impetus to the processes of social mobilization and women are reinventing gender roles in private and public spaces. Interestingly, due to their increased visibility, the gender-based distinction between the private and public space is becoming blurred.

From "Women's Empowerment in the Context of the Constitution (Seventy-third and Seventy-fourth Amendments) Acts: An Assessment" by Mohanty and Mahajan.

Areas in which government policies could be strengthened to foster the empowerment of women include the following:

- Education programs to improve knowledge about critical issues such as health, hygiene, sanitation, purity of drinking water, use of modern contraceptives and the legal age of marriage.
- Development of innovative and replicable health programs using the assistance of NGOs and the private sector.
- Increased efforts to universalize primary education for girls and to retain girls in schools up to secondary level.
- Formation of self-help groups (SHGs) for women.
- Enhancement of women's income and earning opportunities

through improved access to credit, training, technology, market support, etc.
- PRIs should be strengthened to focus on women and children.
- Policies and laws should be strengthened to deal with violence against women.

The First UN World Conference on Women held in 1975 in Mexico City, marked the beginning of the International Decade of the Woman (UN Development Decade for Women, 1975-85). Since then, World Conference on Women have been held in Copenhagen in 1980, in Nairobi in 1985 and in Beijing, China, in September 1995.

While stressing on equality of rights/human rights, the Mexico Plan of Action (POA) called for the ratification and implementation of the United Nations Convention on the Elimination of all forms of Discrimination Against Women (CEDAW) referred to earlier. It declared 1975 as the International Women's Year and called for measures to grant and protect women's rights, including property rights within marriage, reallocate Government funds through programmes elevating the status of women, formulate polices and programmes for equal opportunity and treatment of women workers and equal pay for equal work, adhere to standards for equality and conditions set by the International Labour Organization, accommodate family and work responsibilities through adequate child care and transportation facilities and recognize the substantial role of women in development and place higher value on domestic/family work.

The Copenhagen World Conference of 1980, interpreted equality not only as legal equality but also as equality of rights, responsibilities and opportunities for the participation of women in development both as beneficiaries and as active agents. It urged States to enact legislation guaranteeing women the right to vote, to be elected or appointed to political office and to exercise public functions on equal terms with men. It also called for placing value on women's unpaid work for inclusion in GNP, Provision of maternity and parental leave, protection against any sexually oriented practice that endangers a woman's access to jobs or undermines her job performance.

The Nairobi Forward Looking Strategies for the Advancement of Women, 1985 emphasized integration of Women in the development process and the need to establish specific targets at each level to increase the participation of women in professional, management and decision-making positions in their countries. They also call for promotion of women to position of power at every level within all political and legislative bodies in order to achieve parity with men. The document urges recognition of the extent and value of women's unpaid work, inside and outside the home, and its inclusion in national accounts and economic statistics. Further it calls for sharing of domestic responsibilities and establishment of flexible working hours to encourage the same.

CHART 12.1

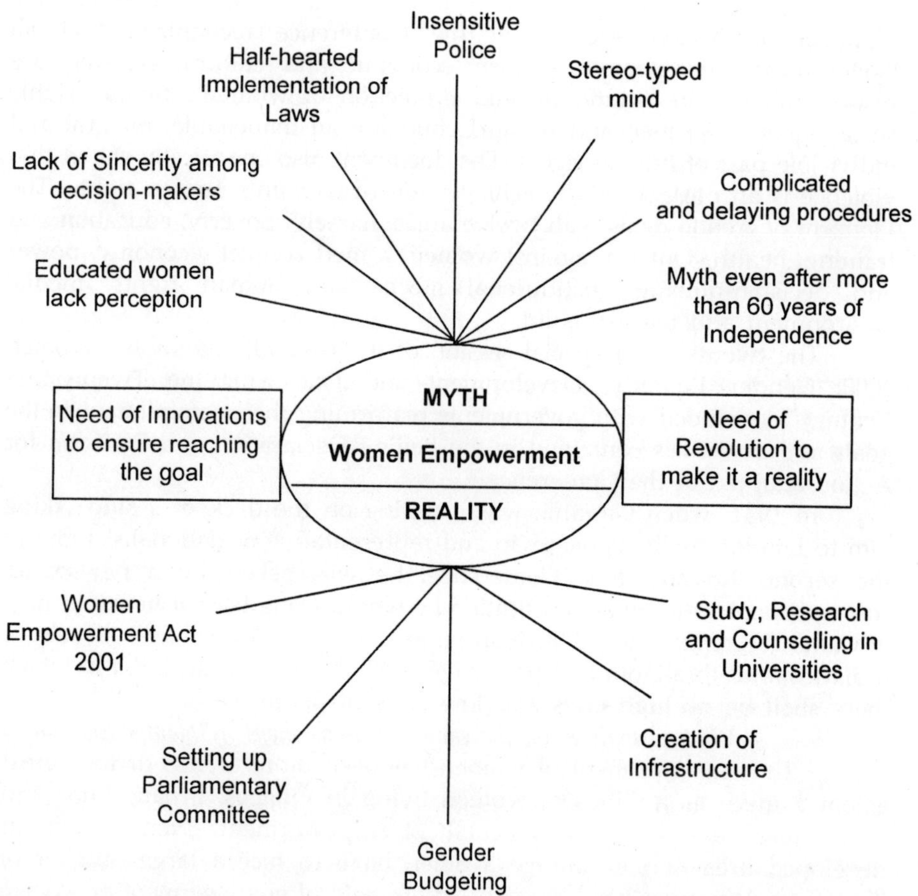

The International Conference on Population and Development (ICPD) at Cairo in 1994 affirmed that women's rights are an integral part of all human rights. It stresses that the population and development programme are most effective when steps have simultaneously been taken to improve the status of women. ICPD was the first international forum to acknowledge that the enjoyment of sexual health is an integral part of reproductive rights. Men's rights and responsibilities to their partners were noted. The conference established an international consensus on a comprehensive approach to population stabilization where in family welfare services are to be provided in the context of Reproductive Child Health Services. It calls for efforts to reduce infant mortality by one-third and maternal mortality by one-half by 2000. According to its principles, advancing gender equity and equality and the empowerment of women, the elimination of all kinds of violence against women and ensuring women's ability to control their own fertility are cornerstones of population and development related programmes.

The United Nations Fourth World Conference at Beijing 1995, and the Platform of Action adopted at the Conference recognized that all Governments, irrespective of their economic and cultural systems, are responsible for the promotion and protection of women's human rights since rights of women and the girl child are an inalienable, integral and indivisible part of human rights. The document also specifically stated that violence is an obstacle to the achievement of women's human rights. The Platform of Action deals with twelve areas, namely, poverty, education and training, health, violence against women, armed conflict, economy, power and decision-making, institutional mechanism, human rights, media, environment and the girl child.

The twenty third special session of the General Assembly "Women 2000: Gender Equality, Development and Peace for the Twenty-first Century" concluded with governments reaffirming their commitment to the goals and objectives contained in the Beijing Declaration and Platform for Action adopted at the Conference .

In 1931, when Gandhiji was standing on the deck of a ship taking him to London as the spokesman and representative of nationalist India to the second Round Table Conference, he was asked by a newspaper correspondent as to what constitution he would bring back if he could help it. Gandhiji's reply was:[1] "I shall strive for a Constitution which will release India from all thralldom and patronage—I shall work for an India in which there shall be no high class and low class of people.[2]

—Women shall enjoy the same rights as men. . ." (emphasis added)

The empowerment of women has been more or less or to a great extent a myth as millions of women living in villages, urban slums and tribal areas have not got any benefit of empowerment. Even in cities or developed area of the country, women have to face a large number of limitations. Whatever has been done in the field of empowerment of women has not trickled down to women but is simply locked in official documents/field, law books, government circulars, etc. There has been little effort on the part of the legislature, executive and judiciary to ensure empowerment to women.

How have the women of India fared in this grand enterprise of economic and social change? On the one hand, one sees exciting developments like women becoming Supreme Court Judges, Chief Ministers and even the Prime Minister. They have become presidents and CEOs of large business enterprises and many have distinguished themselves in the fields of literature, science and arts. Yet others have flown aircrafts and driven train engines. On the other hand, one reads about large multitudes of women suffering indignities at home and outside. Even physical violence and criminal assault on women have become so routine that one just reads the reports in the national and vernacular press and then dismisses them as non-events. One is tempted to ask: what has freedom meant to this five hundred million strong mass of Indian womanhood?

Dr. Poornima Advani rightly observed (New Grade equity making it happen, 2001) Admittedly, there is no shortage of laws and constitutional provisions guaranteeing a place of honour and equality to women. There is no dearth of schemes designed to eradicate every conceivable evil and solve every imaginable problem concerning women. There are large bureaucracies at the central and state levels and an elaborate network of institutions like the National and State Commissions for Women, the Human Rights Commission and Boards and Corporations with schemes and budgets to elevate the status of women, socially and economically. Yet, at the turn of the millennium, does the Indian woman stand, tall and confident, like the menfolk of this country: The crime statistics speak eloquently that they cannot. The complaints cell of the National Commission for Women, as indeed many other monitors of social health and hygiene, show that women, not only those belonging to the deprived or depressed sections of the society but even those, who are economically independent and seemingly liberated, suffer from the assaults of a patriarchal social order within and outside the family circle.

In consonance with its mandate, the National Commission deliberated intensively on the plight of women to evaluate the causes for their low status despite a multitude of legal and constitutional guarantees to safeguard their rights.[3]

Politics of Gender-Ideological Underpinnings

The journey towards equality necessarily involves dismantling structures of power and oppression. This necessitates re-engineering of social relations emphasizing a shift in power relations, which in turn challenge the *status quo* and give a blow to the vested interests thriving upon them. At the macro-level, the need to maintain *status quo* gets manifested in an approach where State only pays lip service to not only the international commitment but also Constitutional obligations. Toning down the commitment is at the outset apparent in the declarations and reservations placed by India when it ratified CEDAW. India had made declarations with respect to Article 5(a)[4] and 16(1)[5] CEDAW. With regard to both the provisions India has declared that it will "abide by and ensure these provisions in conformity with its policy of non-interference in the personal affairs of any Community without its initiative and consent." The declaration seeks to restrict the application of one of the most significant provisions of CEDAW. The wedge CEDAW seeks to drive into the most prominent cause of discrimination by imposing an obligation on the States to address the ideological underpinnings in the form of gender stereotypes manifested in norms which may be social, religious, cultural *et al.* thus stands abandoned. It is lamentable that despite international recognition in CEDAW and existence of Constitutional mandate to secure equality, "personal affairs" are granted such a sacrosanct stature. Secondly, it is not clear as to what would amount to community initiative and consent in this regard. Whether a demand from a marginalized group like women within the community would be considered as demand from the community or only the one which is made by the leaders of the community would qualify the test. The ambiguity only appears to be a way to maintain the *status quo*. The demand from women of Christian community to amend the Indian Divorce Act, which was discriminatory was a mute testimony to the ambiguity of this declaratory clause.

The citizens of India have been witnessing the strong resistance put up by Parliamentarians to thwart even the attempts to table the Bill providing for reservation of 33% seats for women in Parliament and state legislatures. The instances of backlash against women who challenges *status quo* in any sphere of life are rampant. The most recent instance of the rhetoric of gender equality is manifested in the initiative to amend the Hindu Succession Act, 1956. Purportedly, one of the main objectives of the Hindu Succession Amendment Bill, 2004 is to give "equal rights to daughters in the Hindu Mitakshara coparcenary property as the sons have."[6] However, as Professor Bina Agarwal points out that it excludes "significant interests in agricultural property", introduces inequalities within different female heirs mentioned as class I heirs in the Act and leaves the testamentary rights over one's property unrestricted thus leaving an option with the people to exclude women from inheriting property.[7]

None of the pillars of the State—the legislature, executive and the judiciary has remain untouched from the hegemony of the ideology of gender. The obligations that CEDAW imposes on the State Parties are not restricted to one of the pillars of the State but it binds all of them equally in making efforts towards ushering equality. The obligations to respect, protect and fulfil relate to all the three pillars of State. The legislature has the most prominent role to play in recognition of rights of women in order to fulfil its obligation to respect, while the judiciary has the most prominent role in protecting rights by offering redress against actual or threatened violation and the executive has a duty to fulfil by offering people institutional structures to ensure enjoyment of rights by women. In India, as discussed above, the legislature has failed to enact laws with respect to many issues affecting women or has failed to repeal laws that are discriminatory towards women. The judiciary has at times stepped in to fill the legislative vacuum and has also made attempts to strike down or tone down provisions that are discriminatory. The role of judiciary in this regard has been ambiguous. It has been very proactive with regard to certain issues like sexual harassment at workplace,[8] developing jurisprudence with respect to compensation to rape victims for violation of their rights,[9] certain cases relating to discrimination in the matters of employment[10] whereas it has persistently followed the policy of either non-interference in addressing discrimination writ large in personal laws,[11] or where it has attempted to consider issue of discrimination in certain provision the redress has been partial.[12]

Partial success in providing redress in case of violation of certain rights, only rhetoric of the legislature towards its obligation to ensure respect for rights, piecemeal efforts by the executive to create conditions for enjoyment of rights of women coupled with the real and artificially created barriers at the normative level pose a great challenge to the practical realization of women's rights in India. All these factors when supported by the deep-rooted ideology of gender make the challenge much more formidable thus necessitating a persistent long drawn out struggle led by women for the practical realisation of women's human rights.

Women and Poverty

- An estimated 260-300 million people remain below the poverty line, more than half of them being women and girls. The implementation and monitoring of gender equality and rights-based policies and programmes with a view to reducing the feminization of poverty, needs to be a priority.
- Eradicating poverty requires improvement on many fronts—not just improving access to income generating opportunities. The challenge is to combat hunger and malnutrition, provide avenues for employment ensure adequate wages for work, reduce drudgery and provide sustained access to drinking water and sanitation.
- The impact of macro-economic policy on the incidence of poverty needs to be carefully assessed.

Gender Budgeting

Gender responsive budgeting or gender analysis of budgets is a very useful tool being used in India to promote gender mainstreaming. Gender budgeting refers to presentation of budgetary data in a manner such that the gender sensitivities of budgetary allocations are clearly highlighted. Gender budgeting includes carrying out an impact analysis of government programmes and its budgetary allocations on the overall socio-economic status of women in the country. The Tenth Plan states that 'The Tenth Plan will continue the process of dissecting the Government budget to establish its gender differentiated impact and to translate gender commitments into budgetary commitments. . . .' 'The Tenth Plan will initiate immediate action in tying up these two effective concepts of Women's Components Plan and Gender Budgeting to play a complementary role to each other, and thus ensure both preventive and *post facto* action in enabling women to receive their rightful share. . .[13]

Gender sensitization training of personnel of executive, legislative and judicial wings of the State, with a special focus on policy and programme framers, implementation and development agencies, law enforcement machinery and the judiciary are in progress. Gender sensitization forms part of the training given to judges by the national Judicial Academy. Most of the State level training institutions have included a gender sensitization module for the orientation of officials. National

Research Training Center at the Lal Bahadur Shastri National Academy of Administration for the training of administrators imparts training in gender concerns, and gender budget analysis is a part of the syllabus.

Medical officers who are responsible for implementing the Pre-Conception and Pre-Natal Diagnostic Techniques (Prohibition of Sex Selection) Act, 1994 (PNDT) Act are sensitize through regional seminars with collaboration of UNFPA, Ministry of Health and Family Welfare and State Governments. Gender sensitization is also included in the training module of health functionaries under phase II of the Reproductive Child Health (RCH) Programme. The Department of Women and Child Development has undertaken several training and orientation programmes in this regard. The Department has enlisted significant support of various civil society organizations. The civil society itself is very active in gender sensitization and is playing a very effective role in promoting gender awareness.

The Government has undertaken various measures, through law, policies and programmes in the last 7-8 years to address gender inequality and to eliminate discrimination against women and girl children. Many laws and programes are still being reviewed to repeal the discriminatory provisions. There are significant improvements on various indicators, which have been discussed at length, in the above paragraphs. With the general poverty level reducing to 26 percent and the marked increases in female literacy level, slight improvement in sex ratio and the entry of women into decision-making bodies, the inequalities that exist between men and women have reduced. However, gender discrimination continues to be a daunting challenge and the Government will continue to pursue all measures, in a concerted manner, to eliminate discrimination against women and to translate the *dejure* rights into *defacto* enjoyment of rights and equal results. The Government commits to pursue the National Policy on Empowerment of Women, 2001 and the Plan of Action that is being adopted to give effect to this policy, strengthen gender budgeting and the Women Component Plan and adopt planning strategies that enhance socio-economic gains for women, which in turn would lead to empowerment of women.[14]

The Convention on the Elimination of All Forms of Discrimination Against Women (CEDAW), also called the Women's Convention and the International Bill of Rights for Women, was adopted by the UN General Assembly in 1979, the first, comprehensive internationally binding document on women's rights. Currently, 177 countries 90% of the members of the United Nations are party to the Convention. For the first time, 25 years ago, we had an internationally recognized definition of discrimination against women:

Article 1: The term 'discrimination against women' shall mean any distinction, exclusion or restriction made on the basis of sex which has the effect or purpose of impairing or nullifying the recognition, enjoyment or exercise by women, irrespective of their marital status, on a basis of equality of men and women, of human rights and fundamental freedoms in the political, economic, social, cultural, civil or any other field.

Set against this vision is the reality of many women's lives. Of the 1.2 billion poor people in today's world, an estimated 70% are women. The Convention recognizes that is situations of poverty, women have the least access to food, health and education training, opportunities for employment and other needs. The Convention provides us with a comprehensive framework for turning aspirations to equality and justice into concrete measures to tackle the poverty, discrimination and exclusion that women face.

The Convention seems ever more relevant and urgent to the lives of women at the turn of the 21st century. Indicators show that women are living in increasing poverty. The UN Millennium Declaration, committing all 191 Member States to the Millennium Development Goals, renews the resolution of the international community to tackling the most pressing problems by 2015. Gender issues figure strongly. With this political will, backed up by the tireless work of women's organizations worldwide, we may be able to turn the aspirations of women into realities.

The Convention deals with ten key areas:

- it calls for measures to suppress the exploitation of women in trafficking and prostitution;
- the equal rights of women to full participation in political and public life, including the right to vote, to stand for election, to participate in the formulation of government policy, to hold public office;
- an equal right of women to represent their country at the international level;
- the equal rights of women to acquire, change or retain their nationality, as well as an equal right with respect to the nationality of their children;
- equal rights of women in education, including training and career opportunities;
- equal rights of women in employment, including the right to work, the right to the same employment opportunities, promotion, job security and benefits and conditions of service, the right to equal remuneration, right to safeguard the function of reproduction; a duty of care imposed on states to provide for maternity benefits;
- the equal rights of women to access health care services, including family planning and maternity services;
- discrimination in relation to rural women: to take measures to ensure the equal participation of rural women in and benefit from rural development to access health and education services and to assist economic development, as well as equal treatment in land and agrarian reform as well as in land resettlement schemes;

- equality with men before the law, an equal right to conclude contracts, administer property; and
- matters relating to marriage and family relations: the same right as men to enter into marriage, right to freely choose a spouse, to enter a marriage with free and full consent, same rights and responsibilities during marriage and its dissolution, the same rights and responsibilities as parents, with regard to guardianship, wardship, trusteeship and adoption of children, the same rights to reproductive freedom, the same rights, including the right to choose a family name, profession or occupation, the same right in respect of ownership, acquisition, management, administration, enjoyment and disposition of property.[15]

While violence against women continues to increase in India, the law and the criminal justice system have in many ways failed to respond to or deal effectively with this. Indeed the rate of conviction is reported to be less than 10% in crimes against women.[16] In fact, apart from paying lip service to issues of violence against women from time to time, very little effort has been made in the past few years by the state to actually curb or deal with the violence, both in terms of making the law more sensitive to women and in terms of enforcing it. Women therefore continue to suffer without adequate legal or other redress. Although some amendments took place in the early eighties, the substantive laws relating to violence against women are inadequate and do not reflect the violence women experience.[17]

It is a matter of great concern that the UGC through its study centres wanted to expedite women empowerment through teaching, research and counseling. However, UGC opened most of these centres, in cities where they have not much role to play. In Delhi only, there are 5 women study centres while these must be located in Universities in backward areas where there is a great need for them.

However, there is marginal reality of the concept of empowerment of women which can be ascertained from the plethora of legislation passed to ensure women empowerment.

Institutional Mechanisms for the Advancement of Women

Institutional mechanisms for the advancement of women include institutions of different types—government, non-government, central and state government, local government—which support the cause of women's advancement. Institutional mechanisms for integrating gender perspectives in policy and planning include such innovative features as 'gender budgeting'.

The term National Machinery refers more narrowly to bodies designated by the state to promote the status of women. In India, such government bodies are themselves composed of a set of structures and systems. For the bureaucratic structure, the DWCD can be seen as being at the centre:

- The Department of Women and Child Development set-up in 1985 as a part of the Ministry of Human Resources Development and at present Ministry of Women and Child Welfare is the nodal department in the Government of India to look after advancement of women and children.
- The National Commission for Women was established by an Act of Parliament in 1992 to safeguard the rights and interests of women. It acts as a statutory ombudsperson for women. The annual report of NCW containing recommendations is placed in Parliament by the Government of India with a detailed compliance report.
- The National Institute of Public Co-operation and Child Development assists the Department in the areas of training and research. Objectives of the Institute include the development and promotion voluntary action in social development. It has developed innovative gender training/sensitization modules.
- Rashtriya Mahila Kosh (National Credit Fund for Women), established in 1993, has as its main objective facilitation of credit support or micro-finance to poor women, as an instrument of socio-economic changes and development.
- Central Social Welfare Board is an umbrella organization networking the activities of State Social Welfare Boards and voluntary organizations. It implements a number of schemes including Family Counseling Centres, Short Stay Homes, Rape Crisis Intervention Centres, crèches for children of working mothers, etc.
- State Departments of Women and Child Development, State Commissions for Women and State Social Welfare Boards form part of the institutional system in most of the states. Women's Development Corporations (WDCs) have been set-up in most of the states to help the government implement the programme.
- Gender focal points (Women's Cells) have been formed in the ministries in the development sector, including Education, Rural Development, Labour, Agriculture.
- The Panchyati Raj Institution and urban local self-government bodies provide a framework for women's empowerment in political participation and decision-making all over the country.
- A Parliamentary Committee on Empowerment of Women was constitutes by the Lok Sabha (Lower House of the Parliament) in 1997, and reconstituted in 2004, to review the effectiveness of measures taken empowerment of women. This has 30 members from the Lok Sabha and from the Rajya Sabha (Upper House of the Parliament).
- The Planning Commission carries out periodical reviews of programmes and policies impacting on women.

- Commissions and Committees are set-up from time to time to focus on specific areas. A focal point on the human rights of women has been set-up in the NHRC.
- A number of institutions are in place to help women get speedier justice like wider recruitment of women police cell in police stations and exclusive women police stations. Also Rape Crisis intervention Centres have been set-up in police stations in some big have been set-up. The States are being requested to set-up Family Courts and earmark one Fast Track Court, if there is more than one in a district, to deal exclusively with cases of sexual abuse and cruelty in marriage relating to women.

Partnerships

The agencies listed above draw in persons from the voluntary sector, and the women's movement. Such partnerships have been essential to the formulation and implementation of approaches to gender equality. The country wide network of more than 12,000 voluntary organizations has played a very significant role in the empowerment of women and development of children as they share the major burden of implementing governmental policies and programmes. NGOs have demonstrated viable alternatives in the areas of women's literacy, support services, micro-credit for poor women, employment and income generation, gender sensitization, organizing women into SHGs, fight against atrocities, etc. The various programmes and schemes of the Department are based on the concept of SHG that have been set-up with the co-operation of organizations at the grassroots level.

Different departments of the government also work in partnership with bilateral, multilateral and UN agencies on women- specific and women related projects. Examples include the gender budgeting and gender statistics initiatives, in which UNIFEM played an important role, or the State Human Development reports initiated with the assistance of UNDP.[18]

Realising that there is a wide gap between the goals enunciated in the Constitution, law, policies, plans and programmes and the *defacto* situation, the Government adopted a 'National Policy for the Empowerment of Women' in the year 2001. The goals of this Policy are to bring about the advancement, development and empowerment of women. The objectives of this Policy are to create an environment for the full development of women through positive economic and social policies, enable them to realize their full potential, ensure equal access to education, health care, employment, social security and public office and participation in decision-making in social, political and economic spheres and thereby ensure *defacto* equality to women. It also aims at changing societal attitudes and community practices by active participation an involvement of both men and women, mainstreaming a gender perspective in the development processes and eliminating discrimination and all forms of violence against women and girl children and building and strengthening partnerships with civil society, particularly women's organizations.

The policy prescribes affirmative action in areas such as the legal system, decision-making structures, mainstreaming gender perspectives in development processes; economic empowerment of women through increased access to resources like micro-credit, better resource allocation through Women's Component Plan, gender budget exercises and development of Gender Development Indices; and social empowerment of women through universalization of education, adopting an holistic approach to women's health, etc. The policy takes into account the new development initiated by the process of economic reforms and impact of globalization and liberalization on women, particularly on those in the informal sector.

The operational strategies of the above policy envisages time bound action plans to be drawn up by all Central and State Ministries in consultation with the DWCD and the National and State Commissions for Women, to translate the policy into a set of concrete actions and measurable goals to be achieved by 2010. It will also identify and commit resources, define responsibilities for implementation, put in place budgeting process. This Policy provides for National and State Councils for monitoring the operationalisation of the policy. The Prime Minister will head the National Council and the Chief Ministers, the State Councils. A draft National Plan of Action for implementation of the Policy has been drawn up and is in the process of finalization. The Plan of Action identifies the commitment of resources and responsibilities for implementation and strengthens institutional mechanisms and structures for monitoring.[19]

Critical Areas of Concern: Beijing Platform for Action

- *Poverty*: prevent women becoming the most poor in the world
- *Education*: address illiteracy amongst women and ensure more girls continue school; educate men and boys about inequality and women's rights.
- *Health*: increase women's access to health services, including preventive care; women's sexual and reproductive rights.
- *Violence against women*: make laws which work, policing which is effective in bringing violent men to court and raise awareness.
- *Armed conflict*: bring women into peace negotiations, reduce arms expenditure, protect women refugees.
- *Women and economic activities*: ensure rights at work, help women to combine families and jobs, give women access to credit.
- *Participation of women in decision-making*: promote and enable participation at every level, from home and village to national parliament.
- *National machinery*: strengthen and finance women's ministry, check laws are working equally, keep separate statistics for each sex so that progress can be monitored.
- *Human rights of women*: implement CEDAW and ensure women and men know what it says.

- *Women and the media*: access to the media for women and balanced reporting on women's issues.
- *Environment*: monitor the effect of the environment on women; and promote their participation in decision-making processes.
- *The girl child*: ensure her equal education, improve her status and work against negative practices such as sex determination, child labour and child marriages.

Millennium Development Goals

The Millennium Development Goals commit the international community to an expanded vision of development, one that vigorously promotes human development as the key to sustaining social and economic progress in all countries and recognizes the importance of creating a global partnership for development. The goals have been commonly accepted as a framework for measuring development progress. The key focus areas of MDG are:

- Eradicate extreme poverty and hunger,
- Achieve universal primary education,
- Promote gender equality and empower women,
- Reduce child mortality,
- Improve maternal health,
- Combat HIV/AIDS, malaria and other diseases,
- Ensure environmental sustainability, and
- Develop a global partnership for development.

http://www. undp.org/mdg/

International Women's Day (8 March)

International Women's Day (8 March) is an occasion marked by women's groups around the world. This date is also commemorated at the United Nations and is designated in many countries as a national holiday. When women on all continents, often divided by national boundaries and by ethnic, linguistic, cultural, economic and political differences, come together to celebrate their Day, they can look back to a tradition that represents at least nine decades of struggle for equality, justice, peace and development.

Conclusion

To realize economic empowerment of women, the Tenth Plan envisages to ensure provision of training, employment and income generation activities with both forward and backward linkages with the ultimate aim of making all women economically independent and self-reliant. The Plan aims to achieve this through: (1) organizing women into SHGs under various poverty alleviation programmes and offering them a range of economic options and support measures to enhance their capabilities and earning capacities; (2) ensuring that the women in the informal sector are given special attention with regard to improving their working conditions; (3) ensure that the benefits of training and extension in agriculture and allied activities reach women and also issue joint titledeeds for the spouses under social forestry and joint forest management programmes; (4) ensure that employers fulfil their legal obligations towards women workers; (5) retraining and upgrading skills of women displaced by technology so that they can take up jobs in new areas of employment and formulating appropriate policies and programmes to promote alternate self and wage employment; (6) initiating affirmative action to ensure atleast 30 percent reservation for women in services in the Public Sector; and (7) increasing access to credit for women.[20]

Why do we tolerate violence?

The solution to violence against women lies not just in making rules, holding conventions, etc. This requires a change in the attitude. Every adult—parent, teacher, sibling, etc. should take the responsibility of making the child understand the equality of genders, the need to respect a person irrespective of gender. We can have rules and legislations and laws to punish the guilty but that can not serve the purpose in the long-run because every rule has a loop hole. Although the laws and punishments are extremely useful as deterrents and they should be in place to punish the guilty but the real change can take place only when there is a change in the mindset—not only of men but also of women! Boys and men need to realize that they can not get away with any wrong behaviour, that a woman will not take it lying low and girls and women should get rid of the 'I'll tolerate anything' mode. Only when you respect yourself can you expect others to respect you. Therefore, the solution is—make every child aware, make every adult responsible and accountable. Guide, teach, punish if guilty.[21]

The need to ensure women empowerment needs sincerity, dedication, earnestness on the part of decision-making authorities and especially by women occupying high offices.

Women empowerment mission is firmly rooted in the Constitution of India. The constitution does not change but in response to new challenges, the programme based upon women empowerment, must move foreward in a state perpetual evolution. This evolution is not only continual but also geared and committed to the real needs of women empowerment. This would make the women empowerment movement a reality. However, if all the ideals enshrined in the Constitution of India, laws enacted by legislature are not implemented in letter and spirit, the process of women empowerment will remain ornamental and a paper tiger indicating thereby that women empowerment is only a myth.

Union and State Government of India must become practical in the process of translating the concept of women empowerment into reality otherwise a lip service to the concept would make women empowerment a myth as is true of our country.

On the huge hill,
Cagged and steep
Truth stands, and,
he that will reach her,
about must, about must goes.

—*John Donne (c. 1593), Satyre 111-179*

Notes and References

1. Artee Agarwal, Initiatives State in Gender Empowerment : A Study of Uttar Pradesh, IDRC and CRDI International Development Research Centre, Workshop Report, A Decade of Women's Empowerment through Local Govt. in India, Oct. 20-21, 2003, New Delhi, pp. 8, 9, 16.
2. National Commission for Women, 2001, Gender Equity—Making it Happen, pp. 29-30.
3. *Ibid.*, p. vii
4. State Parties shall take all appropriate measure : (a) To modify the social and cultural patterns of conduct of men and women, with a view to achieving the elimination of prejudices and customary and all other practices which are based on the idea of the inferiroty or the superiority of either of the sexes or on stererotype roles of men and women".
5. This provision relates to elimination of discrimination in all matters relating to marriage and family relations.
6. The Hindu Succession Amendment Bill, 2004, Statement of Objects and Reasons, Clause 3.
7. Bina Agarwal, Far from Gender Equality", Lawyers Collective, Feb. 2005, pp. 16-18.
8. Vishaka *v.* State of Rajasthan, AIR 1997 SC 3011.
9. Chairman Railway Board *v.* Chandrima Das, AIR 2000 SC 988.
10. C.B. Mudhamma *v.* Union of India, (1979) 4 SCC 260, Air India *v.* Nargesh Meerza AIR 1981 SC 1829, Govt. of Andhra Pradesh *v.* P.B. Vijaykumar, 1995, II CLR 1128.
11. Ahmedabad Women Action Group (AWAG) *v.* Union of India, AIR 1997 SC 3614.
12. Ms. Githa Hariharan *v.* Reserve Bank of India, AIR 1999 SC 1149.
13. Platform for Action—10 Year after India: Country Report, Deptt. of Women and Child Development, Ministry of Human Resource Development, GOI, p. 58.
14. Deptt. of Women and Child Development, Ministry of Human Resource Development, GOI, 2005, pp. 7, 98.
15. Ann Stewart, British Council, The Women Studies Network—A Collaborative Initiative of British Council and Women Studies Centres of Universities in India, July 2005, pp. 1, 2.
16. "Crime in India", National Crime Record Bureau, Ministry of Home Affairs, Govt. of India, 1997.
17. Kirti Singh, "Law, Violence and Women in India, Study Supported by UNIFEM/UNICEF, New Delhi, p. 1.
18. Platform for Action—10 Year after India: Country Report, Deptt. of Women and Child Development, Ministry of Human Resource Development, GOI, pp. 55-56.
19. Deptt. of Women and Child Development, Ministry of Human Resource Development, Govt. of India's II and III, Periodic Report on the Convention on the Elimination All Forms of Discrmination against Women, (CEDAW), 1997-2005., GOI, 2005, pp. 7, 21.
20. Deptt. of Women and Child Development, Ministry of Human Resource Development, GOI, 2005, pp. 7, 65.
21. British Council of India, Discussion on Forum, p. 7.

APPENDIX 12.1

Selected Gender Development Indicators

Sl. No.	Indicators	Female	Male	Total	Female	Male	Total
1	2	3	4	5	6	7	8
Demography and Vital Statistics							
1.	Population (in million 1991 and 2001 (Census)	407.1	439	846.3	495.7	531.3	1027.0
2.	Decennial Growth (1981 of 2001) (Census)	24.93	24.41	24.58	21.79	23.93	21.34
3.	Sex Ratio (1991 and 2001) Census	927			933		
4.	Juvenile Sex Ratio (1991 and 2001) Census	945			927		
5.	Life Expetancy at Birth (in years of 1991 and 2001) Census	58.1	57.1		65.3	62.3	
6.	Mean Age at Marriage 1981 and 2001 (Census)	17.9	23.3		19.3	24.0	
Health and Family Welfare							
7.	Birth Rate (per 1000 in 1981 and 2002) SRS			35.6			25.0
8.	Death Rate (per 1000 in 1981 and 2002) SRS	12.7	12.4	12.5	7.7	8.4	8.1
9.	Infant Mortality Rate (per 1000 live birth in 1990 and 2002) SRS	81	78	80	65	62.	64
10.	Child Mortality Rate (per 100 live births in 1990 and 2002) SRS	40.4	36.6	38.4	71.6	70.5	71.1
11.	Maternal Mortality Rate (per 100000 live births in 1997 and 1998) SRS	408			407		
Literacy and Education							
12.	Literacy Rate (1991 and 2001) in percentage (Census)	39.29	64.13	52.21	53.67	75.26.	64.48
13.	Gross Enrolment Ratio (1990-91 and 2002-03)						
	Class I-V (Ministry of HRD)	85.5	114.0	100.1	93.1	97.5	95.3
	Class VI-VIII (Ministry of HRD)	47.0	76.6	62.1	56.2	65.3	61.0
14.	Dropout rate (1990-91 and 2002-03) in %						
	Class I-V (Ministry of HRD)	46.0	40.1	42.6	33.7	35.8	34.6
	Class I-VIII (Ministry of HRD)	65.1	59.1	60.9	52.3	53.4	52.8

(Contd.)

1	2	3	4	5	6	7	8
15.	Work Participation Rate (1991 and 2001) in percentage	22.3	51.6	37.8	25.6	57.6	39.2
16.	Organized Sector (number in Millions in (1981 and 2001) (DGE & T)	2.80	20.50	22.85	4.83	23.20	28.11
17.	Public Sector (number in millions in 1981 and 1999) (Employment Review)	1.5	14.0	15.5	2.8	16.8	19.4
18.	Government (number in millions in 1981 and 1997)	1.2	9.7	10.9	1.6	9.1	10.1
	Women's Representation in Decision-making						
19.	Administration (No. in IAS and IPS in 1997-2000)	579	7347	8036	645	7860	8460
20.	PRIs (No. in Figures in 1985 and 2001)	318	630	948	725	1997	2722
21.	Parliament (No. in 1991 and 2004)	77	712	789	72	712	784
22.	Central Council of Ministers (No. in 1985 and 2001)	4	36	40	8	66	74

Source: Office of the Registrar General of India.

Bibliography

Abraham, A., English life and manner in the latter, Middle Ages (London, 1913).

Achar, M.R. and Venkanna's T., Dowry Prohibition Act and Rules (1990), The Law Book Company Pvt. Ltd., Allahabad.

Aggrawal, Nomita, Handbook on Lok Adalat in India (1991); Interest Publications, New Delhi.

Agrawal, Raj Kumar, Matrimonial Remedies Under Hindu Law, N.M. Tripathi, Bombay.

Agrawal, S.K. (Dr.), Public Interest Litigation in India, A Critique (1985), Indian Law Institute, New Delhi Publications.

Agresto, Hohn, The Supreme Court and Constitutional Democracy (1986).

Aiyar, A.K., Law and Practice Relating to Marriage in India and Burma, University Book Agency, Lahore (1937).

Alexander, Robert. J., *The Entrepreneur, The Manager and Economic Development,* MacMillan Company, New York, 1962.

Allen, C.K., Law in the Making (1958).

Allen, L.L., *Starting and Succeeding in Your Own Business,* Grosset and Dunlop, New York, 1968.

Altekar, A.S., The Position of Women in Hindu Civilisation, 1974, Verry Lawrence Inc. Connecticut.

Amit Sarkar, Social Justice—Rhetoric and Reality (1987).

Anand, C.L., Equality, Justice and Reverse Discrimination in India (1987).

Anderson, J.N.D., Islamic Law Reforms in Muslim World. Anirudh Prasad: Social Engineering—Constitutional Protection of Weaker Sections in India (1979).

Anderson, Robert Lee and Dunkelbert, John D., *Entrepreneurship,* Harper and Row Publishers, New York.

Anna, V., Socio-Economic Basis of Women Entrepreneurship, *SEDME,* Vol. 17, No. 1, 1990.

Anthony, M.J., Women Rights (1985), Dialogue Publication, New Delhi.

Arora, S.K., Economic Development and Female Participation in Work: An Interdistrict Analysis of Haryana, *Kautilya,* 1(1-2), 1980, pp. 50-65.

Aryar, A.P., Perspective of Welfare State (1979).

Ashmore, M. Catherine *et. al., Programme for Acquiring Competence in*

Entrepreneurship, National Centre for Research in Vocational Education, Ohio State University, Columbus, Ohio, 1983.

Austin, Granville, The Indian Constitution—The Cornerstone of a Nation (1966).

Azad, Gulab Singh, Development of Entrepreneurship Among Indian Women, *SEDME,* Vol. XVI, No. 3, 1989.

Azad, Maulana, Abul Kalam, Tarjuman-ul-Quran, Sahitya Academic, New Delhi.

Banerjee, D.N., Our Fundamental Rights—Their Nature and Extent (1960).

Banga, T.R., *Project Planning and Entrepreneurship Development,* C.B.S. Publishers and Distributors, Shahdara, Delhi, 1984.

Barett, Constitutional Law Cases and Materials (1959).

Baron, A.S., Women in Management, Another Look, *Personnel Administrator,* Vol. 29, August 1984, p. 14.

Basu, D.O., Shorter Constitution (1988).

Batla, M.L. and Batla, S., Maintenance, Marriage and Divorce (1978).

Baty, Gordon B., *Entrepreneurship, Playing to Win,* D.B. Taraporevala Sons and Company, Bombay, 1979.

Baumback, Clifford M. and Mancuso, Joseph R., *Entrepreneurship and Venture Management,* D.B. Taraporevala Sons and Co. Pvt. Ltd., Bombay, 1981.

Baxi, Upendera (Dr.), Alternatives in Development: Law—The Crisis of Indian Legal System (1982), Vikas Publishing House Pvt. Ltd., New Delhi.

Baxi, Upendera (Dr.), Laches and the Right to Constitutional Remedies (1975).

Baxi, Upendera (Dr.), Law and Poverty—Critical Essays (1988), N.M. Tirpathi Pvt. Ltd., Bombay.

Baxi, Upendera (Dr.), Towards A Sociology of Indian Law (1986).

Bhagat, D.P., Beauty Parlours, *Women's Era,* New Delhi, 1988.

Bhandari, Arvind, Women Deserve a Better Deal, *The Tribune,* March 8, 2000.

Bhanushali, S.G., *Entrepreneurship Development: An Interdisciplinary Approach,* Himalayan Publishing House, Bombay, 1987.

Bhat, Tushar, Entrepreneurial Skill of Gujarat Women, *Economic Times,* 13 August 1978, p. 4: 1-5.

Bhatia, B.S. *et. al.,* Women Entrepreneurship: Explored and Unexplored Opportunities, *Gender Sensitivity,* TTTI, Chandigarh, 2000.

Bhatia, B.S., New Industrial Entrepreneurs: Their Origin and Problems, *Journal of General Management,* Vol. 2, No. 1, Autumn 1975.

Bhatnagar, S., etc., Social Justice and Equality in India (1987).

Bhatt, Ela *Rt.*, Organising Self Employed Women: The SEWA Experiment, *Indian and Foreign Review,* 21(21), August 1984, pp. 22-25.

Bhattacharya, S.K. and Akhouri, M.M.P., Profile of Small Industry Entrepreneur, *SEDME,* June 1975.

Bisht, N.S., Mishra, R.C. and Srivastava, A.K., *Entrepreneurship: Reflections and Investigations,*. Chugh Publications, Allahabad, 1989.

Bisht, Narendra S. and Sharma, Pamila K., *Entrepreneurship: Expectations and Experiences,* Himalaya Publishing House, New Delhi, 1991.

Blackstone, Commentaries on the Laws of England (1925).

Borala, P.T. (Dr.), Human Rights and Social Justice (1981).

Brownell, A., Legal Aid in U.S.A.

Brush, Candida G. and Hisrich, Robert D., Women Entrepreneurs: Strategic Origins Impact on Growth, *Frontiers of Entrepreneurship Research,* Massachusetts, USA, 1988.

Bryce, Modern Democracy, Vol. II, 1921.

Burns, Paul and Dewhurst (Eds.), *Small Business and Entrepreneurship,* MacMillan Education Limited, London, 1990.

Cannon, T. *et. al., The Nature, the Role and the Impact of Small Business Research,* Glower, Alder Shot, 1989.

Cappelletti, M., Access to Justice: A World Survey, Vol. I (1981).

Chagla, M.C., Law, Liberty and Life (1950).

Carter, Nancy, *Reducing Barriers between Genders: Deterrence's in New Firm Start ups,* Paper presented at the National Academy of Management Meetings, Entrepreneurship Division, Dallas, Texas, USA, 1994.

Carter, S. and Cannon, T., *Women as Entrepreneurs: A Study of Female Business Owners, Their Motivations, Experiences and Strategies for Success,* Academic Press, London, 1992.

Casson, Mark, *The Entrepreneur: An Economic Theory,* Martin Robertson, Oxford, 1982. .

Chandra, Shanti Kohli, *Development of Women Entrepreneurship* in *India,* Mittal Publications, New Delhi, 1991, p. 70.

Chaturvedi, Maheshwar Nath, Liberalizing the Requirement of Standing in Public Interest Litigation.

Chaudhary, P.K., Bhaiji, S. and Asokan, Citicorp/Citibank serves women entrepreneurs, *Management Review,* Vol. 74, February 1985, p. 6.

Chaudhary, P.K., Bhaiji, S. and Asokan, M., Banks and Women's Enterprise Development: A Comparison of Approaches in India and U.K., *SEDME,* 1997.

Chittley, Commentary on the Constitution of India.

Chowdhury, S.B., Public Interest Litigation and Status of Locus Standi in Different Legal Systems (1981).

Choudhary, K.V.R., Successful Characteristics of Rural Entrepreneurship, *SEDME,* 1980.

Clarke, P., *Small Business: How They Survive and Succeed,* David and Charks Publishers Limited, Great Britain, 1972.

Cordozo, The Nature of Judicial Process (1957).

Cunningham, J. Barton and Lischeron, Joe, Defining Entrepreneurship, *The*

Journal of Small Business Management, Vol. 29, No.1, January, 1991, p. 45.

Curran, J., Bolton fifty years on : *A Review and Analysis of Small Business Research* in *Britain*, 1971-86, Small Business Research Trust, London, 1986.

Daftary, Sharayu, Women and Business: An untapped potential, *Journal of the Indian Merchants Chamber*, 75(12), December 1981, pp. 9-10.

Dangwal, R.R. (Dr.), New Focus Towards Social Justice (1996), Raj Publishing House, Lucknow.

Dant, Rajiv P. *et. al.*, Participation Patterns of Women in Franchising, *The Journal of Small Business Management*, April 1996.

Dayal, S.R., Law Relating to Dowry (1995), Premier Publishing Company, Allahabad.

Denning Sir, Alfred, Freedom Under the Law (1949).

Desai, Justice Ashok, A., Justice *Vs.* Justices (1994), Taxmann Allied Services Pvt. Ltd.

Deshpande, Manohar U., *Entrepreneurship Development of Small Scale Industries*, Deep and Deep Publications, New Delhi,1984.

Deshta, Kiran, Uniform Civil Code: Retrospect and Prospect (1995), Deep and Deep Publications, New Delhi.

Deshta, Sunil (Dr.), Lok Adalats in India (1995), Deep and Deep Publications, New Delhi.

Desingu, Setty, E., Developing Entrepreneurship Among Women, *Man and Development*, 2(3), September 1980, pp. 92-96.

Desingu, Setty, E., *Developing New Entrepreneurs*, Entrepreneurship Development Institute of India, Ahmedabad, 1987.

Dhagamwar, Vasudhu, Woman and Divorce (1987), Somaiya Publication Pvt. Ltd., Bombay.

Dhameja, S.K. and Sharma, D.O., *Opportunities and Challenges of Women Entrepreneurs*, TITI, Chandigarh, 1995.

Diwan, Paras, Dowry and Protection to Married Women (1995), Deep and Deep Publications, New Delhi.

Diwan, Paras, Indian Constitution—A Document of Peoples Faith and Aspiration (1981).

Diwan, Paras, Modern Hindu Law, Allahabad Law Agency, Allahabad.

Diwan, Paras, Torture and Right to Human Dignity (1981).

Dolinsky, Arthur L., Caputo, Richard K. and Pasumarty, Kishore, Long-Term Entrepreneurship Patterns: A National Study of Black and While Female Entry and Stayer Status Differences, *Journal of Small Business Management*, January, Vol. 32, 1994.

Doraiswamy, R., Women and Self Reliance, *SEDME*, September, 1995.

Dowling, Colette, *Cinderalla Complex—Women's Hidden Fear of Independence*, Fontana Paperback, 1981.

Dr. Sinha Niraj, Woman and Violence, Vikas Publishing House Pvt. Ltd., 1984.

Dracker, Peter F., *Innovations and Entrepreneurship: Practice and Principles,* Willian Heinemann Limited, London, 1985.

Drost, P.N., Human Rights and Legal Rights (1982).

EDII Faculty and Experts, *A Handbook of New Entrepreneurs: With Special Reference to Science and Technology Target Groups,* Entrepreneurship Development Institute of India, Ahmedabad, 1986.

Ewener, J.A., Portrait of Two Artists as Young Entrepreneurs, *Canadian Business,* Vol. 58, September 1985, p. 166.

Finney, S. Ruth, *Towards a typology of Women Entrepreneurs—Their Business Venture and Family,* East-West Centre, East-West Technology and Development Institute, Honololu, Hawaii (USA), 1977.

Flerida Ruth P. Romero, Women and Law, U.P. Law Centre, The Asia Foundation (1983).

Freidmann, Law in a Changing Society (1950), University Broth. House, Delhi.

Gajendragadkar, P.B.J., Law, Liberty and Social Justice (1962), Asia Publishing House, Bombay.

Gajendragadkar, P.B.J., Rule of Law, Indian Parliament and Fundamental Rights (1959).

Gandhi, Indira, Self-Employment for Women, *Social Welfare,* 28(10), January 1982, pp. 1-2.

Gautam, Vinayshil (Ed.), *Technical Entrepreneurship: Issues of Research and Application,* Global Business Press, New Delhi, 1992.

Ghicklich, P., Women's Management Training in a Ghetto, *Personnel Management,* Vol. 17, September 1985, pp. 39-43.

Ghosh, S.K., Women and Crime, Ashish Publishing House, New Delhi.

Gilder, George, *The Spirit of Enterprise,* Viking Publishers, London, 1985.

Goffee, R. and Scase, R., *Women in Charge: The Experiences of Female Entrepreneurs,* Allen and Unwin, London, 1985.

Gomes, F., Why Women Must Make a Choice Between Business and Home Life?, *International Management* (Europe Edition), July 1985, pp. 40-52.

Goode, William J., The Family (1960).

Govind Das, Supreme Court in Quest of Identity (1987).

Gupta, D.P., Dimensions of Social Justice (1983).

Gupta, M.C., *Entrepreneurship in Small Sector Industries,* Anmol Publications, New Delhi, 1987.

Gupta, R., *Industrial Entrepreneurship,* Printwell Publication, Jaipur, 1992.

Gupta, R.S., Windening the Rules of Locus Standi.

Gupta, Uma, Supreme Court and Civil Liberties (1988).

Hakim, C., *Occupational Segregation,* Department of Employment, Research Paper No. 9, London, 1979.

Haksar, R.N., Constitutional Problems of Federal India (1988). Halsbury's Law of England; (Third Edition) (1921).

Halshouse, L.T., The Elements of Social Justice (London, George Allen), pp. 114-15.

Hamilton, Hedayas, 1945.

Harbison, F. and Myers, Charles A., *Education, Manpower and Economic Growth: Strategies of Human Resources Development,* New York, McGraw Hill Service in International Development.

Harbison, F., Entrepreneurial Organisation as a factor in Economic Development, *Journal of Political Economy,* 1956, 64, pp. 364-79.

Harper, Malcolm, *Entrepreneurship for the Poor,* Intermediate Technology Publications, London, 1984.

Harper, Uschi Kraus, Towards a Typology of Enterprising Women in Poor Communities, *Frontiers of Entrepreneurship Research,* Massachusetts, U.S.A., 1992.

Hate, Chandrakala, Hindu Women and Her Future, New Book Co., Bombay (1948).

Heggade, O.O., Development of Women Entrepreneurs; Problems and Prospects, *Economic Affairs,* Vol. 26, No. 1, Jan.-March, 1981, pp. 39-50.

Hidayatullah, M., Highways and Bye-Laws of Justice (1983).

Hisrich, Robert D. and Brush, Candida, G., Women Entrepreneurs: A Longitudinal Study, *Frontiers of Entrepreneurship Research,* Massachusetts, USA, 1987.

Hisrich, Robert D. and Fuldop, Gyula, Women Entrepreneurs in Controlled Economies: A Hungarian Perspective, *Frontiers of Entrepreneurship Research,* Massachusetts (USA), 1993.

Holmquist, Carin and Sundin, Eli Sabeth, *Indian Economic Survey (1999-2000),* Govt. of India, New Delhi, March 2000.

Holmquist, Carin and Sundin, Eli Sabeth, Indian Women in Business, *Indian and Foreign Review,* 18(4), December 1980, pp. 19-21.

Holmquist, Carin and Sundin, Eli Sabeth, International Conference on *Women Entrepreneurs,* 1981, November 27, New Delhi.

Holmquist, Carin and Sundin, Eli Sabeth, Women as Entrepreneurs in Sweden: Conclusions from a Survey, *Frontiers of Entrepreneurship Research,* Massachusetts, USA, 1988.

Imam, M., The Indian Supreme Court and the Constitution.

Iyer, V.R. Krishna, Equal Justice and Forensic Process—Truth or Myth (1986), Eastern Book Company, Lucknow.

Iyer, V.R. Krishna, Human Rights and the Law (1984).

Iyer, V.R. Krishna, Indian Justice-Perspective and Problems (1984), Vedpal Law House, Indore. ,

Iyer, V.R. Krishna, Indian Social Justice in Crisis (1983), Affiliated East-.West Press Ltd., New Delhi.

Iyer, V.R. Krishna, Judicial Justice—A New Focus Toward Social Justice (1985).

Iyer, V.R. Krishna, Justice and Beyond (1982).

Iyer, V.R. Krishna, Law and the People (1972).

Iyer, V.R. Krishna, Law and the Urban Poor in India (1988).

Iyer, V.R. Krishna, Law in India: Some Contemporary Challenges (1982).

Iyer, V.R. Krishna, The Social Dimensions of Law and Justice in Contemporary India-The Dynamics of New Jurisprudence (1981).

Iyer, V.R. Krishna, Law *versus* Justice—Problems and Solutions (1981), Deep and Deep Publications, New Delhi.

Iyer, V.R. Krishna, Law, Freedom and Change (1980).

Iyer, V.R. Krishna, Law, Lawyers and Justice (1989).

Iyer, V.R. Krishna, Processual Justice to Poor (1973).

Iyer, V.R. Krishna, Social Justice: Sunset or Dawn (1987), Eastern Book Company, Lucknow.

Iyer, V.R. Krishna, Socialist Humanism and People's Justice (1983).

Iyer, V.R. Krishna, The Social Mission of Law (1976).

Iyer, V.R. Krishna, Islamic Law in Modern India.

Iyer, V.R. Krishna, Judicial Justice: A New Focus Towards Social Justice (1985), N.M. Tripathi Pvt. Ltd., Bombay.

Jaffar, S.M., Entrepreneurial Skill of Gujarat Women, *Economic Times*, 13 August 1978, p. 4:1.

Jain, Deviki, British Constitution (1950).

Jain, Deviki, Indian Women.

Jain, Deviki, Some Characteristics of Indian Constitution (1953).

Juneja, P.C., Equal Access to Justice (1993), The Bright Law House, Rohtak.

Jain, Deviki, The Law of Constitution (1948).

Jain, Gautam Raj and Ansari, M. Akbar, *Self-made Impact Making Entrepreneurs,* Entrepreneurship Development Institute of India, Ahmedabad, 1988.

Jain, M.P., Indian Constitutional Law (1987), N.M. Tripathi: Bombay.

Jayakar, Roshni, First Lady of Indian Shipping, *Economic Times,* 24 March 1985, pp. 4:1-4.

John, Usha Emerging Corporate Women, *Economic Times* (Supplement), 25 November 1981, pp. 11:1-5.

Jyothi, V. and Prasad, G., A Profile of Potential Rural Women Entrepreneurs, *SEDME,* Vol. XX(I), 1993.

Kagzi, M.C. Jain, Present Constitutional Issues and Views (1988).

Kane, P.V., History of Hindu Dharmshastra.

Kalam, A.P.J. Abdul, *20th J.P Memorial Lecture* delivered at Jawaharlal Nehru University, New Delhi, Dec. 7, 1999.

Kanitkar, Ajit and Contractor, Nalinee; *In Search of Identity—The Women Entrepreneurs of India,* EDI(I)., Ahmedabad, 1992.

Kaplan, Eileen, Women Entrepreneurs: Constructing a framework to examine venture success and failure, *Frontiers of Entrepreneurship Research,* Massachusetts, USA, 1988.

Kaur, I., Status of Hindu Women in India, Chug Publications, Delhi (1983).

Kaur, Jaspreet, How Free is the Women of Today, *The Tribune,* March 8, 2000.

Keith, A.B., Constitutional Law (1966).

Kelkar, R.V., Maintenance Denied to Tribal Wifes?

Kelsen, Hans, What is Justice? (1957).

Kidvai, Sheikhs M.H., Women Under Different Social and Religious Systems (1978).

Kilby, Peter (Ed.), *Entrepreneurship and Economic Development,* The Free Press, New York, 1971.

Kirve, Harsha and Kanitkar, Ajit, Entrepreneurship at the Grass-roots: Developing the income generating capabilities of Rural Women, *The Journal of Entrepreneurship,* Volume 2, No. 2, 1993.

Klein, Uta, Returning to Work: A Challenge for Women, *World of Work,* I.L.O., No. 12, May/June, 1995.

Kolvereid, Lars, *et. al.,* Is it equally Difficult for Female Entrepreneurs to Start Business in all Countries, *Journal of Small Business Management,* October, Vol. 31, No. 4.

Kumar, S. Ashok, *Entrepreneurship in Small Industry,* Discovery Publishing House, New Delhi, 1990.

Laski, H.J., Encyclopaedia of Social Sciences (1946).

Laski, H.J., Liberty in the Modern State (1951).

Laski, H.J., Reflection on the Constitution (1950).

Lasser, J.K., *How to Run a Small Business,* McGraw Hill Book Co., New York, 1963.

Layman, A., Women in Family Business: An Untapped Resource, *Advance Management Journal,* Vol. 50, Winter.

Letournean, C.H., The Evolution of Marriage and the Family (1891).

London Business School, *Small Business Bibliography,* 1983.

Lugmanul Haq, "The Plight of Women in Industrial Sector", *Social Welfare,* 31(2), May 1984, pp. 12-14.

Manu Smriti IX, p. 104.

Marshall, T.H., Sociology of Crossroad (1963).

Martin, J. and Roberts, C., *Women and Employment: A Life Time Perspective,* Report of the 1980 DE/OPCS Women and Employment Survey, HMSO, London, 1984.

McClelland, D.C., *et. al., Motivating Economic Achievement,* The Free Press New York, 1969.

McClelland, D.C., *The Achieving Society,* Princeton, New Jersey, D. Van Nostrand Co., 1961.

Mehan, K.K., *Small Industry Entrepreneurs Handbook,* Productivity Services International, Bombay, 1973.

Menon, N.R. Madhav, Legal Aid and Legal Education. : Legal Aid and Justice for the Poor (1986).

Mercar, Peter Phillip, The Gounet Case—PIL in Britain and Canada (1979).

Meredith, Geoffrey G., *The Practice of Entrepreneurship,* International Labour Office, Geneva, 1982, p. 3.

Mikalachki D.M. and Mikalachki, A., Women in Business Going for Broke, *Business Quarterly,* Vol. 50, Summer 1985, pp. 25-32.

Mill, John Stuart, On Liberty (1926).

Mitra, A., The Status of Women—Literacy and Employment, Vol. II.

Mitra, Srimany and Pathak, The Status of Women—Household and Non-household Ecoactivity.

Mohiuddin, Asghari, Entrepreneurship Development among Women: Retrospects and Prospects, *SEDME,* 10(1), March 1983, pp. 1-8.

Mookerji, More Business are Owned by Women, *Advance Management Journal,* Vol. 49, Summer 1984, pp. 55-56

Mookerji, Tapati and Mondal, Uma, Spirited Entrepreneur, *Eve's Weekly,* 18, November 1978, p. 23.

Mukherji, P.B., Civil Liberties (1963).

Nadkarni, Sulochana, Women Entrepreneurs: Socio-economic Study of Pune City, *Economic Times,* 14 September, 1983, p. 5, 15 September, 1983, p. 5.

Nagaiya, D., Impact of liberalisation on small scale Sector and the unfinished Agenda, *SEDME,* Vol. XXIII, No. 1, March, 1996.

Nair, Tara S., Entrepreneurship Training for Women in the Indian Rural Sector: A Review of Approaches and Strategies, *The Journal of Entrepreneurship,* Vol. 5, No. 1 (1996).

Naisbutt, John, *The Future of Franchising: Looking 25 years ahead to the year 2010,* Washington, D.C., International Franchise Association, 1985.

National Conference on 25 years of Entrepreneurship Development in India: Retrospect's and Prospects—Background Papers, National Institute for Entrepreneurship and Small Business Development, New Delhi, 23-25 January, 1990.

Nayak, Nalini, A struggle within the struggle, 1986, Programme for Community Organisation, Spener Junction, Trivandrum.

Nelson, Blossom O' Meally, Small Business Opportunities for Women in Jamaica, *SEDME,* Vol. 18, No. 1, 1991.

Nelson, Blossom, *Networking for Entrepreneurship Development,* UNDP/ILO/INTERMAN Inter-regional project for Entrepreneurship Development and New Enterprise Creation, ILO, Geneva, 1999.

Nelson, Blossom *New Economic Realities: The Rise of Women Entrepreneurs, "A Report of the Committee on Small Business,"* House of Representatives, Second Session (June 28, 1988), Washington, D.C., US Government Printing Press.

Olson, Shirley F. and Currie, Helen, M., Female Entrepreneurs: Personal Value Systems and Business Strategies in a Male-Dominated Industry, *Journal of Small Business Management*, January 1992.

Paise, See Suzanne Panandiker, Surekha, Management of Enterprise, *The Economic Times*, Delhi, 26 Dec. 1985.

Paise, See Suzanne, Lessons for LDCs from Japan's Experience with Labour Commitment and Sub-Contracting in the Manufacturing Sector, *Bulletin of the Oxford Institute of Economics and Statistics*, 33, No. 2 (May 1971).

Pal, B.K., Problems and Concern of Indian Women, 1987, ABC Publishing House.

Pandey, J.N., Constitution of India (1990), Central Law Agency, Allahabad.

Pant, Niranjan, Status of Girl Child and Women in India (1995), A.P.H. Publishing Corporation.

Pappu, S., Legal Provisions—An Assessment of Indian Women.

Paul, Harrison, Third World Tomorrow (1978).

Pareek, Udai and Rao, T. Venkateswara (Ed.), *Developing of Entrepreneurship: A Handbook*, New Delhi, Learning System, 1978.

Parlee, M.B., Getting a Word in Sex-wise: Business Women's Conversational Style, *Across the Board*, Vol. 21, September 1984, pp. 7-10.

Parry, E.A., The Law and the Poor (1914).

Patel, V.G., *Entrepreneurship Development Programmes in India and its Relevance to Developing Countries*, Entrepreneurship Development Institute of India, Ahmedabad, 1987.

Patel, V.G., *Women Entrepreneurship Development*, National Convention of Women Entrepreneurs.

Pathak, H.N, *et. al.*, *Management of New and Small Enterprises*, IGNOU, New Delhi, 1991.

Paul, Burns and Jim, Dewhurst (Eds.), *Pre-workshop Papers—National Workshop on Employment Generation through Entrepreneurship Development*, National Science and Technology Entrepreneurship Development Board, Department of Science and Technology, Govt. of India, New Delhi, 1988.

Paul, Burns and Jim, Dewhurst (Eds.), *Small Business and Entrepreneurship*, Macmillan Education Ltd., London, 1990.

Paul, M.C., Dowry and Position of Women in India, Inter-India Pub., New Delhi, p. 16, pp. 66-98.

Pie, Administration of Criminal Justice.

Pound Dean Roseue, Introduction to the Philosphy of Law (1934).

Prasad, Anurudh, Social Engineering and Constitutional Protection of Weaker Sections in India (1980), Deep and Deep Publications, New Delhi.

Prasad, Hanuman, Suppression of Immoral Traffic in Women and Girls—A Case Study.

Price, Courtney and Fleming, Dick, Four year study of 'Colaredo Entrepreneurship with Minority and Women Business Owners, *Frontiers of Entrepreneurship Research,* Massachusetts, USA, 1991.

Price, Courtney and Monroe, Stuart, Proceedings of *12th Annual Conference of Canadian J. Council for Small Business and Entrepreneurship,* Ontario, Canada, 25-27 October, 1995.

Price, Courtney and Monroe, Stuart, *Proceedings of 25th European Small Business Seminar on Excellence* in *Small Business Management,* Nicosia (Cyprus), 20-22 September 1995.

Price, Courtney and Monroe, Stuart, *Proceedings of Fourth ENDBC World Conference on Dynamic Entrepreneurship,* Nanyang Technological/ University, Singapore, 15-17 July, 1993.

Price, Courtney and Monroe, Stuart, *Proceedings of Global Conference on Small and Medium Industry and Business,* SDM Institute for Management Development, Mysore and Indiana University—Purdue University, Fort Wayne, USA at Bangalore, 3-5 January, 1996.

Price, Courtney and Monroe, Stuart, *Proceedings of National Conference on 25 years of Entrepreneurship Development in India—Retrospects and Prospects,* 23-25 Kamiaru, Ahmedabad, 1990.

Price, Courtney and Monroe, Stuart Proceedings of *National Seminar on Current Research in Indian Entrepreneurship,* EDI(I), Ahmedabad, 29-31 March, 1994.

Price, Courtney and Monroe, Stuart, *Proceedings of National Seminar on Intrapreneuring and Entrepreneurship,* TITI, Chandigarh, 25-26 November, 1993.

Price, Courtney and Monroe, Stuart, *Proceedings of National Seminar on Researches and Innovations in Indian Entrepreneurship,* TITI, Chandigarh, 8-9 December, 1994.

Price, Courtney and Monroe, Stuart, *Proceedings of National Seminar on Industry, Institute Partnership and Small Business Development,* TITI, Chandigarh, 6-7 September 1995.

Price, Courtney and Monroe, Stuart, *Proceedings of National Seminar on Entrepreneurship Development and Small Business Development,* TITI, Chandigarh, 21-22 August, 1997.

Price, Courtney and Monroe, Stuart, *Proceedings of Seventh ENDEC World Conference on Globalisation and Entrepreneurship,* Nanyang Technological University, Singapore, 5-7 December, 1996.

Price, Courtney and Monroe, Stuart, *Proceedings of Sixth ENDEC World Conference on Entrepreneurship in Transitional Economies,* Nanyang Technological University, Singapore, held at Shanghai, People's Republic of China, 7-9 December, 1995.

Price, Courtney and Monroe, Stuart, *Proceedings of the National Seminar on Entrepreneurship Development in Small Scale Industries,* Development Commissioner, Small Scale Industries, New Delhi, 26th and 27th May, 1975.

Price, Courtney and Monroe, Stuart, Promotion of Credit to Women Entrepreneurs, *Reserve Bank of India Bulletin,* 35(12), December 1981.

Price, Courtney and Monroe, Stuart, Quick Advice for Women Entrepreneurs, *Training and Development Journal,* May 1985, p. 39.

Price, Courtney and Monroe, Stuart, Educational Training for Women and Minority Entrepreneurs Positively Impacts Venture Growth and Development, *Frontiers of Entrepreneurship Research,* Massachusetts, USA, 1993.

Rajula Davi, A.K., Women Entrepreneurs, *Yojana,* 22(13), 16 July 1978, pp. 19-22.

Ranadive, Vimal, Multinational Companies and their Impact on Working Women, *Social Scientists,* 9(5-6), December 1980-January 1981, pp. 62-70.

Rani, C., Potential Women Entrepreneurs—A Study, *SEDME,* 13(3), pp. 13-32, 1986.

Rao, B.N., India's Constitution in the Making (1948).

Rao, C. Harinarayana, Promotion of Women Entrepreneurship, *SEDME,* Vol. 18, No. 2, March 1991.

Rao, J.V. Prabhakara (Ed.), *Entrepreneurship and Economic Development,* Kanishka Publishers, New Delhi, 2000.

Rao, K. Subba, Social Justice and Law (1974).

Rao, P. Subba, *Entrepreneurial Challenges,* EDP Series, Kanishka, New Delhi, 1993.

Rao, T.V. and Pareek, Udai (Eds.), *Developing Entrepreneurship: A Handbook,* New Delhi learning systems, 1978.

Rao, V.V. and Rao, N., Marriage, The Family and Women in India, Heritage Publishers, New Delhi (1982).

Rathore, B.S. and Chhabra, Rama, Promotion of Women Entrepreneurship—Training Strategies, *SEDME,* Vol. 18, No. 1, March 1991.

Rathore, B.S. and Dhameja, S.K. (Eds.), *Entrepreneurship in the 21st Century,* Rawat Publications, Jaipur, 1999.

Rathore, B.S. and Saini, J.S. (Eds.), *A Handbook of Entrepreneurship,* Aapga Publishers, Panchkula, 1997.

Ravindran Nair, G., International Conference of Women Entrepreneurs, *Social Welfare,* 27(9), December 1980, pp. 7-8.

Rawal John, A Theory of Justice (1972).

Rayden, Divorce, Butterworths (London) (1971), p. 1101.

Reddy, C.R., Changing Status of Educated Working Women—A Case Study, B.R. Publications Corporation, Delhi, pp. 63-68.

Reddy, V.N., Right to Counsel *vis-a-vis,* "The Poor Under the American and Indian Constitution", 162 MIR (1982), p. 31.

Reginald, H. Smith, Justice and the Poor (1919).

Romero, Florida Ruth, P., Women and the Law (1983), U.P. Law Centre, The Asia Foundation.

Sahasranaman, Meenakshi, Special Problems of Women Entrepreneurs, *Women's Era* (India), 2 April 1978, pp. 17-21.

Saini, J.S. and Dhameja, S.K. (Eds.), *Entrepreneurship and Small Business*, Rawat Publications, Jaipur, 1998.

Saini, J.S., Dhameja, S.K. and Gupta, S.K., *Case Studies of TTTI Trained Entrepreneurs*, TITI, Chandigarh Publication, 1990.

Saini, J.S., *Effectiveness of Entrepreneurship Development Programmes in Northern India*, unpublished thesis, Deptt. of Business Management, Punjabi University, Patiala, 1993.

Saini, J.S., *Entrepreneurship Development*, Deep and Deep Publications, New Delhi, 1996.

Saini, J.S., Gurjar, B.R. and Rathore, B.S., *Facilities and Incentives to Entrepreneurs*, TITI, Chandigarh, 1998.

Samson, K.T., Motives as an Elements of Cruelty in Divorce (1948) II MLA 88. '

Sarkar, Lokita, Crime and Women, Vikas Publications, New Delhi.

Sarkar, Pauper Suits in C.P.C.

Sathe, S.P., Public Participation in Judicial Process: New Trends in Law of Locus Standi with Special Reference to Administrative Law.

Saxena, Shobha, Crimes against Women and Protective Law, Deep and Deep Publications, New Delhi.

Schumpeter, J.A., Self-Employed Women, *Hindu*, 10 September 1978, p. 8:1.

Schumpeter, J.A., *The Theory of Economic Development*, Cambridge, Massachusetts, Harvard University Press, 1949.

Schwartz, Bernard, Constitutional Law of America (1982).

Seervai, H.M., Constitutional Law of India (1988).

Sen, Amartya, *Gender and Co-operative Conflicts*, WIDER Working Paper No. 18, 1987.

Sengupta, N.C., Evolution of Ancient Indian Law (1950), Eastern Law House, Calcutta.

Sethi, Jyotsna, Women Entrepreneurship in India: A Brief Comment, *SEDME*, Vol. 21, No. 4, 1994.

Sethi, Narendra K., Women in Business, *Integrated Management*, 15(9), September 1980, pp. 39-46, 15(10-12), October-December 1980, pp. 32-37.

Shah, H. and Pathak, C.H., *Women Entrepreneurship Development Programmes: Trainers' Manual*, International Centre for Entrepreneurship and Career Development, Ahmedabad, 1990.

Shah, Hina, *Fostering Women Entrepreneurship—A Study of Distinctive Features*, Research Report, Serial 3, National Institute of Entrepreneurship and Small Business Development, New Delhi, 1990.

Sharma, D.D., Dhameja, S.K. and Gurjar, B.R. (Eds.), *Entrepreneurship, Strategic Management and Globalisation*, Rawat Publications, Jaipur, 1998.

Sharma, S.S., Legal Aid to the poor (1993), Deep and Deep Publications, New Delhi.

Sharma, V., Protection to Wowen in Matrimonial Horne, Deep and Deep Publications, New Delhi, 1996.

SIDBI Report on Small Scale Industries Sector, Lucknow, 1999.

Singh, K.P., Women Entrepreneurs: Their Profile and Motivation, *The Journal of Entrepreneurship,* Vol. 2, No. 1 (1993).

Singh, N.P., Sehgal, P., Tinani, Madan and Gupta, Rita Sen, *Successful Women Entrepreneurs-their Identity, Expectations and Problems,* Research Report Serial 2, National Institute of Entrepreneurship and Small Business Development, New Delhi/Management, Development Institute, Gurgaon Collaborative Study published, 1990.

Singh, N.P. and Gupta, Rita Sen, *Potential Women Entrepreneurs.*

Singh, Nagendra P., *Role of Financial Institutions* in *Entrepreneurship and Development,* Development Banking Centre, New Delhi, 1982.

Sinha, Niroj, Women and Violence, Vikas Publishing House Pvt. Ltd., 1989.

Sinha, Ramesh P., Entrepreneurship Development: Problems and Prospects, *Man and Life,* 8(1-2), January-June 1982, pp. 48-56.

Sirajual Islam, Directive Principles of State Policy in Indian Constitution (1988).

Smith, The Right to Life (1964).

Srivastava, A.K. and Chaudhary, Sanjay, *Women Entrepreneurs—Problems, Perspective and Role Expectations from Banks,* unpublished thesis, Panjab University, Chandigarh, 1991.

Srivastava, S.B., *A Practical Guide to Industrial Entrepreneur,* Sultan Chand and Sons, New Delhi, 1981.

Stevenson, L., *'An Investigation of the Entrepreneurial Experience of Women: Implications for Small Business Policy* in *Canada',* Acadia University, Wofville, Nova Scotia, November 1983.

Stone, Juilius, Human Law and Human Justice (1961).

Stoner, James A.F., Freeman, R. Edward and Gilbert Jr., Daniel. R., *Management,* Prentice Hall of India Pvt. Ltd., New Delhi, 1996.

Sugumar, M., Entrepreneurial Competencies amongst Small Entrepreneurs, *SEDME,* Dec. 1996.

Surti, K. and Surupia, Psychological Factors Affecting Women Entrepreneurs: Some Findings, *The Indian Journal of Social Work,* 44(3), pp. 287-95, 1983.

Surtton, C.D. and Moore, K.K., Executive Women—20 years Later, *Harvard Business Review,* Vol. 63, September-October 1985, pp. 42-44.

Tayabji, F.B., Muslim Law, N.M. Tripathy, Bombay.

Their Profile, Vision and Motivation, Research Report, Serial 1, National Institute of Entrepreneurship and Small Business Development, New Delhi/Management Development Institute, Gurgaon, Collaborative Study, 1990 (first published 1985).

Thomas, P., Indian Women Through the Age (1964).

Tinani, Madan, *Trainer's Manual on Entrepreneurship Development*, Singapore, Technonet Asia, 1981, p. 7.

Tinani, Madan, Women Entrepreneurs, *The Economic Times*, 10 April, 1988, Bombay, p. 5.

Tope, T.K., Constitutional Law of India, Eastern Book Co., Lucknow.

Venkataramaya, M., Human Rights in the Changing World (1978).

Verghese, Jamila, Her Gold and Her Body, Vikas Publishing House Pvt. Ltd. (1980).

Vinze, Medha Dubashi, *Women Entrepreneurs* in *India: A Socio-Economic Study of Delhi*, 1975-85, Mittal Publications, Delhi, 1987.

Wade and Bradley, A.W., Constitutional Law (1965).

Watson, E.D. and Hodgson, R.C., Women in Management: Reducing the Price of Success, *Business Quarterly*, Vol. 49, September 1984, pp. 137-43.

What Prospects for Women Entrepreneur?, *Hindu*, 17 May 1981, p. 4:4.

Wheare, K.C., Modern Constitutions (1960).

White, J., The Rise of Female Capitalism: Women as Entrepreneurs, *Business Quarterly*, Vol. 49, September 1984, pp. 133-35.

Winston, Sandra, *The Entrepreneurial Women*, Newsweek Books, New York, 1979.

Women and Small Business, International Women's Tribune Centre, New York, November, 1985.

Women Entrepreneurs, *Economic* Times, 10 March 1985, pp. 4:1-8.

Women's Wing of NAYE, Gujarat Chapter, Ahmedabad, February 6-8, 1986.

Working Women: Problems and Unionisation, *All India Trade Union Congress (AITUC) Publication*, Education Series-7, New Delhi.

World Executive Digest, Hong-Kong, June 1984. Zapalska, Alina M., A Profile of Women Entrepreneurs and Enterprises in Poland, *Journal of Small Business Management*, Vol. 35, No. 4, October 1997.

Zhang, Yon Yun, A high priced slot in the world of work. *World of Work*, 110, No. 12, May/June 1995.

Zinkin, Maurice, "Entrepreneurs: Key to Growth," *Stanford Research Institute Journal*, Second Quarter, 1961.

Index